"We, Too, Are Americans"

WOMEN IN AMERICAN HISTORY

Series Editors
Anne Firor Scott
Stephanie Shaw
Susan Armitage
Susan Cahn

A list of books in the series appears at the end of this book.

"We, Too, Are Americans"

African American Women
in Detroit and Richmond, 1940–54

MEGAN TAYLOR SHOCKLEY

University of Illinois Press

URBANA, CHICAGO, AND SPRINGFIELD

∞ This book is printed on acid-free paper.

Library of Congress Cataloging-in-Publication Data
Shockley, Megan Taylor.
We, too, are Americans : African American women in Detroit and
Richmond, 1940–54 / Megan Taylor Shockley.
p.   cm. — (Women in American history)
Includes bibliographical references and index.
ISBN 978-0-252-02863-2 (cloth : alk. paper)
1. African American women—Michigan—Detroit—Political
activity—History—20th century. 2. Civil rights movements—
Michigan—Detroit—History—20th century. 3. Social classes—
Michigan—Detroit—History—20th century. 4. African American
women—Virginia—Richmond—Political activity—History—20th
century. 5. Civil rights movements—Virginia—Richmond—History—
20th century. 6. Social classes—Virginia—Richmond—History—
20th century. 7. Detroit (Mich.)—Race relations. 8. Detroit (Mich.)—
Politics and government—20th century. 9. Richmond (Va.)—Race
relations. 10. Richmond (Va.)—Politics and government—20th
century. I. Title. II. Series.
F574.D49N4825   2004
305.48'896073077434—dc21   2003000555

Contents

Acknowledgments

Through the various stages of this manuscript I received invaluable support and guidance from a number of people. I must first give my gratitude to Karen Anderson, Sarah Deutsch, and Sharla Fett. Their constant willingness to offer guidance and suggestions through various incarnations of these chapters has enabled me to write a more coherent, more compelling study. They challenged me to think about gender, race, and citizenship in ways that deepened my analysis and made my work much easier. I cannot thank them enough for their efforts. I am also grateful to Eileen Boris, who read various portions of the manuscript and helped me to rethink the effects of UAW politics on black women's activist efforts. I would like to thank Nancy Hewitt and Gretchen Lemke-Santangelo, both of whom offered valuable critiques and helped me sharpen my writing. Laurie Matheson and Mary Giles have been wonderful editors, encouraging me through several revisions and remaining optimistic throughout the review process. I must also thank Francis Foster and Hilda Warden, both of whom taught me much about the racial dynamics of Richmond, past and present. Their knowledge of the African American community in the city enabled me to look for myriad sources, many of which I would never have noticed on my own. I am also grateful to my colleagues at Longwood University who have worked with me to schedule courses around revisions and have cheered me on through the entire revision process. I would especially like to thank Larissa Smith, who cheerfully consulted with me on issues pertaining to local and national civil rights efforts.

In addition, I am indebted to the various librarians and archivists who made my work much easier. Mike Smith and Carolyn Davis of the Archives of Labor and Urban Affairs at Wayne State University cheerfully offered advice, pulled collections, and gave me rides home on cold Detroit nights. Their knowledge of the UAW collections was a tremendous help. William Wallach of the Bentley Memorial Library, Gregg Kimball at the Virginia State Library and Archives, Susan McElrath and Robert Parker from the Bethune Council House, Ray Bonis from the Virginia Commonwealth University Special Collections, and numerous other archivists helped track down elusive sources so I could create an accurate account of African American women's activities.

I was fortunate to receive financial assistance from several sources, including the Borden/Gillette Travel Fellowship from the University of Michigan and the Alpha Chi Omega Emma Griffith Marshall Fellowship. These fellowships enabled me to travel to Michigan and Virginia to conduct my research. In addition, the Alpha Chi Omega fellowship allowed me travel to conferences in order to engage with historians of various disciplines, and they provided questions and comments that enhanced my work.

I could not have completed this manuscript without the help of family and friends. Jennifer Kerns-Robison and Jennifer Fish Kashay read chapters and have offered valuable advice and support over the years. My sisters and parents have been cheerful listeners and supporters throughout the seemingly endless manuscript revision process. My husband Jeff has endured countless jobs, taking care of my beloved pets for weeks at a time while I went on the road to research, acting as copy editor and critic, and being a cheerleader when I felt the pressures of the trials of researching and teaching a heavy courseload. My thanks go to him and all the others whom I have and have not mentioned but who helped me shape the manuscript for this volume into its present form.

"We, Too, Are Americans"

Introduction

In 1943 Detroit erupted into a race riot that paralyzed war production for two days. Although men composed the majority of rioters both white and black, 4.5 percent of the participants were African American women who took to the streets to protest the prejudice they faced on a daily basis.[1] After witnessing the violence perpetrated by women, local members of the historically black sorority Delta Sigma Theta decided to build a settlement house in the Detroit ghetto to provide material and moral assistance to poor young black women who had taken their grievances to the streets because they had nowhere else to turn for help.[2] Two years earlier, in Richmond, Virginia, Helen Johnson had also "taken her grievances to the streets." After enduring countless indignities on the city's segregated bus system, Johnson finally had enough. She slapped a white man who had kicked her and as a result suffered blows from other white male passengers before the driver threw her off the vehicle.[3]

The two cases raise important questions about the nature of class differences among African American women activists, their use of and relation to white-dominated and black-run institutions, and the new political possibilities presented by civilian mobilization during World War II. The context of Franklin D. Roosevelt's "V for Victory" campaign—victory for democracy abroad—presented new political and discursive possibilities for African American women. Encouraged by traditional black institutions such as the National Association for the Advancement of Colored People (NAACP), the National Council of Negro Women (NCNW), and the Urban League, African American women fought for "Double V for Victory," victory over fascism abroad and racism at home. This gave them a new way to articulate citizenship as they called upon the government to recognize them as waged and volunteer workers in the wartime state, deserving of the full rights of citizenship. The women created a conditional claim to citizenship and based it on their contributions to the state. From 1940 to 1954 they asserted their right to full citizenship by attempting to challenge racism, poverty, and underemployment in various ways. Strategies ranged from traditional (e.g., creating settlement houses to "uplift" poor women) to militant (e.g., directly challenging social prejudice by rioting and fighting in the streets when demands for equality went unheard).

Central Questions

This study provides new understanding of activities that helped launch the modern civil rights movement. By looking at black women's wartime protest and exploring how women created templates for activism and networks for the dissemination of new discourses about citizenship, it reveals the gendered roots of the modern civil rights movement. The study will also help articulate how marginalized groups can use state structures in order to promote their own interests and maintain autonomy in the face of an oppressive dominant society. It analyzes African American women's efforts to define and claim citizenship from 1940 to 1954 in Detroit, Michigan, and Richmond, Virginia, cities typical of northern and southern urban centers at the time.

I employ a cross-class analysis within a cross-regional analysis in order to understand how African American women transformed their relationship with the state and gained equality. Detroit and Richmond were two very different cities in two diverse regions of the country. While Detroit typified a midwestern World War II boom city as auto manufacturers geared up for massive production increases, Richmond was a typical Upper South city that benefited by converting its chemical, textile, and tobacco industries to wartime production. In Detroit, a massive labor shortage resulting from stepped-up production enabled black women to engage with employers and unions in order to claim new wartime jobs. Richmond experienced fewer manpower shortages, and legalized segregation kept many black women out of wartime factories.

Black women of different socioeconomic levels found the possibilities for activism framed by the cities in which they resided. Middle-class women experienced many of the same issues in Detroit and Richmond. Being educated, they tended to hold jobs with social services departments and as teachers; being elite, they tended to affiliate with national organizations that had similar agendas in both cities. The middle-class women faced different problems in each city, however, based on racial structures that operated in the North and the South. Women in Richmond faced daily indignities resulting from the state-supported system of segregation. Detroit had no legal segregation, but African Americans still found themselves constrained by white social norms that maintained separate restaurants, neighborhoods, and job opportunities for African Americans. In its failure to enforce the civil rights law, the state tacitly supported de facto segregation.

Working-class women, however, faced different challenges in each city as a result of segregation practices within industries and residential spaces. Their more localized activist efforts reflected the different racial problems they encountered in cities across the country. Richmond's laws designated separate spheres for African Americans and whites, which made the structure of oppression more visible because it was state-sponsored. In Detroit, however, the fact that the white population ignored the existing civil rights law led to the black community's struggle to have that law enforced. Women's class positions and local government structures in each city affected how African American women constructed claims to citizenship and maintained activist strategies to promote equality.

My primary questions are, first, how did African American women define a new discourse of citizenship based on their participation in the vastly expanded wartime state? Second, how did gender, class, and regional differences affect discourses constructing citizenship? And, third, how did African American women balance their historical distrust of state institutions with communitywide efforts to desegregate state-run voluntary associations and other war-based organizations? This study suggests that African American women redefined citizenship during and immediately following World War II by basing it on their real or potential contributions to the wartime state. They entered into negotiations with the state over the meanings of equality, and their actions helped launch the modern civil rights movement.

Gender, Race, Class, and Citizenship

In order to understand how African American women redefined citizenship in a specific moment of change it is important to historicize the meanings that citizenship had for them. Key feminist scholarship asserts that capitalist states construct the meanings of citizenship around a masculine norm in order to promote patriarchal family structures and privilege men's status as leaders in the state. To maintain order, the state needs to create stable economic climates and stable families. In this situation women are called upon to provide service work to the state in the form of reproductive labor. The state represents an amalgam of the interests of the dominant class, and in the United States that means state interests have historically represented the interests of white men. The state represents more than the formal structures of policymaking power; it extends into all levels of society, including the family. That does not mean, however, that the state is fixed and ahistorical. Rather, it is a broad center of power that represents many interests, and the population constantly tests the fluid polity. At various times the state provides entry points so those normally outside it can negotiate for citizenship.[4]

In the early twentieth century, middle-class white women found a point on which to negotiate as they used the power of motherhood to claim authority in policymaking. White maternalist reformers idealized normative structures of white motherhood in order to define motherhood as an important component of citizenship and gain welfare benefits for women. Although social constructions of gender had always been linked with race—white women did not work, black women worked; white women had the potential for virtue if surveilled and constrained by authority figures, black women's bodies were sexualized in order to justify rape—white maternalist reformers further distorted race/class differences to gain legitimacy for themselves within the state. They constructed a typical welfare recipient as a widowed white woman who could potentially sink into poverty and sin if she failed to receive money that enabled her to stay at home with her children. That created a standard that eliminated black women from benefits, because white society had already eliminated them from having any virtue to protect.[5]

This categorization of citizenship placed African American women in a tenuous situation when they attempted to define their own relationships with the state. They were far from state centers of power in terms of having a voice in policymaking efforts, but they were close to oppressive state power structures. State agencies, including welfare officials, health departments, and police, paid close attention to the lives of African American women. Because state agents constructed all of them as deviants, they found themselves subject to surprise visits by welfare officers; moreover, health officials regulated their work, and law and parole officers policed their actions.[6]

In order to enter into negotiations with the state over issues of segregation and inequality, African American women had to construct a new discourse to position themselves as citizens within the wartime and postwar state. They worked from multiple locations that defined their own lives and their relationships with others.[7] Moreover, they experienced multiple oppressions in the United States because of their lack of proximity to state centers of power. A woman's position within her community, in relation to the state, depended very much on social and geographical location. For example, a middle-class African American woman had the resources to create national networks of opportunity that contested domination on a large-scale level, whereas a working-class woman would often have to use individual resistance, kin, and neighborhood networks that grounded her activism at a local level. Although working-class African American women sometimes received help from national unions, many whites who controlled the unions had little or no interest in promoting civil rights. In addition, African American women in the North experienced racial oppression differently from those in the South because most northern states passed few Jim Crow segregation laws.

In general, African American women employed several strategies in order to claim citizenship. First, they relied in large part on the independent judicial branch in order to effect social change. Beginning in the 1880s, they sued transportation companies for the right to sit in first-class seats, a strategy that continued throughout the twentieth century. In addition, African American women fought for suffrage. They viewed the right to vote as a political tool and believed their votes could alter urban conditions, affect decisions on health issues, and pressure school boards to change policies. They often used their clubs in order to create national political networks, and the National Association of Colored Women (NACW) became a serious partisan player in the 1920s, fighting for voter registration and supporting racial moderates. African American women recognized the Constitution as fluid. They fought to be included as citizens by fighting for the vote and using it where available and also by using the courts to establish legal precedents for desegregation.[8]

Often, African American women of varying socioeconomic stratas advanced differing methods of achieving equality. From 1880 to 1920, for example, those in the middle class embraced the politics of respectability in order to claim rights denied them. These women expected that by espousing the ideals of Victorianism—thrift, Christianity, strict standards of sexual propriety, and hard work—African Americans could win the respect of white America and claim rights in that way.[9] Believing that a race could rise no further than its women, middle-class African American women created clubs and sororities in order to form the vanguard of racial uplift in their communities.

In this early period, the NACW formed an umbrella organization that represented all the smaller organizations and coalesced around the ideologies of respectability and uplift.[10] Within that context, African American women politicized gender as they promoted women's importance to reform efforts. By constructing themselves as intrinsic to community uplift by nature of their gender, they claimed space within uplift programs as they attempted to promote race progress and equality. They did so, however, within the confines of normative gender relations, maintaining the ideology that women were first and foremost the mothers and reproducers for the race. That role often put them at odds with their public roles as reformers and leaders, and many middle-class women struggled to maintain balance between domestic roles and public activities.[11]

At times, middle-class and working-class women's concepts of respectability converged. Both focused on the domestic arena as critical to community uplift and the protection of African American women. Women of all classes agreed that respectability could protect them from sexual harassment.[12] Still, middle-class African Americans often viewed the behavior of the working class as pathological, determined by poor education and social dislocation, and exacerbated by economic hardship. Because they believed that such behavior proved detrimental to the progress of the black community, middle-class women set out to change working-class black women's behavior through uplift programs that taught good mothering, nutrition, and personal hygiene skills. The programs provided critically necessary services not furnished by the state but failed to address structural economic inequalities that kept poor women out of jobs that would enable them to provide better for their families. In essence, because African American women reformers saw the necessity to work as a given in a society that underemployed all African Americans, they focused more on community and family development issues and not enough on helping women break into segregated industries.[13]

Although the programs of middle-class organizations were progressive given the oppressive climate under which they operated, many groups failed to advocate direct protest activities, which created a schism between groups like the NAACP and NACW and more radical organizations. At the turn of the century the NACW and the NAACP formed the vanguard of protest, offering an alternative to Booker T. Washington's accommodationist uplift programs by protesting inequalities in educational and other public facilities. The NAACP and NACW sponsored programs that instilled race pride; they also created uplift programs in an attempt to provide financial support to black economic and social institutions.

Many middle-class African Americans, however, felt uncomfortable with demonstrating publicly against inequality, and they disagreed with the more radical activities of the United Negro Improvement Association and the Communist Party. For example, the NAACP clashed with the Communist Party over the former organization's failure to bring more pressure on the city of Scottsboro, Alabama, for the infamous rape trial of nine young black men in 1937. Middle-class African American women also tried to focus more on economic opportunities for professional women and service employees by lobbying for protective legislation rather than by using direct protest movements. Deborah Gray White maintains that middle-class African American women's commitment to maintaining respectability and promoting reform of the working class without understanding the real needs of poor women led to the failure of black women to effect a cross-class alliance and eventually helped cause the decline of the NACW during the 1920s.[14]

During the late 1920s and throughout the 1930s, middle-class African American women moved away from merely promoting respectability, which had failed to win many concrete rewards for the black community, to using their professional status and status within the community to challenge structural inequality. They participated in voter registration campaigns and called upon the federal government to alleviate the plight of poor African Americans. Moreover, they tried to move to jobs that enabled them to promote race relations work as they attacked inequality more openly than they had during the Progressive Era.[15]

Working-class women constructed their own meanings of citizenship from the period immediately following emancipation and continuing through the Great Depression. Because black women in lower economic stratas viewed waged work as absolutely vital to their existence, they often framed constructions of citizenship around equal opportunity to employment, control over their own labor, access to state entitlements like welfare benefits, and better working and living conditions for themselves and their families. Tera Hunter contends that black women's attempts both to thwart oppressive employers and achieve liberation and justice from the 1870s to 1920 came from understanding the importance of controlling their own labor, which is one of the main tenets of American citizenship.[16] Atlanta's black women attempted to do so and better their lives, both inside the workplace and in their communities, by negotiating with employers for better wages and working conditions and creating benefit societies to help each other financially and psychologically. Working-class women even struck together for control over the laundry trade so they could set their own hours and wage standards.[17]

Working-class women in the 1930s and 1940s stressed creating more opportunities in diverse occupational fields and demanding entitlements directly from state officials. During the 1930s, working-class African American women formed relationships with federal government agencies to try to obtain relief and work. Demanding redress for grievances, they became outspoken in their attempt to claim welfare and work rights and often wrote to

President Franklin D. Roosevelt and Eleanor Roosevelt. During the 1940s, women began to use unions to address grievances when they found employment, such as in the meatpacking industry in Chicago. Working-class African American women showed willingness to engage national organizations in a vocal attempt to gain equality in the job market. Although direct negotiations with state agencies and unions occurred during the 1930s, such activity would increase tremendously in the 1940s. The number of benevolent societies for working-class African American women declined in the 1930s, but the women continued to support each other through boycott campaigns. In addition, they were less likely to try conforming to middle-class standards when demanding help from federal government institutions.[18]

Working-class African American women had few means to organize on a national level before the 1960s, but they still created an oppositional culture that rejected the dominant ideology about race and class while they used segregated work and residential spaces to create collective resistance. Robin Kelley maintains that workers on the margins, without strong political alliances, still struggled to push against the oppressive racial and economic structures that threatened their autonomy, both in collective and individual struggles.[19]

The women found themselves affected by many different power structures. First, regional politics determined how they would be treated in their jobs, what their wages would be, and in which nonservice jobs they could work. In Detroit, for example, working-class women met with less resistance in lucrative war industries than in Richmond, where factories maintained strict segregation. In addition, urban settings altered experiences. These women, unlike their counterparts in the country, who often had fewer choices, could quit at any time and look for new jobs. Both Hunter and Kelley see this as the ultimate statement of control over the labor process. Women in cities could choose among more employers and from different types of jobs, although their choices were, of course, constricted by the structural racism that kept them in low-skilled jobs.

Gender also played a key role in how African American workers saw the terrain of power relations. As Elsa Barkley Brown and Gregg Kimball assert, Richmond's working-class African American women traversed the city as they moved from their homes to the homes of employers as domestics or laundresses. They understood how power structures operated and how to exploit them. Hunter discusses the women's willingness to wear their clients' clothes and "pan-tote" leftovers home as a form of activism and survival because their incomes could not stretch to support families.[20]

To working-class African American women, citizenship meant not only voting rights and abstract ideals of citizenship but also equal access to jobs and welfare benefits, decent housing, fair treatment on the factory floor, and control over their own labor. During World War II, they took the opportunity to merge claims for equal opportunity with demands for recognition as citizens who bought war bonds, voted, and participated in other home-front activities. To these ends, they negotiated the terrain of welfare officials and employers, substandard housing, and segregation in public places in order to claim citizenship.

World War II and the Possibilities for Citizenship

Most historians agree that World War II created a watershed moment for the civil rights movement. Deborah Gray White, John Dalfiume, Neil Wynn, and others maintain that disruptions in southern agriculture—together with the mass movement of millions of people to urban centers across the country, the increase in federal government programs that focused on helping peoples of color get hired in war industries, and the rhetoric of a war fought for democracy abroad—enabled African Americans to claim rights and opportunities previously held only by whites.[21] The federal government tripled in size, and its focus on food and metal conservation, neighborhood defense blocks, and other local wartime programs brought it in contact with the smallest units of the state—families. In addition, changes wrought by mass mobilization, including the necessity of all civilians working for victory on the home front, enabled African American women specifically to claim civil rights based on a new definition of citizenship that enabled them to negotiate with the state.

Wartime shifts in polity and ideology enabled African Americans to step forward and actively claim rights, but often the state and others viewed their activities as suspicious. The state needed to repress social conflicts during the war and had to call upon all Americans in order to mobilize the entire home front. State support of women's mass movement into industry provided an impetus for black women to press for equality; at the same time, however, the state viewed with suspicion any activities that would threaten social peace. Because the Roosevelt administration wanted to put off dealing with race and class conflict until the war was over, its policies cut two ways. It gave concessions to black organizations and labor, and it maintained controls over both groups in order to suppress any activities considered subversive. Although the administration supported labor organizations, for example, it imposed a no-strike pledge that angered many workers. Those who violated the pledge, however, were considered dangerous to the state's wartime goals.[22] The administration conceded to black concerns over equal work opportunities by creating the Fair Employment Practices Committee (FEPC), but it also surveilled black organizations, namely the NAACP's and Urban League's magazines and newsletters, and partially blamed the black press for the 1943 riots in Detroit and Harlem.[23]

World War II enabled African Americans to claim rights based on the wartime rhetoric of fighting to preserve democracy in Europe. In order to justify entering the war, the Roosevelt administration created the V for Victory campaign. Roosevelt called upon all citizens to support the war, both in the field and on the home front. Encouraged by the wartime rhetoric, the *Pittsburgh Courier* created the Double V campaign—victory for democracy abroad and at home. African Americans pointed out the hypocrisy of fighting to preserve democracy abroad when so many people of color faced discrimination and oppression at home. As Neil Wynn maintains, "From the very beginning, the duties and the privileges attached to citizenship were thus linked together and demands for participation in the war effort were coupled with specific demands relating to civil rights."[24] Organizations such as the Urban League, the NAACP, and the NCNW converged to promote equality by claiming citizenship based on black participation in the wartime state.[25]

Although many historians have acknowledged the positive impact of World War II on the civil rights movement and the establishment of full citizenship for all African Americans, they have largely ignored the impact of black women on the redefinition of citizenship, focusing instead on the experiences of black soldiers. Wynn, Dalfiume, and others observe that soldiers learning to understand equality in Europe, staging sit-ins on bases, and rioting against injustice in segregated camps redefined citizenship in the black community. These historians suggest that war duty, for black leaders, equaled citizenship and that returning veterans formed the vanguard of the civil rights movement as they demanded rights based on their obligations to defend their country.[26] Although these historians depict an important component of the redefinition of citizenship, they obscure the actions of black women in an attempt to equate military service with citizenship. In her work on women and the obligations of citizenship, Linda Kerber explains that taking up arms to defend the country at war is normally reserved for men, excluding women as citizens if one considers bearing arms a quid pro quo for citizenship.[27] In times of war, however, women become vital to the operation of the home-front state despite the fact that few bear arms for the country.

Although scholars make valid arguments about the importance of World War II to the struggle for equality, they do not locate the efforts of African American women from 1940 to 1954 specifically within the modern civil rights movement. Aldon Morris maintains that the movement, which he believes began in 1953, was marked by the widespread movement of African Americans into direct confrontations with institutions of oppression, sustained for long periods in the face of severe repression, and characterized by the use of nonviolent protest tactics.[28] If one uses this definition, it is clear that African American women participated in modern civil rights activities from 1940 to 1954. During World War II, they became involved in gendered efforts to redefine citizenship—they employed established community networks to spread information and broaden understandings of their relationship to the state, and they participated directly in civil rights activities.

As a result of opportunities opening for all women on the home front in both paid and voluntary work, African American women positioned themselves at the forefront of the civil rights movement by claiming citizenship for themselves and their communities based on real and potential contributions to the wartime state. Moreover, they empowered the organizations they needed to pressure employers and government at all levels to secure their rights and opportunities; they staged sit-ins and engaged in personal and broad-based nonviolent efforts to desegregate public facilities; and they contested directly the institutions of segregation on local, state, and federal levels in order to claim rights previously denied them.

Black women used the Double V program to redefine the goals of citizenship for themselves as volunteers and as potential war workers for the state. They "en-gendered" the Double V effort by applying the program's tenets to efforts to equalize social relations. Although they could not bear arms and "prove" their patriotism, for example, they demanded to be included in all home-front war efforts on an equal basis with white women. They criticized racist policies of groups such as the Red Cross and USO that often kept black women's participation at a minimum in order to maintain strict segregation and lower the costs of supporting black troops. They also questioned the hiring practices of industries that, despite facing tremendous manpower shortages, were still reluctant to hire black women.

African American women still based their new constructions of citizenship on a notion of reciprocity. They agreed to serve the state but demanded full citizenship based on their participation in the wartime state. In this way their goals were similar to the goals of men, but their methods of achieving full citizenship—based on gendered contributions to the state—were different in that they focused on home-front activities rather than military service. The conditional basis of citizenship put tension on the tenets of race progress and the ideology of unquestioning service to the state because it required African Americans to support a state that did not guarantee them equality.[29]

World War II posed specific challenges for African American women. Although white women made gains in industries during the war, only six hundred thousand of the seven million women in war industries were black. Only 18 percent of black women worked in production jobs during the war years.[30] Black men gained jobs in factories, in part because they had already established footholds in production jobs like those of the auto industries before the war. White society's construction of black women as disreputable and oversexualized creatures, however, created barriers in the workforce when they attempted to gain lucrative wartime jobs, because often white women employees refused to work in proximity to black women. Some employers used the excuse that white women could not or would not work with black women and thus hiring black women would impede war production.[31] Faced with employer objections, many African American women sought assistance from federal agencies and civil rights organizations in securing workplace opportunities. They created a new definition of citizenship based on their potential importance as workers for victory in order to negotiate with the federal government and gain the right to work.

African American women who attempted to enter factories had to engage with the state in order to bolster their power. Repeated visits to hiring gates sometimes wore down employers, but the women still needed the power of institutional structures in order to coerce industry to equalize hiring practices. In her study of women in the United Auto Workers Union (UAW), Nancy Gabin finds that African American women appeared much more willing than men to employ the power of the state and the union in order to break into factory work. She suggests that because the women were the last hired and faced the most resistance from employers, workers, and union locals, they exhibited more militancy than men in trying to gain entry onto the factory floor. In addition, because of problems they faced in obtaining lucrative war jobs, working-class African American women also had to contend with creating community networks in places that were dangerous, dirty, and overcrowded.[32]

The women had new institutional structures that bolstered their negotiating power. Franklin Roosevelt had created the FEPC to investigate claims of unequal hiring practices after staving off a march on Washington threatened by A. Phillip Randolph, the noted black leader of the Brotherhood of Sleeping Car Porters. Although elite black leaders denounced the 1941 march, it was the actions of a working-class group that effected change, not pressure from the NAACP or other elite groups.[33]

Although wracked with the problems of bureaucracy—namely slow procedural policies and a lack of enforcement power—the FEPC proved especially useful for African American women, who used their potential as war workers to attempt to define themselves as citizens who had the right to equal employment. Industries became increasingly willing to hire black men by 1942 as the worker shortage reached nationwide crisis proportions, but they remained steadfastly against employing African American women. In fact, many more women than men complained to the FEPC, because neither unions nor black organizations seemed to be able to help them gain a foothold in industries. In 1942 the first FEPC probe into Detroit specifically addressed African American women's complaints. According to a national newspaper, the women "were being refused employment even by those firms which employ colored men." The same industries, the women pointed out, had sought out white women for employment even as African American women stood by the gates and waited to speak with employment officers.[34]

The fact that women's work became an important component of the new gauge to equality contradicted traditional gendered uplift efforts by taking the focus away from domesticity. The shift in focus to working rights resulted from the formation of the FEPC, which placed workers in a different relationship with the state and, in so doing, made work-related issues more central to definitions of inequality. The old understandings of women's work existed in an uneasy tension with the support of women's entry into heavy factory work, especially for middle-class black women who came to recognize the importance of equal opportunities for working-class women as intrinsic to the advancement of civil rights. In effect, the new focus on women's paid labor created tension between the politics of respectability and the politics of responsible patriotism, which middle-class women tried to alleviate by taking control of the labor issue. Middle-class clubwomen promoted opportunities for others while continuing to make discrimination in volunteer work central to their understandings of social inequality.

Middle-class African American women also faced discrimination during the war. Because they provided most of the volunteer services needed to keep up troop morale and produce clothing and medical supplies for troops overseas, they were at the forefront of the fight to desegregate voluntary associations. Barred from certain Red Cross and USO facilities as a result of nationwide segregation in the volunteer home-front organizations, African American women who volunteered sought to point out the inequalities they faced as they helped work for victory and legitimized state goals by showing willingness to sacrifice husbands and sons for the war effort.[35]

Virtually every community in the country experienced residential segregation, which both the Red Cross and the USO justified by locating units in neighborhood centers. A Mrs. Price, head of Richmond's Red Cross sewing units, for example, commented, "'There's a nice spirit of democracy in the knitting groups that does [sic] Red Cross work. All churches and schools are represented. Knitters are all ages and live in all sections of town. . . . Girl reserves at Maggie Walker and sub-debs at St. Catherine's both work for the Red Cross.'"[36] In 1942 no African American women attended the exclusive St. Catherine's prep school in the West End, and Maggie Walker High School was situated in the heart of the black district. Local residential segregation enabled the Red Cross to maintain the appearance of equality by providing everyone with a place to volunteer yet still retaining strict racial barriers.

National sororities and the recently formed NCNW contested discrimination in voluntary organizations as a symbol of discrimination practiced in larger society. They constructed a discourse of responsible patriotism in order to claim positions within the state and fight for civil rights. African American clubwomen demanded the right to volunteer so that their services would define them as citizens by nature of their important contributions to the wartime state. In 1940, for example, Dorothy Boulding Ferebee, national president of Alpha Kappa Alpha (AKA) sorority, wrote, "War contributions must not be thrust aside because we are women or because we are Negroes."[37]

The tone Ferebee used marked a subtle break within the ethic of service that women espoused during the Progressive Era. African American clubwomen no longer felt willing to be anonymous and invisible when supporting their community and their country—instead, they sought compensation in the form of equal treatment. Their organizations had begun to move toward a more fully articulated citizenship that went beyond maternalism in the 1930s; the NCNW's goals included lobbying for black women's economic and political advancement. Deborah Gray White contends that Mary McLeod Bethune, founder of the NCNW, believed that the federal government could be the black community's best advocate in the fight for equality. As a result, the NCNW focused on obtaining protective legislation for domestic workers and equal opportunity for all women workers as well as petitioning the government to hire more black professionals in federal positions. NCNW members used their networking skills to lobby for change at the highest levels of government.[38] Although middle-class reformers had been active in making claims on the state before World War II, the war gave immediacy and urgency to their struggle.[39]

As they claimed the responsibilities of citizenship by demanding to be included in volunteer efforts, middle-class African American women politicized the nature of respectability by bringing it into negotiations with the state. The expanded wartime state made the boundaries between public and private permeable, and African American women recognized that the state could not achieve its purposes without their contributions of unpaid labor. They agreed to supply such labor, legitimizing the war in the process, but demanded compensation by calling on the state to grant them full citizenship for those contributions.

While African American clubwomen's discourse of responsible patriotism included demands for electoral participation, equal pay, and equal opportunity in the workforce, middle-class women maintained a sense of class status and power in their abilities to become leaders in the black community and represent the interests of disadvantaged women. Paula Giddings stresses that during the war Delta Sigma Theta sorority members decided to use their leadership abilities to educate workers, to give "advice and guidance" to potential employees, and to use their influence to highlight inequalities to a national audience. National president Mary McLeod Bethune maintained that "'our intellect, our abilities, and our strength must now be used in a supreme effort of giving maximum service to the nation and in preserving those values which make democracy worth fighting for.'"[40]

Gendered volunteer efforts, which included knitting and sewing for the Red Cross, servicing and comforting soldiers in USO facilities, and providing food through canteen services, reinforced the values of domesticity and respectability. Such actions became quite subversive, however, when coupled with the demands for equality that emerged through the discourse of responsible patriotism. African American women threatened to overturn Jim Crow practices by demanding equality in volunteer organizations. In addition, they suggested that African Americans were willing to contest the state at a time of national crisis in order to promote their own interests.

Based on their contributions to the home front, middle-class and working-class African American women took advantage of new wartime rhetoric and structures to redefine themselves as active citizens. Although each group chose to define citizenship in a different way, based on either voluntary or paid work experiences for the state, they maintained a militant fight against inequality on the home front throughout the war. In addition, they maintained claims to citizenship long after the war was over and bolstered their discourse with actions, including staging sit-ins in restaurants and stores and making complaints to unions and the FEPC in order to carry out civil rights programs from 1940 to 1954. These combined actions formed the basis of the modern civil rights movement as women espoused discourse and methods that broke with the more moderate civil rights protest activities of previous eras.

Race, Region, and Citizenship

Race, class, and gender are not the only factors that shape definitions of citizenship. Before the Civil Rights Act of 1964, citizenship for African Americans had varying meanings in the North and the South. This study examines Detroit and Richmond, cities representative of their regions during and immediately following World War II, in order to understand how different structures of racial oppression defined citizenship in each region. In addition, a local study of two representative cities enables an understanding of how the national policies of groups such as sororities, the NCNW, the FEPC, and unions played out in women's locally organized campaigns for equality. Detroit and Richmond shared the characteristics of residential and commercial segregation and a wartime boom based on contracts to preexisting industries, but their racial structures diverged from that point and defined the parameters within which African American women struggled to define the rights of citizenship.

Richmond and Detroit experienced massive in-migration during the 1940s. Between 1940 and 1950, Richmond's black community grew by over 20 percent to a total of 73,087, or approximately 32 percent of the city's total population. Detroit experienced an even greater in-migration of African Americans as a result of the war. Its black population grew 48 percent between 1940 and 1943, and by 1950, 300,506 African Americans—16.2 percent of the city's total population—lived in Detroit.[41] These numbers were significant in both cities because mass mobilization of the black community affected the politics in each.

Richmond and Detroit also enjoyed the presence of powerful chapters of historically black institutions. The Richmond NAACP involved itself in major state litigation, including the equal pay for teachers case that began in Norfolk during World War II. Led by Oliver Hill and other highly competent lawyers, the NAACP in Richmond received national recognition for its efforts. The local chapter boasted an impressive 2,672 members by 1951. Detroit's NAACP assisted Dr. Ossian Sweet, a victim of violence when he bought a home in an all-white neighborhood in 1925. Sweet's brother shot a man participating in a violent mob activity outside the house, and the NAACP defended both his right to protect the house and the family and the right of the Sweets to live in the home. The criminal case was thrown out of court in 1927, which signified a significant victory for the NAACP, the Sweets, and the effort to desegregate neighborhoods. During the 1930s the NAACP became a reluctant supporter of union activities, and by World War II the chapter was the largest in the country, with twelve thousand members. Richmond's Urban League, founded in 1913, and Detroit's Urban League, founded in 1916, both assisted thousands of workers to find jobs. Richmond's chapter also helped establish a neighborhood community house and began a campaign to pressure the city to hire African Americans, 366 of whom had been engaged for various jobs by 1950. Detroit's Urban League–trained workers formed the first recreational program for African American youths, founded a baby clinic that served thousands of babies and mothers a year, established a summer camp program in 1931, started block clean-up units, and helped newcomers to adjust to city life. By the early 1920s the Detroit Urban League was the most prominent institution for African Americans in the city.[42]

In addition to the NAACP and the Urban League, each city had its fair share of local African American women's clubs that were affiliated with national organizations. In 1912 and under the auspices of Maggie Walker, a prominent African American businesswoman, Richmond's local NACW chapter was founded, and Walker and her friend Janie Porter Barrett founded the Industrial School for Girls. Clubwomen from the Woman's League were responsible for founding the first black hospital in Richmond as well. The Detroit NACW chapter, called the Detroit Association of Colored Women's Clubs (DACWC), was established in 1921 to focus on civic reform, provide recreational opportunities to youths, and investigate health issues in Detroit. By 1945 the association had more than seventy-three clubs, three thousand individual members, and had bought a clubhouse to be used for meetings and receptions. African American women also founded the Housewives League of Detroit, which in turn launched the National Housewives League. The organization started in 1930 to support black business owners and to pressure employers to hire black workers. Members used their power as consumers to boycott discriminatory businesses and patronize those that were black-owned; they had also branched out into political work by the 1940s, supporting candidates for office and working to get out the vote. Each city also had active local sorority chapters, including Delta Sigma Theta and Alpha Kappa Alpha.[43]

Similarities between Richmond and Detroit end with a massive influx of African Americans resulting from manpower shortages during the war, residential segregation, and the presence of strong local chapters of historically black institutions. Richmond represented the possibilities a New South city could achieve. Boosters promoted its tobacco and iron foundry industries and boasted about its benign race relations, but their words belied the reality of a strict racial hierarchy enforced daily by rituals of racial etiquette and maintained by segregation laws. Before World War II, Richmond was the most industrialized city in the South, with a growth rate second only to Atlanta, and produced more tobacco products than all North Carolina factories combined. It was also home to several light industrial factories, such as textile and chemical manufacturers and the famous Reynolds Aluminum Company, a corporation that began as a by-product of the tobacco industry. Richmond claimed that its racial tensions were eased by such concessions as an all-black adjunct city council, which basically promoted black business ventures and black voting participation. In reality, however, Richmond was one of the most stratified cities in the South.[44]

Richmond's laws ensured strict racial segregation.[45] African Americans lived in three areas: Jackson Ward, Fulton, and the Seventeenth Street Bottom area. In order to keep them from moving beyond the borders of the black district, the city council studied each block of the city and zoned it black or white by city ordinance, creating institutionalized neighborhood segregation. African Americans felt the brunt of city "improvements" during the Progressive Era, when the city moved its landfills to Jackson Ward. Moreover, the Richmond city council refused to pave or improve neighborhoods in black districts, a problem as well in the black districts of many other southern cities, including Atlanta and Memphis.[46]

During the New Deal, when southern cities like Atlanta prevailed upon the federal government to build low-cost housing projects for African Americans, Richmond leaders could not decide where to put such a project in order to halt black advancement into white neighborhoods. Moreover, black homeowners fought against the destruction of their homes to make way for housing projects, a move that represented class conflict between them and subsidized housing recipients. Finally, in 1941, the city moved hundreds of African Americans from Jackson Ward in order to build Gilpin Court, its first housing project, for black Richmonders. When war rationing threatened the acquisition of materials for the project, however, city officials turned Gilpin Court into a housing project for black war workers. Only twenty-five of the original families moved from their homes qualified for occupancy in the segregated project under this new statute, because most Richmond war production industries refused at this early date to hire African Americans.[47] Residential segregation thus enabled Richmond city leaders to weaken the power of the black vote and maintain the city's racial codes.

Richmond's hierarchy extended beyond residential segregation. Virginia constructed its Jim Crow laws fairly late in the twentieth century. Leaders enacted a ban against interracial marriage in 1924, against integrated seating at all functions in 1926, and against integrated seating in public transportation in 1932.[48] Moreover, Richmond's industries were segregated. Although African American women worked in the tobacco factories, they found themselves located far from white women, both spatially and in terms of their jobs.[49] Black women had the dirtiest, lowest-paying work, including tobacco stemming and hauling. Although Richmond leaders opposed unionization of industries, workers joined unions during the 1930s under the leadership of the American Federation of Labor (AFL). The Tobacco Workers' International Union (TWIU), an AFL affiliate, gained footholds in several factories, including the American Tobacco Company and Larus and Brother. The TWIU maintained strict segregation within its locals by creating black auxiliary locals within each factory. The AFL was widely known for its discriminatory policies, and despite pleas from A. Phillip Randolph and other black leaders it refused to pass antidiscrimination policies during its wartime conferences.[50]

In theory, black Richmonders could change racial practices through the vote; in practice, however, prohibitive poll taxes that accrued yearly with each nonpayment discouraged the majority of the black population from voting. In 1936 only 1,527 African Americans voted in Richmond.[51] Of course, African American women had the hardest time registering to vote because, being employed in domestic work and tobacco factories, they were the lowest-paid group of workers in the city. Even the better-paid middle-class teachers made far less than white teachers in twentieth-century Richmond. Richmond's system of spatial segregation and economic and political oppression constructed narrow parameters in which African American women could create definitions of citizenship and promote equality.

An oppressive racial structure shaped class relations within Richmond's African American community. Elsa Barkley Brown and Gregg Kimball maintain that the structured segregation of neighborhoods placed middle-class professionals in close proximity to poor blacks as well as to illicit, less than respectable amusements in Jackson Ward.[52] The middle class was large. Virginia Union University was one of the most respected black universities in the country, and the number of black businesses in Richmond before World War II was second only to that in Durham. Sororities and social clubs flourished in the middle class but so did poverty and dislocation among the poor. Middle-class clubwomen could not help but see the suffering of many poor African Americans, and their social clubs maintained programs to step in and help where possible. For example, the Order of St. Luke founded by Maggie Walker encouraged poor African Americans to deposit whatever savings they had into St. Luke's black-owned and managed bank. The Urban League and the NAACP worked to help African Americans find jobs, and middle-class women took the lead during World War II in trying to promote job opportunities for working-class women. Although these institutions had tried to help the women secure positions in the past, the majority of opportunities had been in domestic work. The war, however, opened up possibilities for middle-class organizations to help train working-class women for skilled positions in industries.

Both middle- and working-class women in Richmond exhibited a propensity for civil action in promoting equality. The middle-class women fought for the survival of black institutions and the destruction of black codes during the 1930s, and in 1939 the working-class women struck against Liggett and Meyers Tobacco Company alongside white women, received pay raises, and then voted to become part of the Congress of Industrial Organizations (CIO)–affiliated United Cannery, Agricultural, Packing, and Allied Workers of America (UCAPAWA) after the strike.

Middle-class women in general tended to see working-class behavior as proof of an inability to become respectable citizens before World War II, and, in large part, they failed to see problems with employment and pay structures. Clubwomen in Richmond, however, did try on many occasions to address working-class issues, both during and after World War II, but with varying degrees of success. The war made middle-class women understand even better how racial restrictions in the hiring process hurt poor women looking for jobs. Yet they still failed to understand the depths of racism within factories, including problems with unions and unequal pay structures, so they could not sympathize completely with working-class views on work and equal opportunities. Despite the restrictions placed on all African Americans in Richmond, black women became leaders in the struggle for citizenship and equality.[53]

Although Detroit suffered many of the same problems as Richmond, including rampant segregation in public facilities and neighborhoods, the city's African Americans had more opportunities to contest racial hierarchy for a number of reasons. Detroit's neighborhoods were racially constructed, and most African Americans lived in the Paradise Valley area west of the main boulevard, Woodward Avenue. African Americans also moved out toward the periphery of the city as they created suburbs in Conant Gardens, the Eight-Mile/Wyoming area, and the West Side around the Ford River Rouge plant. As in Richmond, New Deal policies hurt black homeowners by classifying black residential areas as unsuitable for home loan aid. In addition, real estate agents and residents colluded to keep African Americans out of all-white neighborhoods with written or implied covenants. The covenants were not enforced by law but by ritual; whites sold only to other whites, and black encroachment was protested. Thomas Sugrue notes that although whites became very violent about African Americans moving to white neighborhoods, and police often remained ambivalent about protecting African Americans who tried to break color barriers, African Americans did move in on many white-dominated blocks, which led to white flight after 1940.[54]

The difference between Richmond and Detroit as far as spatial segregation was concerned revolved around each city's methods of enforcing racial structures. Richmond's city council legalized segregation by constructing and forcibly maintaining blocks for each race. In Detroit, whites informally maintained segregation by ritual, which enabled African Americans to stake claims in white neighborhoods as long as they endured the violent outbreaks and continuous hostility that inevitably followed their actions.

Detroit's African Americans enjoyed more freedom than Richmond's because Michigan did not codify racial structures. While Virginia constructed Jim Crow laws to enforce strict racial structures, for example, Michigan passed the Diggs Civil Rights Law in 1918, which outlawed racial discrimination in public areas. That did not mean African Americans in Detroit enjoyed total freedom from segregation from 1940 to 1954, but it did enable them to challenge de facto segregation in restaurants and other public facilities from a place within the state. The fact that the state had already struck down legal segregation allowed many African Americans to take their claims to equality to court in order for the state to uphold a preexisting law. Moreover, African Americans in Detroit voted with no restrictions, giving them a benefit of citizenship denied to most African Americans in Richmond. Nevertheless, Detroit experienced major problems with segregation and prejudice, which coalesced in 1943 and erupted in a riot during the summer of that year. The city's African Americans did have, however, institutional structures in place that could uphold claims for democracy and legitimize their fight for equality.

Workers in Detroit also had the benefit of the unions and the FEPC in their fights against discrimination. While Richmond had few powerful unions and the AFL practiced blatant discrimination, the UAW, a CIO affiliate, claimed to practice complete integration and representation for its black members. August Meier and Elliot Rudwick point out that the UAW worked hard to recruit African American members, who were reluctant unionists as a result of their loyalty to the employers who hired them and because of the hostility of some union locals to integration. By 1941 the UAW had finally won over the black (and predominantly male) population. Moreover, in 1942 and 1943 Detroit's UAW officials worked with the city's NAACP chapter to recruit black factory workers. The growing presence of both African Americans and women in industry helped African American women gain footholds in the union. In fact, Lillian Hatcher and Gwendolyn Thomas, both black, moved up through the ranks of the union from the factory floor to high positions within the Women's Bureau and later the Fair Practices and Anti-Discrimination Department, playing important roles in investigating many African American women's cases, especially after the war.[55]

Although African Americans often faced hostility from locals when they tried to join or address grievances, national leaders remained committed to racial change. By the 1940s the UAW had passed many nondiscrimination clauses at its conferences. Moreover, the FEPC created a suboffice in Detroit, and the city's mayor founded the Detroit Commission on Community Relations to investigate racial problems. Each of these institutions enabled African Americans to make claims against Detroit's white society from a position within the state. Again, African Americans worked hard to obtain the equality they were promised by the UAW and the FEPC, but the structures that helped them were already in place.

It is important to note that working-class African American women in Detroit faced many of the same impediments as women in Richmond. Nancy Gabin argues that although the UAW might have been sympathetic to the plight of black male workers, it was quite hostile to women workers in the 1930s because it privileged male workers as heads of households who needed union protection for seniority and better benefits. The UAW endorsed discriminatory practices such as gender-typing jobs and maintaining separate seniority lists for men and women. As the UAW realized the need to address the issues of women who had entered the workplace in such large numbers during World War II it became more responsive to the women.[56] They could not break into Detroit industries until they received help from both the FEPC and the unions, and once they did enter war factories they remained spatially segregated and in the worst jobs.[57] They fought to make gains in factories and gained UAW support against hate strikes that erupted when they were upgraded. In this way, black women in Detroit had a better structure in place to support claims to equal work and equal pay. Women in Richmond did not have that structure yet still faced considerably more segregation and discrimination than did black men in the same factories. As Gabin notes, "The effort of black women first to gain access to defense jobs and then to attain the same jobs held by white women earned them a reputation for assertiveness and militancy."[58] Their militancy situated African American women at the forefront of the civil rights campaign in the working class.

Class relations among African Americans were not always tension-free in Detroit. The spatial distance between middle-class and poor neighborhoods led to ideological distance on many issues. That distance resulted, in part, from the historic alliance middle-class blacks sought with white elites, which caused them to ignore many issues important to the working-class community.[59] For example, black ministers, the Urban League, and the NAACP had originally fought against the entrance of black workers into unions. Meier and Rudwick suggest that the UAW threatened the close relationship black leaders had with employers at Ford and other factories by criticizing management policies although the leaders finally did embrace the union when it proved loyal to black workers during the 1941 Ford strike.[60] In addition, Sugrue finds that the middle class actually joined whites in protesting construction of the Sojourner Truth housing projects, and then the entry of African Americans into them, because the movement of low-income blacks to Conant Gardens threatened black property values.[61]

Such evidence does not mean that the middle and working classes engaged constantly in an antagonistic relationship, but it does suggest that the classes were not as likely to work together closely for change. In fact, working-class African American women had to fight for the NAACP and the Urban League to recognize their problems during and immediately following World War II. At the same time, middle-class African American women often misunderstood working-class culture as pathological, which led them to ignore some of the economic problems women faced. Still, like the middle-class women in Richmond, Detroit's clubwomen tried to connect on some level with working-class women from 1940 to 1954, and, as in Richmond, they met with varying degrees of success.

Although class relations were not smooth in Detroit, race relations became increasingly worse during 1942 and 1943. The city's racial tensions erupted on June 20, 1943, in a four-day-long riot that left thirty-four people dead and at least 765 injured. Trouble had been brewing for some time, and incidents like the 1942 Sojourner Truth housing struggle and the hate strikes in 1943 at the Highland Park Packard plant exacerbated racial tensions in a city in which everyone struggled to claim space. On the day of the riot the temperature reached ninety degrees, and numerous incidents had broken out among black and white youths fighting over space in the city's largest recreational park, Belle Isle. That night, they fought on the bridge while leaving the island, an incident that sparked widespread rioting as rumors spread that an African American woman and her baby had been tossed off the bridge. The city fell into chaos as white mobs attacked African Americans on the street and African Americans vandalized and looted neighborhood stores. By June 22, Roosevelt sent in 1,900 troops and military police, and two thousand Michigan state troops occupied the city. By June 23, 2,416 more troops entered the city and slowly restored peace, although curfew restrictions were not lifted until June 28. The riot caused $2 million in property damage, cost wartime

industries a million hours in lost labor, and cost another $115,000 per day for
the federal troops. Police arrested over two thousand people, the majority of
them black men. Of the thirty-four people who died, twenty-five were black.
Although authorities blamed the riots on hoodlums of both races, particularly the Ku Klux Klan, "hillbillies," newcomers, and "5th Column activists"
trying to halt the war effort, studies suggest that most rioters were Detroit
residents. African Americans tended to riot in order to express anger at being left out of war industries and decent housing, and white ethnic groups
rioted because they feared the encroachment of African Americans into the
neighborhoods and industries they had dominated for decades. Although
Detroit did not have as many legal impediments to equality as Richmond, it
was wracked by the same kind of racial problems.[62]

The participation of African American women in the riots affected Detroit's middle-class clubwomen because it encouraged them to sponsor more
programs for underprivileged women. The women who participated in the
riot tended to be single. The median age of female rioters was 24.5 years old,
and although 69 percent of the women were employed, 43 percent of those
had jobs in service and domestic work. Clearly, many had found that their
opportunities for employment lagged behind those of black men and white
women. More than half the women committed felonies, because they were
charged with stealing from stores within their neighborhoods. Others found
themselves charged with carrying concealed weapons in order to defend
themselves when they went out on the streets.[63]

The different racial structures of Richmond and Detroit affected how African American women in particular shaped concepts of citizenship from
1940 to 1954. By running USO and Red Cross programs in both cities, wom-
en provided leadership for the gendered volunteer work that supported the
Double V movement and the discourse of responsible patriotism. In Richmond and Detroit, working-class women had to fight harder than men to
gain entry into lucrative war jobs, enabling them to become the militant
vanguard for working-class rights. Each city had strong NCNW and sorority chapters. Richmond women had to define citizenship as the achievement
of rights denied them by the city and state government, whereas Detroit
women fought for the implementation of the rights of citizenship already
granted to them by the government but not enacted by the larger, dominant
society. The fact that they had to fight to obtain rights already granted by the
state reinforces the point that the state is a center of competing power relations and not necessarily dominant in the face of popular dissent against its
laws.

In addition, northern states set more barriers to integration than their laws suggest, either by inability or unwillingness to enforce laws that would up-end cultural norms of segregation. Each city had unions for its major industry and the federal FEPC to help working-class women, but women in Richmond had to work within a segregated union environment in which black work-ers' concerns remained an afterthought. Detroit women found the UAW much more open to their concerns about equality. The FEPC did not main-tain an office in Richmond, and investigators there seemed reluctant to up-end the racial segregation that characterized the city. The FEPC in Detroit, however, took many complaints from African American women and helped them negotiate for the right to work. In Richmond, women defined citizen-ship as the achievement of equality and the gaining of rights owed to them but denied by government structures. In Detroit, women defined citizenship as the overturning of social structures through the enactment of state legis-lation already in place but weakened by employer practices and societal rit-uals and norms constructed to maintain de facto segregation.

African American women provided the leadership, the community net-works, and the template for activism that influenced the civil rights move-ment of the 1950s and 1960s. Although Charles Payne locates black women's activism primarily in their organizing efforts, Belinda Robnett suggests that they acted as formal leaders and "bridge leaders," local leaders who brought their communities into networks of activism. She observes that "women's power was largely derived from autonomous pioneering activities," like their sorority, church, and community club efforts.[64] Robnett, Paula Giddings, and others locate the abilities of black women to create, mobilize, and operate networks as critical to civil rights efforts. Moreover, because women took up leadership positions on the home front they formed the front lines of activ-ism at this time.

National leaders such as Ferebee and Bethune redefined citizenship in a way that placed women in a critical position to negotiate with the state. Lo-cal leaders supported unions and canvassed for voting registration and NAACP memberships. According to Harvard Sitkoff, it was a woman who suggested the march on Washington movement, which Randolph then sup-ported with his large organization.[65] Working-class women also became very active in promoting equality of opportunity through their work with the FEPC and the unions and by resisting oppressive racial constructs at the hir-ing gates and within the factories. They used individual resistance, commu-nity networks of resistance, state agencies, and historically black institutions to further their goals of equality. Given the activities of women in the 1940s and early 1950s, it is necessary to place them at the forefront of civil rights efforts in this period and acknowledge that their efforts launched the more militant phase of the civil rights movement.

African American Women, Citizenship, and Civil Rights

This study reassesses both the role of African American women in the civil rights movement and the impact of World War II on African American women's discourse and activism. Although women had been active in promoting civil rights before World War II, the urgency of the war situation enabled women of all socioeconomic stratas to adjust their language and activist strategies and move from asking for their rights to demanding those rights. Although the war opened possibilities for all women, most women's historians posit that, ultimately, white women did not profit from gains made during the war because national agencies refused to define them as anything but wives and mothers. Their short-term gains in industry led to pink-collar, lower-paying jobs in the postwar world. For African American women, however, the war provided the opportunity to take the civil rights movement to a new, more militant level. Although they largely did not profit from the fact that industries were opening to women, they claimed citizenship based on real and potential contributions to the war. Moreover, they backed their claims with lawsuits, sit-ins, and other demonstrations of significant activism. In some cases, women helped alter the racial hierarchies in their cities. Although the white community often failed to recognize the activities of these women, their efforts tremendously affected the black community.[66]

From 1940 to 1954 African American women provided strong leadership in the fight for citizenship and civil rights, continuing their struggles from decades past into a new wartime environment that expanded the possibilities for definitions of citizenship. Middle-class women had networks in place and national organizations that created the discourse of responsible patriotism and backed their language with programming designed to challenge inequalities in volunteer and paid work as well as in electoral politics and in public accommodations. Local club chapters used this discourse and enacted programming that challenged the racial structures of their cities.

Working-class women continued fighting for better work and better pay, taking advantage of whatever manpower shortages they could and using institutional structures such as the NAACP, the unions, and the FEPC to support claims to citizenship. They also fought for better working conditions, improved living conditions, and state and private entitlements. Their definition of citizenship focused on job opportunities, factory desegregation, and better benefits for themselves and their families, including child care, decent housing, and cash payments for crisis situations.

African American women of all socioeconomic classes in Richmond and Detroit formed a base of activism by maintaining civil rights activities and negotiating for more freedom in their own lives. Because they were the leaders in their community networks and in labor struggles, African American women stood at the vanguard of the modern civil rights movement from 1940 to 1954.

1. Engaging with the State: Middle-Class Women and Responsible Patriotism, 1940–45

In a 1941 address to her Alpha Kappa Alpha (AKA) sorority sisters, President Dorothy Boulding Ferebee urged black women to promote civil rights. She maintained that their most important contribution to home-front defense was "the all-out effort to make America know that we as American citizens want to taste democracy for ourselves while we are making it safe for all. We want to know and feel that real democracy means human freedom, unqualified and unshackled."[1] She also emphasized that African American women were important to the creation of positive race relations because they were prime participants in home-front defense. "Negro women," she observed, "have a unique opportunity to participate in this education of America by utilizing every moment to gain information to become broad and articulate, and actively insistent on the correction of this travesty on democracy."[2] Ferebee warned, however, that merely pointing out inequalities failed to advance adequate change in the new Double V movement. Women had to enroll in home-front organizations like the Office of Civilian Defense (OCD), work for better living conditions for other African Americans, and help the black community attain equality.

Ferebee and other African American women leaders created a new phase in the civil rights movement. They used war discourse—the goal of the war was to save democracy, and all citizens had to be involved in winning—to claim rights as political citizens in a free democracy. African American women's groups had already begun to move toward employing a discourse of citizenship during the 1920s and 1930s, but the urgency of winning World War II enabled middle-class women to give the discourse a sense of immediacy and power that was unavailable to them before 1940.

The Roosevelt administration's specific call for women to participate in the war, both in industrial and voluntary capacities, enabled black women's organizations to engage actively with the state in negotiating new freedoms. As they formed a vital part of home-front defense strategies and made themselves invaluable to the government, African American women simultaneously demanded concrete equal rights, such as the power to vote, the opportunity to take better-paying jobs, and the right to have a voice in the government as contributors to the wartime state. Middle-class African American women worked as volunteers for home-front defense, as civil rights activists, as teachers and social workers, and as advocates for the working class in order to achieve "uplift" within their communities and equality in American society.

Traditionally a haven for middle-class women, the organizations stood continuously at the forefront of equal rights movements. Before World War II, middle-class black women had asked for equal rights by focusing on their position as respectable Christians who were just as morally upstanding as middle-class white women. From 1880 to 1920, African American women promoted equal rights, suffrage, antilynching, and resistance to oppression. The identities they created within the black church reflected a belief that respectability would convince whites of their ability to be first-class citizens. The women tried to convince poor African Americans that traditional Victorian morality, such as temperance and thrift as well as a notion of sexual propriety based on middle-class white standards, would gain them rights.[3] At the same time, black female writers and intellectuals used ideologies that the dominant culture normally associated with the white middle class in order to create oppositional discourses and gain autonomy in the creation of the NACW and other uplift-oriented groups.[4]

The politics of respectability highlighted middle-class African American women's class consciousness. Believing that they had the money, the education, and the correct moral upbringing as Christian women and mothers to head the equal rights movement, they considered themselves as natural leaders of community uplift. They also thought their leadership abilities and moral values would enable them to meet more easily with middle-class white women in order to promote better race relations.

Although the discourse of respectability based claims for equality on African American women's behavior, it had no way to define their citizenship beyond working for the African American community. The National Council of Negro Women (NCNW) developed a language of universal citizenship in the 1920s and 1930s and made it concrete during the 1940s. The language gave black women a chance to focus on the responsibility of women and work both as patriots for the country and as warriors for equality. Black women did not abandon the traditional discourse of respectability; rather, they reshaped it in order to give it a political immediacy that it did not have before 1940.

Middle-class women still believed in the power of moral suasion, but they shifted their focus from Christian sexual purity to political responsibility toward a war-mobilized state. Rather than argue that they deserved equality based on their womanhood, the women insisted that their gendered war contributions as volunteers for the state gave them the right to full citizenship. This marked a new phase in the civil rights movement as African American women entered into direct negotiations with the state over meanings of citizenship.

Ferebee defined a new discourse of "responsible patriotism" as she addressed fellow members:

> We recognize Democracy as the way of life which offers to us, as to all mankind, the greatest vehicle for human freedom. . . . We have prepared ourselves to make contributions to our civilization comparable to those of any group, and we hold as a fundamental principle that these contributions must not be thrust aside because we are women or because we are Negroes. And we as women, must aid Democracy in casting off its defects. Of course, we know that realistically we cannot expect overnight transformations—but never has there been a time in our history when there has been a greater need for the renovation of our institutions, nor a time when it was more important that we strive to salvage the good in them in rejecting their evils, nor when these things required accomplishment with greater dispatch.[5]

Ferebee was identifying women as critical to the movement for equality because they were the guardians of society. Her demand for government compensation in the form of full citizenship for volunteer work suggests that middle-class women understood the power in their unpaid labor.

War gave a strong sense of immediacy to the struggle for civil rights. Women emphasized that for democracy to be successful abroad it must be instituted quickly at home; a disunited home front would never help to win a war for freedom. The discourse of responsible patriotism involved several different demands. First, middle-class black women fought for the simple right to volunteer for home-front organizations. They promoted the power of womanhood and traditional reproductive labor as they cared for soldiers and U.S. citizens. Once they had proved that their unpaid labor was indispensable to prosecuting the war, black women fought hard for political, social, and economic equality. While they worked for the Red Cross and USO, they enrolled

NAACP members, helped instill the values of citizenship in children, and challenged government and industries to desegregate vital war jobs.

The discourse of responsible patriotism placed the onus on middle-class black women to demand equality immediately because they were educated and historically leadership-oriented. Adherents to the new discourse believed in the power of black womanhood to command respect. Black clubwomen would no longer appear to the state as supplicants but as active participants in a war for democracy on the home front, expecting the government to answer their calls for equality. Because they were essential to the fabric of their communities, they believed, they were also essential to the functioning of the wartime state. Their contributions as women volunteers enabled the government to maintain a home-front defense. Mary McLeod Bethune, president of the NCNW and Delta Sigma Theta, contended that "America is our home. We have fought for her in every battle, we have worked for her, we are willing to walk the last mile in defending her."[6] As patriots, African American women leaders maintained, they recognized their duty to make certain that democracy functioned at home. Bertha Black, president of Sigma Gamma Rho Sorority, suggested, "Let us fight with our country. May we not lose an opportunity to correct the injustices that are heaped upon us. Let us not wait until the war is over."[7] Fighting the war and fighting for immediate social and political equality became inextricably intertwined in the discourse of responsible patriotism. In fact, such discourse demanded that middle-class women, as patriots, fight to gain the rights denied their community.

"Responsible patriots" kept many tenets of the earlier focus on respectability intact, especially those involving the power of womanhood to change the course of history. African American women believed that their morality could command respect and that they should continue to situate themselves at the forefront of the equal rights movement. As Marjorie MacKenzie, a Washington, D.C., lawyer, told a convention of NCNW members, "Colored women, particularly, need to work toward the post war goal of a single standard democracy. . . . A task which confronts all colored women is to obliterate the idea among white people that colored people need to prove themselves. . . . We are not on probation in the human race . . . and colored women should constantly be on guard to offset the insidious sabotage of our best efforts based on the prevailing idea that as a group we are lazy, unreliable, and stupid."[8]

In a sense, MacKenzie rejected the old notion of respectability. She maintained that the black community did not need to perform for the government in order to secure its rights; rather, rights were owed to African Americans. Still, she recognized that middle-class women had to combat the white community's negative construction of blacks, which meant that black women would still need to be respectable and responsible in order to display power.

The wartime appeal also borrowed ideas about class privilege from the traditional discourse of respectability. In fact, the language of responsible patriotism could not extricate itself from certain aspects of the Victorian discourse. Clubwomen were self-described middle-class activists. They believed that membership in sororities, exclusive clubs, and certain church affiliations signified membership in the middle class. Moreover, they suggested that homemaker status or certain college-required professions revealed evidence of a woman's middle-class lifestyle. YWCA Business and Professional Girls' Clubs, for example, only allowed teachers, stenographers, librarians, and social workers into their circles. All other professions fell under the Industrial Girls' Clubs.[9] "As women who are privileged beyond the average of our race, we have responsibilities," middle-class African American women asserted.[10] Moreover, they considered themselves specially appointed to deal with the problems of their race, believing that they had superior minds and enhanced status in the community. Bethune told Deltas at a sorority conference, "You sorors are in positions of leadership. You have trained minds and splendid abilities."[11]

Middle-class women also acknowledged that not everyone could be accorded their status, and, consequently, they understood that their status enabled them to help poor black women. "Do not be satisfied with your own success," Bethune warned the Deltas, "but go out into the highways and byways where your less fortunate sisters reside, and endeavor to show them the light and lift them up . . . to continue this fight of making democracy share its privileges and opportunities, as well as hardships, with all persons living under this democratic form of government."[12]

Sometimes, middle-class women struggled with the paradox of speaking out for democracy from organizations that excluded vast numbers of poor African Americans. Often, these black women would try to justify their position in society as leaders. After all, when they were able to raise their own status, the entire black community would benefit. Beulah Whitby, Detroit's Wartime Welfare commissioner, secretary of Detroit's Interracial Commission, and national AKA president, conceded that sororities historically had promoted stringent standards of conduct and made them part of middle- and upper-class culture. She pointed out, however, that AKA had always been socially conscious and had its own scholarship program, cultural contributions, Mississippi Health Project, and Non-Partisan Council. She asked members at a national convention, "Are we willing to give up our C+ and B average requirements, and our rigid black-balling based on whether a candidate conformed to middle and upper class standards?"[13] The answer was an un-equivocal no.

Whitby herself was very much a part of the middle-class elite communi-ty. Born in Richmond, she attended Oberlin College and graduated in 1926 with a degree in sociology. She moved to Detroit, where she joined the po-lice force for a short time before becoming a caseworker for the Detroit Public Welfare Office in 1931. Whitby created a domestic-training class for girls thir-teen to seventeen whose families received welfare, a project that reveals her understanding of where this group would later obtain jobs. Whitby soon became director of DPW's Alfred District, where she oversaw a staff of eighty, including fourteen African American women. In 1942 she became executive secretary of the city's Office of Civilian Defense, and she served as the assis-tant director on the Mayor's Interracial Committee after 1944. In 1944 she became an instructor of social work at Wayne University. Whitby's stature in the Detroit community launched her into national roles, and she served as the national president of AKA from 1942 to 1944.[14]

Although Whitby's efforts clearly served the poor African Americans of Detroit, her class bias was revealed when she was asked during an interview whether the leadership of black organizations was only interested in the middle class. "It was very necessary that the leadership should come from trained people," she replied. "In response to the feeling that many people used to have that in the middle class when a person got educated . . . he forgot about the common people. . . . if it had not been for these people who had some advantages of training being willing to give of themselves in leadership, I think that the Negro group as a whole would be in a much worse position."[15]

Volunteer Work

As volunteers, middle-class women provided the force behind the civil rights movement because they claimed compensation from the state for their un-paid labor. Advocates of the discourse of responsible patriotism believed that volunteer work on the home front would be the key to African American women's entry into negotiations with the state over civil rights. Once the women insisted on being included in patriotic efforts to fight the war, the wartime state would have to listen to their demands for equality on all fronts. Bethune urged Deltas to push hard for the right to volunteer on the home front: "'We must insist that we be given the opportunity to serve, to use our talents and abilities to the utmost during the time when the national welfare requires sacrifice from all of its citizens.'"[16]

As contributors to the war, African American women understood the necessity of demanding equal treatment, especially in the right to volunteer to help the country win the war. Antoinette Bowler, a member of Zeta Phi Beta and the Second African Baptist Church, president of Richmond's NCNW, a lifelong Richmond resident, and a Virginia Union University graduate, wrote to the NCNW that "much has been in the papers requiring volunteer service on the part of women. We have failed to see where Negro women have been asked to participate. We accepted that as our first issue to work on."[17] By 1942 Bowler served as head of the senior hostesses group, or head chaperone, of Richmond's new black USO.

Women of all classes participated in volunteer services, but clubwomen believed it to be their special, primary duty to make an impact on society in this way. Many had time to devote to volunteer services because they were homemakers or teachers; they also believed that their prominence in the black community made them more visible to whites as they performed their patriotic duties. "To support the War Effort becomes a responsibility of major importance to us," Whitby wrote to sorority sisters. "This would include the Bond-Stamp Programs, Drives, and Rallies, the USO programs, the varied Red Cross activities, Canteen Service. . . . Alpha Kappa Alpha with the hundreds in its ranks equipped to render a vigorous leadership should lead the attack on the Home Front for a complete victory. We must be a vital, contributing part of every fight in every local community where Negroes are attacking those things which destroy true democracy."[18]

Clubwomen across the country responded to their leaders' calls. In 1941 Richmond's African American women registered in large numbers to volunteer for knitting, sewing, library and canteen work, motor corps duty, dramatics with various defense agencies, and as casework assistants.[19] In 1943, with Whitby as director, Detroit's African American women created the Women's Agency for National Defense (WAND) through the auspices of the NCNW. Bethune was the "general" of the organization, and although it was open to women of all races it existed to counter discriminatory practices in volunteer groups throughout the country. The NCNW claimed that "the WANDS will serve a great need, and especially in areas where our women are not permitted to serve through other existing agencies."[20] It worked to force openings in other organizations by giving black women experience in voluntary home-front activities. The WAND program was modeled after the OCD and Red Cross, right down to a "snappy uniform with insignia for members who have earned them by rendering some volunteer service in the war program."[21]

African American clubwomen involved themselves in many activities to support the war. Raising money for and purchasing bonds and war stamps tied them to the state. Their fund-raising work made them indispensable to the prosecution of the $3 billion war, and they were aware of the important nature of the work. Nationally, sororities and clubs spent thousands on war bonds. In 1942 Zeta Phi Betas in the mid-Atlantic region purchased $4,000 in stamps and bonds to add to the large contributions of other regions at their annual convention. The Order of the Eastern Star pledged to buy $10,000 in war stamps and bonds by 1942, and AKA and Delta each invested $25,000 in war bonds by 1943. Local chapters worked hard to buy bonds as well. Deltas in Detroit raised enough to buy a $500 war bond, and the Women's Benevolent Club in Richmond purchased a $1,000 bond.[22]

Although investing in bonds was an important activity for club members, African American women also provided the bulk of labor in the black community for war bond sales. After honing their fund-raising skills for scholarships, church building, and community uplift efforts, African American women had community networks in place as they turned to support government efforts. Raising money for war bonds was merely an extension of their previous uplift efforts, although the benefits were directed toward waging war.

As early as 1940, Mrs. W. H. Hughes, Henrietta Segear, and Marion Bell commandeered Maggie Walker High School in Richmond as their headquarters for a massive fund-raising effort for the Red Cross Colored Division for War Relief. They set up booths in theaters and other public places and raised thousands for humanitarian aid. Richmond's AKA chapters led one of the most successful and creative war bond drives in the history of the city's seven war loan drives. During the Third War Bond Rally in 1943 the AKAs held a jamboree to kick off the drive. They had picnics and sold stamps and bonds from booths in black neighborhoods. They then sponsored an event at Skateland Roller Rink featuring skits and talent shows by servicemen and music provided by the Ninth Regiment Band. Admission was, of course, the purchase of stamps. By the end of the drive just two weeks later, the thirty-nine members of AKA were able to double their expected projections by selling $10,000 worth of bonds and stamps.[23]

Clubwomen in Detroit also raised funds for the war. The Molly Pitcher Club, for example, entered the patriotic spirit by dressing in colonial costumes and staging a contest on "Molly Pitcher Day." The fifteen club members, in full Molly Pitcher dress, took to the streets to collect war bond money. By the end of the campaign they had raised more than $20,000. In 1944 members of the St. John CME Gallant Club staged a valiant effort to sell bonds and stamps. Alberta Campbell received a certificate for selling $11,625 in bonds and $3,472 in stamps single-handedly; others in the group sold $7,650 in bonds and $33.75 in stamps.[24]

The women's assistance in bond drives had important implications. As if they were holding stock in a company, they were buying stock in the government and could argue that they deserved a voice in the way that government "conducted business" or created policies. African American clubwomen proved themselves indispensable in raising money very quickly for the costly war. They raised the stakes of citizenship by providing a direct link between the black community's money and the government's financial needs.

The women also provided service work for the Red Cross and the OCD as part of implementing a responsible patriotism program. Although it harbored traditional roots, their work signified implementation of the radical program called for by national club leaders. Knitting and sewing, rolling bandages, and participating in first aid and home nursing classes meshed nicely with clubwomen's ideology of respectability in that such work upheld the normative gender role of woman as comforter and caretaker. Although not every woman working in voluntary services was middle class, the bulk of those who provided these critical services were homemakers or teachers because becoming certified in the classes necessary to participate in the programs was time-consuming and often costly. As editor Frances Leonard explained, "They are doing their bit cheerfully, quietly, unostensibly, but albeit with real courage and merit. . . . They are the home front morale boosters . . . the knitters, the homemakers, . . . the element that helps to maintain some semblance of normalcy in this upside down chaotic world."[25]

Taken in context with African American women leaders' calls to participate in order to prove their patriotism and thus legitimize demands for equality during the war, these actions formed part of a subversive program. Although the activities were awash in traditional constructions of respectability, the fact that middle-class women participated in state activities and criticized state policies was radical given that the government expected full participation in the war but no criticism of the country's social or economic structures.

Although many clubwomen merely attended official units that the Red Cross had set up in Richmond and Detroit, others easily translated knitting and sewing units into social activities. Throughout the war, for example, Richmond women met at the Community House to sew garments for war relief, and by 1942 several were taking knitting classes so they could send sweaters overseas. The work was voluntary, and all women were accepted into the group. The time of meeting, however—from 11 A.M. to 3 P.M. on Thursdays—dictated that most working women could not attend. From June to September 1942, thirteen women formed the core group of regulars, and others dropped in periodically to help. AKAs volunteered to roll bandages as a group project at St. Phillip's Hospital, to be used both on-site and in the war. In Detroit, members of the American Beauty Social Club held potluck dinners while they sewed dresses and other garments in their homes throughout the war, and the Lucy Thurman YWCA held sewing classes for both war relief garments and for "emphasis on remodeling and restyling for wartime economy."[26] Women in the class must have been both stylish and popular with the rationing board.

The Red Cross considered home hygiene, first aid, and volunteer nursing courses to be women's work, and each proved vital to the war effort. African American women took advantage of classes to train themselves to make the home front a safer place and define themselves as a vital link in the national defense chain, especially in the face of a severe shortage of medical personnel caused by war recruitment. As with knitting and sewing units, classes were technically available to all women, but the facts that most courses ran four to six weeks and all volunteers had to pay for their own uniforms prohibited many poorer women from joining. A volunteer nurses' aide course in Richmond, for example, required a high school education, taking a six-month course, and $30 for a registration fee on top of the purchase of books and uniforms.[27] Not only was the cost high by 1943 standards, but time and educational requirements also aimed at attracting a middle-class group of women.

African American women in both Richmond and Detroit volunteered in great numbers for Red Cross classes during the war. In 1941 seventy-six quickly filled the first home hygiene course offered for Richmond's black community. One month later, twenty-seven women qualified as home nurses and waited to be called for defense service after passing the course at the recreational center. Nursing proved so popular that Richmond's Phillis Wheatley YWCA sponsored another class in 1942 in which thirty-nine women prepared for "possible emergency service."[28] Classes in Richmond ran continuously throughout the war; the last group of seven home nurses graduated in 1945.[29]

First aid and nursing were equally popular in Detroit, where twenty-nine women spent twenty hours learning CPR, first aid, and how to set broken bones in order to become members of the Red Cross Hospital and Receiving Corps. In 1942 alone, twenty-one received advanced first aid, and seventy-five received standard first aid certificates.[30] When the Red Cross set up two home nursing "schools" for Detroit's women, especially for "homemakers who are anxious to do the best possible job of taking care of their families,"

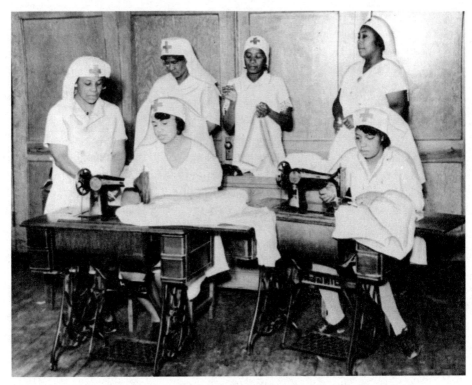

African American women promoted "responsible patriotism" as they worked for the Red Cross during the war. (Courtesy of the Valentine Richmond History Center)

sixty enrolled immediately.[31] Apparently hoping to care for their own families, the Order of the Eastern Star organized a class for members in 1944.[32]

Nutrition classes also formed an important aspect of wartime service. By participating in the government's nutrition awareness campaigns, African American clubwomen showed how they, as homemakers, were critical to the rationing effort. Moreover, by sponsoring nutrition seminars, clubwomen could display themselves publicly as skilled mothers and homemakers as they attempted to "uplift" poorer women and teach them to prepare nutritious foods on a budget.

Clubwomen in both Richmond and Detroit participated in sponsoring nutrition programs in neighborhoods throughout each city. AKAs in Richmond sponsored several nutrition awareness programs in Jackson Ward, a historically black district with many low-income residents. They started by practicing good nutrition during their own meetings and then made presentations to local schools. They also furnished prizes for the best essays on nutrition from each school. Zenobia Gilpin, AKA president, chaired a local committee that sponsored a federal nutrition program in Jackson Ward. She helped organize such courses as "Meats for Victory Meals," in which teachers discussed how to prepare what middle-class women considered a decent dinner on a limited budget that included as much meat as a homemaker could obtain from the rationing board. Others directed efforts toward the Fulton district, another neighborhood that housed many low-income African American families. In cooperation with the Federal Security Administration, the YWCA organized nutrition classes at the neighborhood's Bethlehem Center, and eighteen women enrolled for the first class. Moreover, the Fulton Garden Club and Mother's Club of Bethlehem Center sponsored a series of lectures and canning demonstrations throughout the summer of 1943.[33]

Detroiters did not sponsor as many nutrition and canning classes as Richmond, perhaps because the city was not bordered by farms and did not have the residential space to grow gardens. Still, clubwomen sought to enlighten the community about healthy eating during the war. The Adult Group of the Lucy Thurman YWCA showed films on "nutrition and the war" in 1943 to help teach better nutrition to teenagers, and the Detroit Association of Women's Clubs provided nutrition classes throughout the war at its clubhouse. Later, five African American nutrition instructors gave six-week courses in food conservation at canning centers across the city.[34]

In addition to providing information about nutrition, several groups in Richmond and Detroit focused on how to explain the ration board's often-confusing guidelines in order to make sure that women received their fair share of items. Richmond's Association of Ministers' Wives sponsored a talk by a rationing specialist with the Office of Price Administration (OPA) who traveled to black neighborhood centers across the city in order to explain point rationing and meat pricing. The Housewives League of Detroit trained women to use rationing stamps, taught OPA regulations, and sponsored consumer education classes throughout the war, both at their headquarters and at neighborhood centers citywide.[35]

Although clubwomen attempted to spread the government's message that conservation and good nutrition could win the war, evidence suggests that the training and demonstrations had a class element. By sponsoring rationing and nutrition courses, African American clubwomen told poorer women how to best prepare food. The implication was that the student-prepared meals appeared inadequate to middle-class observers. By teaching cooking skills to working-class women, clubwomen were also proving their knowledge of homemaking and skill at its tasks, a central feature of earlier uplift programs.

Learning first aid, nursing, and sponsoring nutrition awareness and rationing sessions all reflected clubwomen's belief in responsible patriotism, but serving African American troops formed the linchpin of their efforts. By sponsoring canteens, USO dances, and care packages for soldiers, African American clubwomen provided essential unpaid labor, feeding and housing the troops as well as maintaining morale. Moreover, by volunteering in the segregated and often highly inadequate black USO and OCD facilities, they emphasized the effects of segregation on troop and civilian morale while they demanded equality for the black community. In 1941, for example, Jeanetta Welch Brown, the AKA's legal representative to its lobbying committee, the Non-Partisan Council, wrote to the director of the Joint Committee of Army and Navy Boards that six hundred black soldiers had no facilities for recreation at a Texas base. White soldiers, however, had an air-conditioned recreation hall, paid senior hostesses, a movie theater, and a library. Brown emphasized that "our organization is intensely interested in seeing that Negro soldiers are accorded adequate recreational facilities. . . . It is also only fair that equal recreational facilities should be provided for Negro and white soldiers alike."[36]

In addition, African American women could express disgust at the often shoddy treatment they received from national and local USO and Red Cross personnel. Nowhere is that more apparent than in a memo from local Richmond USO Colored Division Director Ada Burroughs: "Red Cross of Richmond refused to convey Negro hostesses to McGuire [hospital] although taking white hostesses. After many conferences between special services and them, the Henrico County Red Cross consented to transport them once a week, eight hostesses to McGuire in a small station wagon. . . . Red Cross needs Christianity."[37]

African American women found themselves not only providing all unpaid labor for the USO Colored Division staff but also finding money to provide facilities for the soldiers. However frustrating it was, helping with the USO provided a real center of power by enabling black women to provide important infrastructure for housing and entertaining millions of troops. Because the USO and Red Cross considered black troop morale an afterthought in their recreation programs, the women raised money to start troop centers in their own cities. The government was well aware of their work, which provided a strong negotiating point for responsible patriots. Richmond women managed to secure $30,000 from the Federal Works Agency to upgrade dormitory facilities for soldiers in that city, because a typical weekend saw more than a hundred turned away from the 150-cot OCD center. The black community raised another $5,000 to add gymnasiums and showers to the center. Detroit clubwomen enabled the expansion of both the city's main center, the John R. USO, as well as USO rooms at surrounding army bases. The Deltas gave $100, and Hester Wilson gave $250, for upgrading the USO, while the Goginnette Social Club sponsored a bridge party to raise $275 for a club room at Fort Brady. Other women's clubs raised $1,200 for Fort Brady rooms. A national consultant for the USO praised the Detroit volunteers' ability to raise their own funds and "plan and execute" programs in accordance with the national USO's wishes.[38]

While Detroit's black community raised enough money and received enough funding from the national USO to create a separate USO structure for troops, Richmond had to house its USO centers in the YMCA and at an old high school. The city council's unwillingness to construct new facilities for black troops suggests the pervasiveness of segregation, under which blacks had to deal with receiving castoffs from the white community or make do with inferior facilities. In this context, the service work of women for the USO became even more important as they struggled to bridge gaps between inadequate funding and entertaining thousands of troops.

Although the importance of serving the troops was stressed, there was no getting around the fact that having eighteen- to twenty-year-old unmarried women provide entertainment made some tenets of "respectability" questionable. Clubwomen stressed the patriotic duty provided by these young women, but the fact remained that USO and OCD junior hostesses literally provided their bodies for men's pleasure at dances and parties. The national USO staff, for example, praised Richmond Girl Service Organization (GSO) members "for the service they have rendered the agency, which is devoted to providing comforts for service men."[39]

Senior hostesses proved very cautious chaperones who monitored just how much "comfort" GSO members provided, but the sexual undercurrent of having teenagers dancing with the troops could not be ignored. Richmond's USO actually held a "Kiss Dance," during which servicemen were invited to dance with hostesses and promised a kiss at the end of each dance. At the close of each, hostesses gave the men Hershey's kisses; later in the evening, however, a lottery determined which lucky soldier could get a kiss from his choice of hostesses lined up for his pleasure. The soldier chose to kiss a senior hostess whose husband was overseas in the war.[40]

Both Richmond and Detroit's USOs put junior hostesses' bodies on display with numerous contests in which "popularity and beauty were qualifications for queenhood."[41] Detroit's USO went so far as to mail pin-up pictures of young women to soldiers in camps. Recipients were to judge a winner based on "beauty, charm, and shapeliness."[42] One cannot help but wonder how accurately soldiers could judge young women's "charm" by merely viewing their pictures.

Moreover, because the dominant society constructed black women as sexually available, the discourse surrounding the young women's service work played into a normative societal definition that African American women had tried hard to dislodge from cultural consciousness. Sociologists, scientists, and military experts all busied themselves with protecting the virtue of young women who worked (and played) with soldiers, and they tried to devise ways to surveil the girls' activities. Serious concerns over the perceived delinquencies of young women led to government interventions to stop the spread of venereal disease. The government saw "victory girls," those who slept with the troops out of a misconceived notion of patriotism, as damaging to the war effort, and many were jailed who violated normative standards of conduct either by staying out late or consorting with soldiers. Given the era's attention to white women's activities, it is understandable that black women would be particularly concerned with maintaining the "respectability" of the young women in their community.[43]

The women used a discourse of conventional respectability in order to solve this sticky problem. Their first solution was to publicize the strong moral character and purity of the junior hostesses. Senior hostesses chose GSO members based on stringent qualifications, almost as if they were conducting a sorority rush. In fact, women in both the senior and junior hostess divisions had to apply for membership, which the incumbent group then decided to accept or reject.[44] A reporter for the *Detroit Tribune* concluded, "We learned in our visit to the servicemen's center that the young women known as junior hostesses are only selected after careful and painstaking appraisal by Mrs. Carrington. . . . they undergo a training which consists of lectures on personality, appearance, topics to be discussed and those to be avoided by the hostesses when in conversation and in general only those things expected of a member of the GSO serving as hostesses."[45] At least one young woman in Detroit, Laura Shumake, determined that a letter from her minister might help her chances of acceptance. The minister of the oldest African American church in the city, the Rev. R. L. Bradby, assured the director of the GSO that Shumake had "fine character . . . good family background . . . [was a] college graduate . . . and is very talented."[46] By casting teens and young adults as beyond reproach, African American women attempted to halt any negative publicity about GSO members' activities.

Senior African American hostesses also publicized their respectability and prominence in the community. In addition, they focused on the power of chaperones to control the behavior of the young people. Many clubwomen involved themselves in the chaperone program. In Richmond, Antoinette Bowler was the head chaperone, as was Rosa Gragg, president of the Detroit Association of Women's Clubs, in that city. Bowler distinguished herself as a teacher at Dunbar school, sorority member, and active Virginia Union alumna. Gragg was extremely well known in Detroit. Born in Georgia in 1904, she graduated from Morris Brown College and pursued graduate studies at Wayne University and the University of Michigan. She became president of the Detroit Association of Women's Clubs, affiliated with the NACW, and in 1941 helped the DAWC to find and purchase a $21,000 building for a meeting site. Under her presidency, the DAWC managed to pay off the mortgage by 1945.[47] Gragg was named one of the "First Ladies of Colored America" by the NAACP in 1942.

Frances Leonard, women's editor of the *Michigan Chronicle,* suggested that the average soldier was "in the presence of decent young women and under the watchful eye of the women who serve as senior hostesses and directors," so parents of young women did not have to worry about their daughters' reputations.[48] In Richmond, the USO entertainment committee urged "all social clubs in the community" to become members of the Defense Service Unit.[49] In response, the Sisterhood of the Second Baptist Church, Zeta Phi Beta, AKA, the Delver Women's Club, YWCA homemakers' clubs, and the Servicemen's Wives' Club all provided many senior hostesses for various functions.[50] In Detroit, members of many clubs, including the Detroit Sophisticates, War Widows, Sapphire, and the Entre Nous, chaperoned USO functions.[51] The importance of senior hostess chaperones revealed itself when Richmond's GSO members went to a function in Petersburg and Richmond's black newspaper assured the community that the girls were "chaperoned by prominent matrons from that city."[52]

African American clubwomen who sponsored USO functions kept entertainment light. Most parties and dances resembled sorority functions, and—reflecting the prominence of both junior and senior hostesses—chaperones reported infinite details of events to the press in order to receive mention in the society pages. Richmond's and Detroit's USOs each held many theme dances for which GSO members appeared in costume after decorating the halls according to the theme of the night. The young women wore white and green, for example, and couples danced in shamrock-bedecked halls on St. Patrick's Day. The GSO also held "barnyard frolics," "kiddie parties," game nights, garden parties, and Halloween dances. In Richmond, a "Sweater Girl

Dance" saw junior hostesses dressed in the popular (and rather tight) sweater sets of the day. Not surprisingly, the event drew the highest attendance of servicemen to the USO to date in Richmond.[53]

Several hostesses in both Richmond and Detroit came up with clever ideas to host servicemen and help contribute to the war in other ways. Richmond's senior hostesses sponsored a "Scrap Dance" to which GSO members had to bring scrap paper for admission. They also held a dance to collect cigarettes for men overseas. Each junior hostess had to bring two packages of cigarettes, and senior hostesses decorated the dance hall with displays of various cigarette brands from Richmond companies. All participants in a Christmas party sponsored by Detroit's Co-Ette Club had to bring groceries for the poor or cigarettes for care packages.[54]

Hosting soldiers in USOs remained a relatively safe activity, but clubwomen worked hard to protect the reputations of the young women who traveled hundreds of miles a year to attend dances at army bases across Virginia and Michigan. Dozens of chaperones accompanied each trip. Hundreds of young women from Richmond, for example, attended holiday dances, picnics, parties, formals, and garden parties at Camp Lee, about forty-five minutes outside Richmond. Army bases held dances at least once a week, but Camp Lee managed to hold seven in two weeks for men about to go overseas. In Detroit, GSO members gave shows and sponsored game days, teas, and dances at numerous camps throughout southern Michigan, including at Fort Brady and the Grosse Ile Naval Base.[55]

Othelia Brown, executive secretary of the Colored Division of Richmond's OCD, made sure that enough chaperones signed up for each event as she planned parties with military personnel.[56] Chaperones also worked with the military to ensure the girls' safety. In a report of activities at Fort Eustis, the *Afro-American* reported, "Mom and Pop don't need to worry because their Nell volunteered to become a hostess at a dance for soldiers, if this and other camps follow the army's general pattern."[57] Chaperones insisted on armed guard units to accompany the busses filled with women to the recreation halls where military police would see they stayed during the dances. After the events, the soldiers would remain in the halls until MPs had escorted the women safely off-base. Again, African American clubwomen refused to take any chance regarding reputation and respectability.

Richmond's and Detroit's black presses recorded positive public reaction to these efforts. The press enthusiastically listed the chaperones for each function and detailed the security measures in place if functions occurred at the bases. In addition, black newspapers took pictures of well-dressed, well-coiffed young women dancing with dashing soldiers, creating the perfect convergence between respectability and patriotic duty. USO activities were described in the society pages, further enhancing the participants' status and advancing the concept that the chaperones and volunteers were not only above reproach but also at the pinnacle of elite black society in Detroit and Richmond.[58]

Chaperoning and hosting USO dances remained an activity of younger African American clubwomen, but older middle-class women found many other ways to comfort soldiers. By serving food, helping to find housing, and generally mothering them, Richmond and Detroit's clubwomen reinforced the power of respectable womanhood in helping wage war by maintaining troop morale. The *Afro-American* recognized that middle-class women were acting as stand-in mothers of a sort when it called Othelia Brown "'mother' to the hundreds of men who have availed themselves of the facilities of the [Monroe] center."[59] Hundreds of women from church and civic groups turned out every weekend to make and serve breakfast to the men, help them find rooms for the night, sew on buttons and mend clothing, and staff the USO lounge that provided cigarettes, candy, and cookies to soldiers passing through Richmond. The Homemakers' League and the Women's Unit of the Fifth Street Baptist Church proved particularly instrumental in providing this unpaid reproductive labor. In addition, the Red Cross canteen unit sponsored an enormous and elaborate Christmas dinner for hundreds of soldiers stationed around Richmond. Leah White, wife of Richmond's NAACP president Walter White, was in charge of the unit.[60]

Detroit did not have the volume of soldiers that Richmond did, so clubwomen there turned much of their attention to caring for troops on bases throughout Michigan. The Deltas, Choicettes, War Widows, and American Beauty Social Club all spent Christmas holidays during the war packing boxes for soldiers. The Deltas also sponsored a massive, citywide book drive for those stationed at Selfridge Air Base, and the Lucy Thurman YWCA Girl Reserves held a fashion show and collected books as admission. Ultimately, the two groups netted 210 volumes, well above the expected quota. In addition, the Deltas volunteered at the Red Cross canteen, which served four hundred soldiers at a concert on Belle Isle in one day and a total of two thousand troops during several months during 1943. Under the guidance of a Mrs. Jones and a Mrs. Witt, the Girl Scouts of Ebenezer Baptist Church gave cookies and candy to men at the USO. The Housewives League of Detroit, the Berea Church Ladies' Society, and the Sapphire Club all provided food to soldiers staying at the USO.[61]

African American women's unpaid labor had a strong effect on USOs, and participating within USOs enabled women to determine how soldiers could best be supported. It also helped them position themselves as important home-front volunteers who filled a tremendous need to house and feed soldiers by performing traditionally gendered work. In Richmond, 480 women clocked enough hours to be listed on the honor roll of the Leigh Street USO. In Detroit, forty-three clubs staffed the USO and chaperoned more than two hundred junior hostesses.[62] These women put in countless hours in the service of African Americans whose needs had not been addressed adequately by either the USO or the military. African American women's traditional reproductive labor—cooking, entertaining, sewing, and comforting—nicely meshed the ideology of respectability with a new discourse of responsible patriotism. By maintaining traditional gender roles in volunteer work, African American women protested against inequalities as respectable women who deserved a voice in the wartime state.

Civil Rights Work

At the same time they created a new definition of responsible patriotism and proved themselves invaluable to the wartime state black women focused on how to secure their rights. As they demanded the right to volunteer in the prosecution of the war, they wrote to the government to get blacks on wartime administrations and committees, sponsored panels dealing with racism, raised money and recruited members for the NAACP, and demanded equal job opportunities for themselves and for working-class women. National organizations created civil rights programs that clubwomen worked to implement on a local level.

In their program to promote civil rights nationwide, sororities and other national groups looked to reduce discrimination against blacks in national government. African American clubwomen's prominence enabled them to be heard by whites in power even if Roosevelt's administration ignored their demands. In 1941 and 1942, AKA's 147 chapters sponsored several campaigns designed to get prominent blacks appointed to federal positions. Chapters across the country flooded him and Secretary of Labor Frances Perkins with telegrams and letters demanding that black women be appointed to the Women's Bureau. When Women's Bureau Director Mary Anderson replied to the chapters and claimed she had no more money to hire anyone and that the bureau had temporarily employed several African American women as clerical workers, AKA took the story to the black newspapers. Doing so enabled the women to secure the support of the national black community, which could then pressure the government to change the policy. The women charged Perkins with personally snubbing prominent sorority members.

The AKAs were fully aware of the fact that the bureau was, in fact, hiring new workers and had passed over qualified African American women already employed in other government bureaus. The sorority called the situation "ridiculous."[63] The AKAs then wrote to Roosevelt, urging him to appoint both blacks and sympathetic whites to the War Manpower Commission. AKA's Non-Partisan Council challenged the president's seriousness about changing race relations. Jeanetta Welch Brown reminded him of Executive Order 8802 and made it clear that AKAs expected him to keep his word: "WE REALIZE; 1. That you, too, are most anxious to Demonstrate to the world that democracy can be made to work in America. 2. That a step was made in that direction when you issued Executive Order 8802. 3. That in order to make democracy work, members of every race must feel that they share fully in all places of their government."[64]

Like AKA, the NCNW took an active role in attempting to make both its own position and the position of black women in general more secure by negotiating with the government for more representation. Bethune sent a "stinging rebuke" to Henry L. Stimpson, secretary of war, for being "deliberately snubbed by the women's interest section of the bureau of public relations of the War Department" when the NCNW found itself among the many black women's groups not invited to participate in a council on soldiers' welfare. "'We are not blind to what is happening,'" she fumed. "'We are not humiliated. We are incensed! We believe what we have asked is what we all desire—a unity of action, thought, and spirit. We still seek this end and urge you that colored representation be included in this advisory council.'"[65] Bethune, a master at using the discourse of responsible patriotism, was accusing the War Department of promoting disunity and hampering the war effort by continuing racism within its own administration.

National African American women's groups also sought to educate white Americans about the persistent inequalities faced by middle-class black women and the black community as a whole by using a nonconfrontational model of protest designed to appeal to white citizens. By creating programs to "enlighten" whites, African American women listed all the racial problems in the nation without blaming whites directly for creating them. The NCNW held a We Serve America Week right after the riots in Detroit, Harlem, and Mobile in order to show the daily humiliations their community faced and what it had contributed to the war despite skepticism about American society in general. The NCNW called upon all "Negro wives and mothers" to telegram FDR to request formal investigations of the riots and promote interracial meetings in their cities in order to educate white society about discrimination.[66]

Richmond's NCNW chapter took up the national headquarters' challenge by parading in their volunteer uniforms, sponsoring mass meetings and teas to protest discrimination, and holding interracial programs to promote better race relations.[67] Whether whites attended the meetings is not known, but it would have been impossible to ignore the parade of black women walking through the streets of Richmond in OCD and Red Cross outfits. AKA also sponsored a Listen America Week to make whites aware of the black community's feelings. They spoke about fighting discrimination in government agencies and overturning white supremacist myths in nationwide radio broadcasts designed to reach a wide audience. Thomasina Johnson, legal representative to the Non-Partisan Council, spelled out the desires of all African Americans in her interpretation of the week's message: "The test of democracy in America is a test of color. . . . We are still being discriminated against in war industries . . . we don't want to be lynched. . . . we are tired of exploitation and disfranchisement, and inferior schools and being politically lynched."[68]

The organizations sponsoring these weeks effectively spread their messages to the entire country by advertising in newspapers and, most important, on the radio in a determined but not accusatory manner. The policy of low confrontation was tied to concerns about responsibility and wartime citizenship. Clubwomen's criticism of American social relations could be construed as divisive to a state that demanded unity on the home front, and so they moderated the message with a less aggressive tone.

National women's organizations also concerned themselves with maintaining the Fair Employment Practices Committee (FEPC) as legitimate and powerful. Throughout the war they urged Congress to make the panel a permanent commission rather than a subcommittee of the War Manpower Commission destined to end with the end of the war. Deltas poured money into their Committee to Establish a Permanent FEPC, and Sigma Gamma Rhos also sponsored members' trips to Congress to lobby for FEPC continuance. Beulah Whitby went to testify for the FEPC. As Detroit's commissioner of wartime welfare she was eminently qualified to speak of the economic climate in that city. She argued before the House that economic insecurity and unfair competition for jobs created a racially antagonistic climate for black workers that could be tempered only by a permanent and powerful FEPC.[69]

The fact that Whitby testified before Congress in 1944 suggests that African American women were gaining some power within the state as a result of their actions during the war. In reality, Whitby was continuing a trend started during the 1930s by Mary McLeod Bethune, whose close relationship

with Eleanor Roosevelt enabled her to engage state officials at the highest
level. Black women had come far in those few years. Whitby held a captive
audience of white men in a congressional hearing, ensuring that her negotiations reached the center of American state power.[70]

Richmond and Detroit's local sorority chapters and clubs continued their
national organizations' fights by promoting improved race relations and citizenship issues in sponsored panel talks, helping with NAACP membership
drives, and registering voters. In Richmond, the Queen Esther Temple, auxiliary of the Elks, sponsored a civil liberties day featuring music and speakers from the NAACP. Teachers brought Virginia Union professors to talk to
students about interracial cooperation in industry.[71] The YWCA held a citizenship rally that addressed abolition of the poll tax, teachers' pay equalization, and "local legislation to prevent the denial of civil rights in national
defense." The Du Bois Circle Women's Club brought in the dean of women
from Howard University to speak to a large audience about the role of women
in promoting civil rights. AKA sponsored lectures by Jeanetta Welch Brown
and Thomasina Johnson at Virginia Union and Leigh Street Methodist
Church, respectively. Each spoke about current legislative issues, education,
and democracy in general.[72]

Detroit's clubwomen began to promote civil rights and race relations panels and public meetings in 1943 after an outbreak of riots that paralyzed the
city in June of that year brought a barrage of programs for the general populace.[73] Detroit's YWCA Homemaker's Club sponsored a representative from
Michigan's Unemployment Commission, Geraldine Bledsoe, to speak on
"Women's Place on the Home Front," and its Business and Professional Girls'
Clubs created an interracial series dealing with how to promote better race
relations. Deltas held a forum on how to alleviate racial tensions and "un-
teach" racial prejudices, and the annual program of Iota Phi Lambda sorority focused on how to participate more effectively in the war effort. AKA held
a tea for its members and other prominent women in order to introduce them
to the local FEPC staff, and the YWCA leadership held an interracial program
series dedicated to teaching about various races and cultures.[74] By holding
lectures and panel discussions, clubwomen spread the discourse of responsible patriotism to the broader community, both white and black. These
panels continued the work of progressive women who attempted to bridge
gaps between middle-class black and white women.

In addition to sponsoring civil rights programs for the public, African
American clubwomen promoted civil rights by signing up members and
holding fund-raisers for the NAACP. Because the NAACP needed funds
during the war to finance lawsuits against industries, schools, and election

boards as well as fight segregation in the military, it sponsored massive yearly membership drives nationwide that brought in the bulk of the money for its operating costs. Although women were not the only ones involved with membership drives and fund-raisers, they vastly outnumbered men in NAACP recruitment ranks. As in war bond sales, they used connections gained through existing networks to reach the greatest numbers of people in their communities.

In Richmond's 1940 drive, seventeen women led general soliciting (neighborhood canvassing) and school soliciting teams. They managed to enroll 1,300 new members, and by 1942 dozens of women had enrolled 1,790. In 1943 canvassers enrolled 3,350 women, and 3,452 people had joined the NAACP by 1944. By then, Senora Lawson, a prominent African American, chaired the NAACP membership committee. Born in Wilmington, North Carolina, in 1898, Lawson graduated from Virginia Union University, served on various committees, and sang in the choir of Hood Temple AME Church. She was also active in the State Federation of Colored Women's Clubs and helped the NAACP to establish a youth branch. Under her direction the increase in membership greatly enhanced the financial status of the local NAACP.[75]

Detroit's NAACP chapter remained the largest in the country, so it did not need to publicize its membership drive as much as Richmond's chapter did. Women, however, were still at the forefront of fund-raisers. Beulah Whitby, for example, chaired the NAACP's Anniversary Ball. In 1945 canvassers had enrolled 3,474 members in one week, which counted toward their goal of twenty-six thousand members.[76] African American women's work for the NAACP was important not only because it brought much-needed funds to the organization but also because it helped educate the black community about NAACP goals and programs.

In Richmond, women raised money for the NAACP, and local teachers worked with the organization to fight for civil rights within their own profession. From 1940 to 1942 the Richmond Teachers' Association involved itself in a battle over salary equalization. By calling on the NAACP for help and taking an unequal wage lawsuit through the court system, the teachers eventually gained enough strength to be in a good bargaining position, and they won their battle for equal pay. In 1938 the average white teacher received $1,848, whereas the average black teacher's salary was $1,098.[77] In 1940, after Norfolk's black teachers won salary equalization through an appeal decision in the Federal District Court, the Richmond Teacher's Association met to test the court's decision in its city. More than two-thirds of the city's 330 black teachers attended a meeting and unanimously asked the school board to drop the color differential in the wage scale. Their petition employed the discourse of responsible patriotism: "democracy would be strengthened by favorable action and . . . the law of the land would be fulfilled."[78]

The teachers suggested an equalization plan that in five years would bring salaries in line with yearly increases costing $45,305. The white teacher's association, the Teacher's League, suggested a nine-year plan to better spread the costs. Each group submitted the plans to the board in the summer of 1941.[79] When the school board countered with a fifteen-year plan to raise salaries overall but not dislodge the color barrier, Richmond's black teachers went to war. First, they asked the NAACP to sponsor anti-school board rallies. Then, three-fourths of the black teachers appeared at a board meeting, threatening a lawsuit if the board did not accept their plan. In addition, the lawsuit would ask for immediate salary equalization at great cost to the school system.[80]

The teachers needed a plaintiff for the test case, which proved a difficult decision because of the problems the association in Richmond faced. The teacher had to be someone with courage and moderate wealth, because many plaintiffs in Norfolk had lost their jobs as a result of the suit; someone prominent in the community, because publicity was important to the case; and someone respectable, patriotic, and generally above reproach, because the plaintiff had to make the white community sympathetic to the teachers' plight. The association decided to accept Antoinette Bowler's offer to stand as plaintiff. In addition to her other duties, she served as assistant secretary of the local NAACP.[81]

Although the teachers had the ideal candidate for the lawsuit, their actions still angered whites. The *Richmond Times-Dispatch,* generally known for its more moderate views on race, urged dropping the suit. It employed an old excuse for racism in the New South when it declared in an editorial, "Our Negro citizens must realize that there are many white Richmonders who do not regard the Supreme Court's order for salary equalization in the Norfolk case as either equitable or sensible. . . . The attitude on this issue of the unreconciled and unreconstructed element of white Richmonders may be deplored. That does not change the fact that the attitude exists."[82]

Despite massive opposition from the white community, the teachers did file the lawsuit. With its back against the wall and knowing the Norfolk precedent virtually guaranteed a loss on appeal if not immediately, the school board agreed to a friendly settlement. Although it refused to equalize salaries at once, it did accept the original five-year plan, which the teachers accepted 151–68. Some in the black community believed the teachers had "sold out" the struggle by not fighting for immediate equalization. The president of the local NAACP contended that they had set the equal rights movement back by many years.[83] The teachers, however, were happy. Not only had they secured the promise of equal pay, but they also forced the removal of the color differential. And, as part of the friendly settlement, the school board had to sign an admission of having discriminated against the teachers racially and assure them that would never happen again.[84]

The board's statement, and the battle itself, proved an enormous step forward in the struggle for equality both in Richmond and for teachers across the nation. By demanding that the school board admit to a history of discrimination, Antoinette Bowler and the other teachers forced Richmond to acknowledge publicly the history of racism in the city. Moreover, by testing the waters of equal pay using the Norfolk precedent, Richmond schoolteachers reinforced the District Court's ruling, which led the way for other teachers in Virginia and elsewhere to fight discrimination in their communities.

Social Work

African American clubwomen believed that in order to promote and finally achieve equality they would have to raise the next generation to respect both democratic principles and themselves as black Americans in order to create a new vanguard of responsible patriots who would take up the fight for civil rights. Class-oriented in their youth programs, middle-class black women attempted to keep children of working-class mothers, especially very young mothers, out of trouble. Although middle-class children took part in the clubwomen's programs, particularly through the YWCA and the schools, working-class children were targeted as the main recipients of efforts. As teachers and community leaders, middle-class women took over the reigns of leadership for programs that would yield children who would be respectable citizens while helping to win the war.

In both Richmond and Detroit many teachers promoted the ideas of responsible patriotism in their classrooms in order to make an impression on their cities' young people. When teachers at Richmond's Maggie Walker High School involved students in selling bonds, they both bought and sold $13,846 worth in six weeks—enough to buy sixteen Jeeps for the army. Teachers also sponsored the Girl Reserves Club of the YWCA, which honored the winner of a bond-selling contest at a formal dance (which soldiers attended, of course). The teachers also invited Grace Matthews, assistant district information officer of the OPA, to discuss the rationing program with young women at Armstrong High School. The girls were shown how to develop into "respectable" and patriotic homemakers by supporting the wartime conservation program in daily household management. Richmond high school girls also formed a Victory Corps that participated in twenty-six different volunteer activities, including first aid and home nursing. Members managed to collect 7,317 tin cans for scrap; one girl collected 1,117 cans on her own. Younger children also became involved in the war conservation movement, and members of playground recreation groups collected twenty-one pounds of tinfoil.[85]

Detroit's teachers also played a major part in helping children practice responsible patriotism. Theoretically, Detroit's schools were integrated. In reality, however, strict neighborhood race barriers created a segregated school system in which black teachers labored for less money and under worse facilities than white teachers, much as they did in the southern school system. Under the guidance of teachers, elementary school children raised $117 for the USO Christmas fund, and students at Garfield Intermediate School raised $42,000 in bonds, enough to buy the army a tank. Under the auspices of volunteer teachers, a group of "popular teenagers" formed a junior civilian defense group. Like Richmond's Victory Corps girls, the group participated in many home-front activities, including selling stamps and collecting scrap material.[86]

Concerned about the growing rate of juvenile delinquency during the war, middle-class women attributed the problem to the large number of mothers who worked full time. In order to curb the growing crisis, clubwomen in Richmond and Detroit used a twofold approach. First, they tried to support programs that would stop youths from becoming delinquent at all. If they provided recreational activities for children, they thought, then the children would spend their time participating in wholesome and healthy programs rather than running the streets with no guidance. Second, they held programs for teens who were borderline delinquents but who, they believed, could be "fixed."

Middle-class women were not happy that the need for day-care centers skyrocketed during the war, but they acknowledged that centers not only were critical to the livelihoods of working women but also could help young children receive guidance and learn about good values at an early age from respectable, trained teachers. AKA's Non-Partisan League fought unsuccessfully for the equal distribution of Lanham Act funds ($20 million in 1943) to day-care centers for blacks as well as whites.[87] Because the funds were not distributed equally—a problem resulting in generally inadequate funding for day care in the black community—clubwomen furnished supplies for, funded, and often staffed their own centers for the children of working women. Richmond's College Women Club and Thor Club gave supplies to the Seventeenth Street Nursery, and the Zeta Phi Beta chapter gave a "supply shower" to the Baker School nursery day care center. Not to be outdone, Phi Delta Kappa, a teachers' sorority, opened an after-school recreation room for children six to fourteen. They also staffed the center and planned all of the programs.[88]

Because more African American women entered war industries in Detroit than in Richmond, that city's clubwomen faced an even more pressing concern with child care. Detroit's black community had a major nursery school, Peter Pan Nursery, begun by middle-class women in 1936 to promote socialization among children on a weekly basis. The board of directors was dismayed about changing the center into a facility for wartime workers: "It was with a great deal of reluctance in 1943 that the Board of Directors . . . changed the type of program from one of co-operation and self-help to one of service to working mothers."[89] Nevertheless, Peter Pan Nursery did change its focus, made admission for children of working mothers its main priority, and even received government subsidies for "scholarship" students. As in Richmond, Detroit's Phi Delta Kappa chapter started its own recreation center for elementary school children at Brewster Homes, a low-income housing project for war workers. Club members included a book and toy lending library at the center, and their programs included education in black history and Bible study, both topics intended to promote the tenets of race progress and Christian values.[90]

Richmond and Detroit's middle-class women also concerned themselves with the problems of teenagers, especially girls, in light of the influx of soldiers into the area. They tried hard to provide wholesome activities in order to keep the young people chaperoned and away from "dangerous" situations. Middle-class women disdained women whom they believed to be lax working mothers and attempted to raise the girls correctly by serving as program directors and chaperoning activities. A Detroit reporter warned mothers about the problems of mixing full-time work with parenting: "Facts show that juvenile delinquency is greatest among children left neglected by working parents. . . . Tragedy may be the outcome of parental neglect."[91]

The Richmond and Detroit YWCAs both operated youth canteens, where teenagers could interact in a supervised setting on weekends. In addition, both held classes in dancing, arts and crafts, sewing, home economics, and charm for young women in order to teach them the skills necessary to become homemakers and the values needed to be a productive member of the middle class. The Detroit Urban League's Chestnut Community Center, located in a very low-income area, held classes in charm, positive attitude, skin and diet, makeup, hairstyling, and party planning. These classes were attempts to indoctrinate children of the working class in the values of middle-class clubwomen.

They also served a purpose for the war effort, because behind efforts to promote "charm," "makeup skills," and "positive attitudes" were other efforts to surveil the activities of young women. By ensuring that these women embraced the tenets of respectability, clubwomen tried to prevent teenagers, often left alone by working mothers, from becoming sexually or morally delinquent and creating problems for the Office of Community War Services, which was responsible for monitoring their activities in communities across the country in an effort to halt the spread of venereal disease.[92]

But what about the children who had already been charged with delinquency or who appeared to show the first signs of delinquent behavior? Both Richmond and Detroit's middle-class women attempted to thwart their troubling behavior by means of intensive programs. Aided by many black female social workers, Richmond's Friends Association for Colored Children found temporary foster homes and permanent adoptive situations for those in danger and whose parents could not adequately care for them. In 1940 alone the association placed 138 children in foster homes and saw that six were adopted to permanent homes.[93]

Teenaged girls' actions in the Detroit riot of 1943 sparked perhaps the largest local volunteer effort in the history of African American clubwomen's activities.[94] Dismayed by what they determined to be the activities of uncontrolled and poorly parented young girls, Detroit's Delta Sigma Theta chapters decided to build a foster institution for young women whom they deemed delinquent but not criminal. Delta's 166 Detroit members discovered that although three homes existed for troubled white girls, black girls either went to the state institution outside Lansing or slid through the cracks of the welfare system. The Deltas decided to buy and operate a supervised home for girls who had behavior problems, "those girls whose environment has contributed to acts of truancy from home and school, late hours and association with undesirable companions."[95]

Delta's ideology indicted the ability of poor women to parent daughters: "These girls, through no fault of their own, have been victims of broken homes, inadequate parental influence, and improper housing."[96] The Deltas would see that the girls would learn proper behavior and become respectable young ladies under the strict scrutiny of sorority members in a supervised living situation. As they explained, "The members of the sorority, who are librarians, social workers, teachers, nurses, business and home women will be able to take care of many of the personal needs of the girls."[97]

Fund-raising for the home began in 1944, and the sorority ran into problems almost immediately. After applying to many local and national grant-giving groups, they found that the idea of a home that catered to both black and white girls was not popular with the powerful white community. One prospective donor offered to give the sorors $20,000 in cash if only they would limit access to the home to black girls. The Deltas refused the money and turned to the black community for help, and by 1947 enough had been raised to open the Delta Home for Girls.[98] Although the facility was interracial by name, it housed only African American girls; the welfare department would not recommend white girls for it.

By trying to teach young children how to be upstanding, respectable, and patriotic citizens, middle-class women revealed an inherent class bias. Such children, they implied, had failed to learn the proper skills and values for becoming responsible patriots. Many working-class women in Richmond and Detroit were single mothers, and they were often blamed for the problems their children experienced. Institutions like the Delta Home for Girls were necessary in most communities, but the message sent out was ambiguous. The implication was that working-class parents were guilty of irresponsible behavior. In reality, however, if these women did not work full time they could not give their children the basic necessities.

Working-Class Advocacy

African American clubwomen were not only interested in solving the problems faced by working-class youths but they also believed they had the ability to help working-class women gain job opportunities. Although many focused on increasing equality in their own professional fields, they aimed the bulk of their efforts from 1940 to 1945 toward opening the war industry fields for working-class women. Because of their education and position in society, middle-class women believed that they were naturally suited to speak about the needs of other black women. Moreover, home-front defense activities had provided them an entry point from which to engage the state on issues of job equality. The clubwomen's program of responsible patriotism enabled them to claim rights by nature of their efforts for the state, and as a group they stressed that working-class women found themselves denied the right to participate in the war because they were not allowed to work in many defense industries.

Middle-class women recognized that because of gender, race, and economic prejudices, working-class women had the most difficult struggle for equality in the black community and also viewed the problems they faced as indicative of women's problems in society as a whole. As Jeanetta Welch Brown noted, "Our enemies still try to keep us in unskilled jobs and in many instances to keep us out of jobs, so that today, we Negro women have no assurance of adequate or stable income now or after the war. . . . our future is bound up with the future of women of all races and with the masses of women within our own group."[99] Many programs that African American club-women instituted in order to help working-class women gain job equality were based on a structural analysis of black women's economic oppression. Many were not.

The clubwomen understood that in order to solve working-class women's employment problems they needed to identify the kinds of discrimination the women faced and identify with the women themselves. At a NCNW-sponsored workshop on employment, housing, and the economic structures that threatened jobs for black women, members determined that "the persistent and dominating part of all the discussions was the responsibility that all women have for being in the forefront of struggle and the necessity for identification and working with organizations, labor and education movements devoted to securing better standards of living for all workers."[100] AKA set up a national vocational guidance program that included unions on the planning level, and it also worked to encourage black women to become qualified for training and helped them secure jobs.[101] In their national program the Deltas emphasized securing job openings for women, setting up job clinics, and helping find day care for working women.[102]

Clubwomen attempted to find government support for the needs of working women by creating and enforcing nondiscrimination policies. They understood that the FEPC was not effective enough to serve the millions of women left out of the wartime employment boom. Representing AKA's Non-Partisan Council, Jeanetta Welch Brown went before the House Committee Investigating National Defense Migration to complain about the lack of opportunities for working-class women. She demanded that the "vast labor market" of black women be given equal opportunities to train and work in war industries. She also reminded the committee that many of the women had been trained during World War I and were thus pre-qualified for war jobs and that many had secured work in foundries, sheet metal factories, and other heavy industrial jobs. She used the discourse of responsible patriotism as she warned representatives that "any failure to train and employ the vast reserve of Negro women will definitely affect the successful prosecution of our Victory program."[103] The policies of AKA and the NCNW demonstrate that the groups concerned themselves with helping working-class women get ahead in industry and believed they had the power to go to the highest levels of government to attain their goals.

Detroit's and Richmond's job markets differed slightly, which led club-women to promote different strategies to help working-class women. Because the labor shortage in Detroit proved seriously acute, clubwomen there had an easier time pointing out the inconsistencies of government policy and hiring practices. Rosa Gragg went directly to the president with a plan to help the thirty thousand black women in Detroit and millions of others around the country who wanted to break into war industries. The self-titled "Gragg Plan" called for the government to force industries to train and employ ten thousand women in Detroit. In Gragg's opinion, Roosevelt needed to use the War Production Board, the War Manpower Commission, and the United States Employment Service for initial meetings with industry. Then the FEPC should be sent in to investigate industries and punish them quickly and severely for any violations against the policy.[104] The government refused to accept these radical programs because the administration believed that such policies would slow war production. Still, Detroit's labor shortage facilitated Gragg's attempt to implement policies that would help working women.

Clubwomen in Richmond and Detroit attempted to make young men and women aware of job opportunities and encourage them to fight for entry into industry. Most activities focused on job clinics and institutes, which highlighted opportunities in each city's industries. In Richmond, AKA, Zeta Phi Beta, Delta, and the Entre Nous Club worked with the Urban League to sponsor an annual vocational opportunity campaign. They accompanied high school students on field trips to factories and stores, showed movies about job opportunities, and made presentations on how to interview for jobs. In 1942 the vocational drive expanded to include programs on broader vocational training courses and information on securing municipal employment. The YWCA held an Institute on Worker's Education, which addressed how to enhance job performance, especially in household employment. In Detroit, Deltas helped sponsor Urban League vocational opportunities campaigns, and they focused specifically on how to increase opportunities for women and how to deal with job discrimination. AKAs in Detroit surveyed black businesses and war industries to gauge the job market for women and then held a vocational conference to publicize their findings.[105]

While clubwomen aimed their programs at helping working-class women get jobs, they also attempted to alter the women's behavior, an endeavor that, clubwomen believed, would help them keep the new jobs. Such efforts were patronizing and intrusive, not to mention unrealistic. During the war, middle-class African American women determined that other black women undermined gains made by the entire community by displaying bad behavior in public. It was a matter of upholding the respectability of the race and maintaining good race relations. As Lillian Payne of the Order of St. Luke in Richmond bemoaned, "Our highest colored citizens are daily bearing the

burdens thrust upon them by ignorance or conduct of our lowest."[106] Emma
Harris of the Women's Council of Second Baptist Church complained to
Detroit's NAACP that the association needed to effect "improvement in the
demeanor of colored persons on conveyances and rest rooms. . . . Mrs. Harris
had observed a growing tendency toward loose and boisterous conduct."[107]

Both Richmond and Detroit clubwomen attempted to change the behavior of working-class women. Richmond's YWCA held a charm school for
those in cafeteria work, as well as for beauty operators, waitresses, and factory and laundry workers. The women would be taught "charm in dress,
charm in personal appearance, charm in speech and poise, charm in man-
ners."[108] Detroit's AKA chapters held a charm school for senior girls as part
of their vocational training conference, and the local YWCA held a school
to show for adults the proper dress for business and industrial work and
provide "personality help."[109] The Housewives League of Detroit distribut-
ed flyers to working women for a "Double V Begins with Me" week in 1942.
Participants were required to pledge "I will . . . do my best on the job; go to
work every day; take active part in my labor union; make friends with my
fellow workers—we are fighting the same war; dress properly to command
respect; not have a chip on my shoulder."[110]

Although middle-class women failed to understand all the issues facing
women in factories, it is important to note that Detroit clubwomen made a
point of supporting labor unions. In particular, they backed the UAW, which
had a positive effect on hiring practices related to black men during the 1930s.
Black clubwomen understood well enough that the union, because of its
bargaining power and liberal national officers, was one of the few institutions
that could threaten to subvert the structural racism that existed within factories.

Beulah Whitby and Geraldine Bledsoe (wife of a prominent attorney) were
the first on the Urban League board to support the UAW in 1940. The following year, AKA helped initiate a sea change in the relationship between
black leaders and the union as it became involved in the movement to condemn Ford's use of black strikebreakers at the River Rouge plant.[111] African
American clubwomen became strong allies of the union in the struggle for
working women's rights, perhaps because they understood that black women
who tried to enter factories encountered many more problems than did black
men.

Along the same lines as the Housewives League of Detroit but on a much
larger scale, the NCNW "sought the assistance" of workers in promoting
responsible patriotism through maintaining standards of respectability.
NCNW chapters across the country, including in Richmond and Detroit,

participated in the national "Can You Hold Your Job Campaign" in 1943. The NCNW directed the effort at working women as an answer to concerns about female employees. In Detroit, acting as executive secretary of the NCNW, Jeanetta Welch Brown informed Rosa Gragg that "some manufacturers have already said that they are just waiting for the time to let them [black women] go because of their conduct." The goal of the campaign, therefore, focused on making women aware of the fact that in order to keep their jobs they must be "clean, courteous, punctual, and affable."[112]

The NCNW used employment clinics to make working women aware of their tenuous situation in industries and ensure they did their part in promoting responsible patriotism. As Bethune said, "It is our task to make plans concretely and in every community so that the employer will welcome her, so that the community will make provisions to absorb her as a full citizen."[113] By the 1940s, it is clear that middle-class women such as Bethune began to equate citizenship with work opportunities for women outside the middle class. Instead of focusing on better training, working with union representatives, and addressing other pressing issues that working women faced, however, NCNW members maintained that respectable women would be successful workers.

The wartime clinics laid out several objectives: proper dress and behavior, discouraging absenteeism, and urging women to take advantage of self-improvement opportunities. Moreover, employers were to introduce new workers to jobs properly so they would do the best work possible.[114] In order to influence workers to attend the clinics, NCNW members circulated a memo to working-class women:

> Wake Up! Your Job Is In Danger! Check up on—Your Personal Appearance: Do not offend others by being careless. Bathe frequently and insure against body odors. Dress neatly and sensibly. Be attractive! Your Behavior on the Job: Girls, be kind and not "catty." Lose that chip-off-of-your-shoulder. Avoid "showing-off" and being loud and boisterous. It is better to be seen at your work station quietly doing your job than to be heard or seen all over the place. Your Attitude: It is important the way you feel about your—Employer: He has his problems, too. Be cooperative. Supervisor: He has a job to do and you're hired to help him do it. Fellow-worker: Get along with the other workers on the job. Work with them, not against them. Your health: Eat, sleep, rest, and play sensible. Avoid indulgence in anything. It lowers your efficiency. Your attendance: Get to work every working day and on time. Don't loaf on the job. Monday and the day after payday are not legal holidays.[115]

Once war workers attended the clinic, NCNW sponsors required them to sign a pledge to uphold all of the tenets described in the pamphlet.

The program to "help" working-class women retain their jobs remained awash both in middle-class Victorian morality and modern notions of efficiency and management. It had less to do with helping the women than with encouraging them to put on the best face for white society. They were not to protest conditions, but they were to work hard and quietly and get along with employers. Because most middle-class women did not visit factories as a general rule, they could not be expected to understand that working-class women usually toiled in the most labor-intensive, dirtiest, and most degrading jobs. Working-class women could no more afford to hold fast to all the recommendations laid out by clubwomen than they could join one of the exclusive clubs that were dictating how to exhibit "respectable" behavior on the job.

* * *

Middle-class African American women's discourse and activities during the war period fundamentally altered the relationship of the black community to the state and enabled the modern civil rights movement to emerge. Their language, demanding the rights owed them as first-class citizens who provided valuable services to the state, created a sense of immediacy never before seen in the history of civil rights. African American clubwomen's direct civil rights activism also had an astonishing effect on the overall national struggle for equality. NAACP membership skyrocketed from fifty thousand in 1940 to more than 450,000 in 1946.[116]

That growth provided the NAACP with the support and funds necessary for civil rights litigation against local, state, and national structural inequalities. When Richmond teachers tested the Supreme Court decision to equalize teacher salaries, they reinforced the fact that lawsuits could advance equality. They also set the NAACP on a course to test many Jim Crow laws, from all-white primaries to restrictive neighborhood covenants. In focusing on the rights of working-class women, clubwomen helped bring national attention to the problems of structural employment segregation in war industries as well as the everyday problems working-class women faced concerning child care and making adequate provisions for their families. The activities placed middle-class African American women on the front lines of the struggle for equality.

2. Working for Democracy: Working-Class Women and Wartime Opportunities, 1940–45

Louise Thomas was tired. She had worked hard for no pay at the Commerce School, learning riveting in a defense training class. She spent 120 hours in the classroom, sacrificing weeks of no income for a chance at a war job that would pay much more than the average job an African American woman in Detroit could obtain. She passed the riveting course with flying colors and went to Ford's Willow Run bomber plant to secure employment in 1942 because she had heard the factory desperately needed female riveters. On two separate occasions she spent money on bus fare to the site, about fifteen to twenty minutes outside town, only to sit and wait in employment offices. Finally, two different personnel officers told her that they could not place her. When Thomas returned to the school to question her riveting instructor about the situation, she overheard him telling other teachers that "the school was not for colored girls and that they were not going to get any employment." She heard him tell another black woman that black women who had left jobs to take the riveting class had better return to them because Detroit factories would never hire them.[1]

Thomas refused to go back to her former job. She had trained for a war defense position and decided to try for the right to work at a skilled job for decent pay. Moreover, she understood that many women had already complained to the Fair Employment Practices Committee (FEPC) about Ford's hiring practices but nothing seemed to have been done to alleviate the discrimination. Thomas took her story to one of Detroit's major black newspapers in order to publicize the situation African American working-class women faced in that city. She spoke for many when she stated:

If the defense plants in Detroit are not going to hire colored women, and if the Government's Fair Employment Practices Committee is not going to enforce the President's order in this matter, why don't they be frank and tell the colored women the facts. I have spent long hours and sacrificed to get this defense training, which time I could have used in other ways, but I have not been hired. If I were a white woman, instead of a Negro, my school credentials and my O.K. slip for work at the Ford Willow Run plant would mean something and I would now be working on a defense job at Willow Run, riveting war weapons to help our nation win the war. It is time for those in authority to get behind these issues and help get a square deal for Negro Women in defense industry. We, too, are Americans.[2]

Thomas's message to the black community suggests that she understood the racial dichotomy in the hiring practices that kept her from a lucrative war position. Her language reflects growing political consciousness on the part of working-class black women who equated war jobs with racial justice and called on the state to support those job claims. Moreover, her demands that "those in authority" support black women's entry into defense jobs reveal that working-class women understood how to use state agencies and unions to negotiate with industries in order to equalize hiring practices.

African American working-class women had always struggled to piece together resources for themselves and their families, and they had experience negotiating with the government to obtain health, monetary, and other benefits. Women of color had consistently organized to gain political and economic rights and counter numerous other forms of prejudice in the United States. In being organized, they sometimes succeeded in making state institutions more responsive to their needs. Moreover, during the 1930s those who had made inroads into certain industries such as meatpacking and tobacco began to use unions to address grievances related to discrimination, particularly in equal pay and fair union representation. African American women struck for better hours and pay at Richmond's Carrington-Micheaux tobacco factory in 1937, for example, and the CIO came to organize them as a result of their activities. In that the issues of equal work opportunities, equal union representation, and equal pay are tied to the civil rights movement, working-class African American women involved themselves in pushing for civil rights throughout the twentieth century.[3]

World War II created an opportunity for the women to advance the civil rights movement to a new level. Government institutions such as the FEPC and the War Manpower Commission (WMC) regulated industries, causing a severe labor shortage that forced the Roosevelt administration to call upon all industries to hire workers of every race and ethnicity to keep up production. As working-class women politicized the meanings of employment, equality in the workplace, and child care during World War II, they created a discourse equating their right to work with their right to be patriots. As they claimed citizenship on the basis of their potential as wartime employees, they raised the stakes in everyday struggles for work and decent child care. As they filed complaints with the FEPC, Franklin and Eleanor Roosevelt, and powerful government institutions, and as they used the NAACP, Urban League, and unions to help them desegregate industry, the women equated work with other forms of citizenship, including the rights to support the country in wartime defense and participate in the electoral process.

When the women demanded better working conditions, promotions, better pay, and membership and seniority within their unions, and when they fought for better wages and child care to provide better lives for themselves and their families, they did so under the rubric of becoming more productive for the war effort. Their attempts to negotiate work and child care, employers, and government officials provided a strong base for a more militant civil rights movement during World War II by creating a sense of urgency in language and action and promoting equal opportunity, pay, and treatment by unions and industries.

Racism and Sexism in War Industries

Black women found it harder to break into wartime industries than their male counterparts. Much of the trouble resulted from employer reluctance to pair them with white women in wartime production jobs classified along gender lines.[4] Evelyn Scanlon, representative of United Auto Workers (UAW) Local 3 (Dodge Main plant), believed that she represented a majority of white women at the Women's Conference in February 1942 and objected to UAW Local 600's support of a desegregation resolution: "I don't think we should bring the problem of negro women into this meeting. I don't think we should consider bringing them into the shops—if we bring them in even in this crisis we'd always have them to contend with. And you know what that means— we'd be working right beside them, we'd be using the same rest rooms, etc. I'm against it."[5]

Scanlon's statement reflects whites' pervasive fear of their space being violated by blacks, deemed dirty, disease-ridden, and impure. Because white women had constructed black women as sexually available and unclean, they resisted sharing factory floors with them for fear of contaminating their own work spaces.[6] Reluctance to work alongside black women was, employers found, an easy excuse to keep them out of factories altogether.

Although Michigan had a civil rights law on the books before World War II, Richmond's Jim Crow laws made desegregating factories not only psychologically trying for the white women already employed in them but also illegal. Segregation laws gave Richmond employers an excuse to not discuss hiring black women. Fr. Richard Roche, a head examiner for the FEPC, found that the personnel director of Richmond's paper company, Wortendyke Industries, "could not" hire black women, although, he claimed, he wanted very much to use them to alleviate the plant's labor shortage. The personnel director admitted that he needed more help but had no extra space to add the required bathroom facilities. According to Roche, the industry's hands were tied. The company, however, was "surveying space" to see whether it could find room for a bathroom.[7]

Although many Detroit companies segregated facilities, they did so under a de facto standard of cultural segregation, flaunting their refusal to adhere to the civil rights law. They as well as Richmond's employers found ample excuses not to hire black women, whether from "fear of reaction" from white women or "lack of space" for the required segregated facilities. In reality, the strict segregation that reached every level of Richmond society kept women out of factories.

Whatever the excuses, in reality employers hired black women only under serious pressure from unions and the government. By the middle of 1943, Detroit's WMC estimated that twenty-eight thousand black women were available for work, but most would only be hired as janitors, matrons (i.e., bathroom attendants and maids), and government inspectors.[8] The Women's Trade Union League (WTUL) acknowledged the difficulties that black women faced, arguing in a monthly newsletter that "Negro women encounter all the prejudice against women in industry and the complication of race."[9] Moreover, the WTUL found that black women's vocational choices had always lagged behind those of white women's. Other than in cases where defense training equalized the applicant pool, hopeful black applicants to war factories had to meet the skill levels of white women. Employers often used their lack of preparedness as an excuse in responding to FEPC charges of racism.

Both Detroit and Richmond experienced a wartime boom, and employment situations for women emerged in each city. Richmond, however, had far fewer manufacturing plants, so African American women there faced greater problems when securing employment in factories. Unlike Detroit, which experienced a desperate need for workers by 1943 that eventually led to the hiring of black women, Richmond's fairly stable economy peaked in 1943 and 1944, but that did not lead to desperate labor shortages. As FEPC investigator Will Maslow admitted in 1944, "The biggest problem in the Richmond area is the employment of Negro women, a group which offers a large available supply." In his report, Maslow told the United States Employment Services (USES) director of Richmond to develop a program that would introduce more black women into metro-area factories.[10] Until 1944, the Federal Security Agency found, most African American women were still employed in Richmond's service sector because of long-standing prejudices against them; a severe worker shortage, however, forced some employers to hire more of the women.[11]

The AFL–Tobacco Workers' International Union (TWIU) had a presence in Richmond, but no local union could come close to wielding the kind of power held by the UAW in Detroit, and Richmond workers had much less protection against corporate policies and hiring practices. The UAW-CIO was often quite liberal in its race policies, encouraged blacks to become active members, and defended their rights to work, but AFL-TWIU locals in Richmond segregated units into white locals with black auxiliaries. That ensured black workers would not have an equal voice in union politics and created an atmosphere in which the union would not fight for equalization of hiring practices.

A lack of job opportunities in Richmond, along with weak unions, hampered the ability of working-class African American women to advance their careers, whereas their counterparts in Detroit had more opportunities to break into and maintain jobs in that city's war industries. Women in Richmond, however, fought where they could and established footholds in industries unrelated to the war, in service work outside the home, and in government jobs. Evidence suggests that they took advantage of every job advancement opportunity available to them and understood that the war enabled them to claim rights to jobs normally held by whites.

Using State Structures to Secure Employment Opportunities

In both cities, African American women tried to use the FEPC to break into industries formerly closed to them. Their letters to the committee suggest that they possessed sophisticated knowledge of how the FEPC worked and believed it existed to help them investigate roadblocks to employment. Detroit's complaint rate vastly outstripped Richmond's, as African American women lodged at least 171 complaints against government and private industries in the city.

Many women complained directly to the FEPC, still others wrote to agents of the government—for example, President Roosevelt, Eleanor Roosevelt, and the WMC director. The women's willingness to take their complaints all the way to the top of the state hierarchy shows they understood that the state had power to help them advance racial justice in the industrial sector. In appealing to the Roosevelts, black workers continued a trend, begun during the depression, of making personal requests to the couple who personalized the state and made the Democratic party more approachable in the eyes of the working class and people of color.[12] Working-class black women may have had little money and no political influence, but they negotiated directly with the most powerful people in the country in order to gain jobs in industry from 1941 to 1945.

African American working-class women's complaints often charged federal agencies with discrimination, because Executive Order 8802 called for the desegregation of government offices. Most likely, the women believed they had a strong chance of success in challenging government segregation because the state had already banned inequality in its bureaucracy. Still, using the FEPC to investigate other state agencies suggests that despite the president's order to desegregate federal agencies, black women were discriminated against at local state offices.

The women placed themselves in a tenuous position by trying to use one part of the state to challenge other state agencies and often failed to effect changes. Moreover, they had few alternatives for appeal efforts. Lela Leverette, for example, told the FEPC that she had passed the Civil Service examination for junior typist with a score of 80–90 percent. When she went to the Detroit Tank Arsenal for her commission, however, the personnel officer twice refused to see her. After finally meeting with two other people for interviews, she still had no job. Noticing that her picture was attached to her file at each interview, she pointed out to the FEPC that, obviously, all personnel decisions were made with full knowledge of candidates' race. Her understanding of the unjust hiring process appeared to make her more determined to break into the arsenal, and she called the FEPC to complain. When the FEPC investigated the Tank Arsenal, the personnel officer replied that the office did not have to hire all commissioned candidates, and the FEPC subsequently dropped the case.[13]

Annie Butler successfully prosecuted her case against Detroit's local Office of Price Administration (OPA). After charging it with discriminatory hiring practices, she obtained a better job as a clerk-typist elsewhere, unbeknown to the FEPC. The agency pressured the OPA personnel director into hiring her because her skill levels were acceptable for the job, but she turned down the offer and formally withdrew her complaint—much to the surprise of the FEPC and the OPA.[14] Her case and Leverette's suggest that no distinct pattern existed on how the FEPC handled complaints against government agencies.

Eight African American women in Richmond focused their complaints on government offices, including the patent office and the very large Quartermaster Depot. Because Richmond's private factories were legally segregated, women understood that gains would not be made in most war industries in that city. Roosevelt had ordered federal government offices desegregated, however, and African American women had legitimate cases for the FEPC when they encountered discrimination in Richmond's government offices. The hiring problems at the Quartermaster Depot became a serious point of contention between the government and Richmond's African American community. Seven women filed formal complaints against the depot, and many articles in the *Richmond Afro-American* detailed the unfair hiring practices at the Bellwood Station Quartermaster Depot. As the editor stated, "A depot like Bellwood needs scores of clerical workers, and a number of young women who passed civil service exams were sent out for jobs only to be told that there were no jobs open while white women who went out were put to work at once." When the editor questioned the depot's personnel director, the official explained that "this is the South, and the white people won't stand for equality of opportunity and treatment."[15] The response reveals the disjuncture that existed between centralized state policies and local racialized politics.

Two women decided to take on the depot by writing to various government officials and seeing who could do the most good. Both used language that reflected their understanding of how working-class women could use the discourse of responsible patriotism. Elizabeth Smith, a janitor at the depot, was tired of seeing hopeful and qualified black female applicants turned away from Bellwood. She wrote to the *Afro-American,* the FEPC, the Civil Service Commission, and the NAACP in order to secure help from state institutions and rally the black community. As she stated:

> I understand that many complaints have been filed with your office about the conditions here at Richmond Quartermaster Depot of which I work here as maid.
>
> It seems as if the patrolman #7 think that the Four Freedom consist of serving the White Lords first and then come out and ask the "Negro Slaves" what in the hell do they want; and then inform them that no maids were being hired at present just as if he thought that all Negro women were looking for maid jobs; also an indication that they at RQM Depot had not seen or know that Negroes could look for jobs as typist, clerks, etc.

It also seems as if your patrolman, number 7 thinks that he is Land Lord over all the Kingdom of the RQM Depot and when ever any one once enter they must obey his throne.

I along with many other persons of our community do wish that you would see that Negroes are not barred from opportunity to participate in the war work at the RQM Depot other then [sic] that of common labor; for we have persons who are qualified for such jobs as stenographers, checkers, clerks, formans [sic], guards, and timekeepers.[16]

For good measure, Smith sent a copy of the letter to patrolman number 7. Her language reveals a connection between middle-class women's discourse of responsible patriotism and working-class women's understandings of patriotic work as fundamental to African American citizenship.

Smith distinguished between democracy and the happenings at the RQM by likening the hiring officer to a tyrant and referring to black workers as slaves, emphasizing what little control African Americans had over the work process there. She also demanded that blacks be given the opportunity to work for the war effort in skilled and well-paid positions.

The Civil Service Commission responded to Smith's complaint only by suggesting that she take the Civil Service examination if she personally wished to apply for the jobs she mentioned in the letter. The office also noted that because she had not furnished evidence to support her contentions, it considered the case closed, effectively negating her power as a leader in the fight for jobs at the base.

Ora Branch was no more successful in her plea for fair treatment at the Quartermaster Depot, an appeal that echoed the same patriotic language Smith used but added a personal plea to the president. The poignant letter suggests that Branch believed the president would personally respond to her complaint because she was a participant in the war effort:

During these perilous times, I realize you are carrying a heavy load, and I have taken every means in order not to worry you, but since my efforts have been in vain, I'm appealing to you. . . . Several whites have been put in at both plants [depot and patent office] but they refuse to take me. President Roosevelt, my problem is, please use your influence and see that I'm put on at the Patent Office or Some War Project here in Richmond, Va. . . . I'm a true American, whole-heartedly and I'm exceedingly anxious to do my share in this great war.[17]

Like Smith, Branch equated participation in the war with patriotism and charged that state agencies kept her from doing her patriotic duty. A subsequent FEPC investigation revealed that Branch did have an interview with the depot but was unfamiliar with the engineering supplies she would need to catalog, and the personnel director refused to hire her. Branch questioned whether white women were expected to know about all the supplies. It was a legitimate query. Black women understood the ploys that kept them from being hired, including being required to have much more experience than white applicants. The director explained to the FEPC that standard procedure had been followed, and Branch did not get the job.[18]

In each letter the authors employed the "Double V discourse" in that they pointed out the irony of a "democratic state" refusing to equalize its own hiring practices. They used patriotic language that reflected their belief that the work women did was work for democracy. This language enabled them to engage with the state over prejudicial practices within its own agencies as potential labor power for the war effort, even if the state failed to respond to their calls for social justice.

Detroit's working-class women also cited many private industries in their complaints to the FEPC, FDR, and Eleanor Roosevelt because the state worked with private industries to increase production for the war effort. Although many women complained about discrimination in various Detroit industries, it was the major automobile manufacturers that received a majority of complaints throughout the period. That is not surprising, given the sheer numbers of manufacturers and suppliers in the city. African American women targeted Murray Body, General Motors, Chrysler, Ford, and Packard in their attempts to desegregate industry. Dorothy Simmons, for example, wrote to FDR about problems she and others had encountered with Murray Body Corporation. She had logged 302 hours of aircraft riveting training, but Murray's personnel directors turned her down because of her weight. Simmons maintained, however, that she had seen "larger" white women hired and that Murray had refused employment to countless other black women. Lillie Trim told the FEPC that Murray turned her down as well, despite her 178 hours of training as a riveter. Further, she noted, Murray hired white women who had sixty-four hours or fewer of training while turning down black women who had 175 to 300 hours. The FEPC investigated both complaints and found that Murray had a plan to begin hiring black women by late 1942. Although there is no evidence that Simmons and Trim were among them, their use of the FEPC enabled other black women to secure jobs at the plant.[19]

Ford, Chrysler, GM, and Packard received a large number of complaints throughout the war because black women saw that these companies always appeared short of workers but continuously refused to hire black women. African American women workers pointed to the problems with racism; they saw factories underperforming because of labor shortages while employment

officers turned black women away at the hiring gate. Ford plants proved especially notorious for turning away qualified black women; three complained
about the Ford Lincoln plant hiring practices in 1944. "Every time I have been
down there," Clarinda Barnett told the FEPC, "they hire white girls and don't
hire any colored girls. On the fifteenth of February Mr. Cook he is the man
that hires picked out twenty-one white girls and told the colored girls there
were no more jobs." Fannie Robinson and Esteria Mayfield concurred. They
had experienced the same discrimination, and their complaints were added
to the evidence against Ford to be used in a larger investigation. In this instance the FEPC failed to help the three women because the company did not
supply the requested information necessary to conduct a large-scale investigation, including the numbers of black women who worked at their plants.[20]

All in all, the FEPC, FDR, and Eleanor Roosevelt received at least forty-
nine complaints against Packard, GM, Ford, and Chrysler between 1941 and
1945. The complaints suggest that black women, in the face of a severe labor
shortage in Detroit, knew that they reflected the best hope for stepped-up
production. The women needed help in securing job positions, however,
because informal systems of racist hiring practices played out in struggles
over employment officers' refusals to interview them. Black women understood that although the FEPC may not have had the kind of enforcement
power to guarantee victories against prejudicial hiring practices, the federal
government was their best ally in making inroads into these industries.

While the FEPC and government officials heard more than a hundred
complaints from Detroit women, FEPC records only reveal eleven complaints
from Richmond. In light of the fact that Richmond was very industrialized
before World War II, that number seems quite low. Richmond's black wom-
en, however, faced more problems than Detroit's in establishing a foothold
in industries. The social space for black and white residents, for example, was
strictly defined by Jim Crow laws, whereas Michigan's established civil rights
act declared segregation illegal. Even though the law was rarely enforced, it
provided a safety net for African American women in Detroit. They knew
they could at least file complaints and be heard based on their accusations.
The law gave them access, at least theoretically, to legal recourse against discrimination, and at this point individuals were using the legislation to contest neighborhood and restaurant segregation.

In Richmond, African American women who tried to break into industry
had no law to support them, and employers made no excuses for failing to
hire them. When the FEPC questioned Wortendyke Industries about pub-
lishing an advertisement for white women aged twenty-five to forty-five, the

personnel director replied, "No colored women are being used, and the company does not believe that they will fit in to the program." Moreover, he asserted that because black women had no experience in anything but tobacco factories they could not work the looms in the Wortendyke plant.[21] The pervasive segregation of the city enabled racist employers to shrug off responsibility for hiring black women, giving failure to fit into factory culture or inadequate preparation because of low-skill jobs as reasons for doing so.

Lack of a strong FEPC presence in Richmond no doubt contributed to the small number of complaints. Because few local industries were considered absolutely essential to the war, they failed to receive the FEPC's attention. In addition, the FEPC failed to place a permanent office in Richmond. In order to file and sign complaints personally, women had to wait until an investigator came to town, which meant that investigations often went uncompleted and employers faced no consistent pressure to change their hiring practices.

African American women complaining to the FEPC also could have faced difficult personal situations. Complainants were required to give much personal information on their forms, including addresses of relatives and personal telephone numbers. Richmond's racially oppressive structure implicitly threatened those who spoke against the reigning ideals of white supremacy. Although no evidence exists to prove it, those who complained to the FEPC might possibly have found themselves targets of white hatred. Moreover, the FEPC had more power when factories employed thousands of workers and had national reputations to lose. Detroit's auto manufacturers, high-profile companies, were essential to the war effort. Richmond industries, however, were not classified as having the highest priority, which led to less regulation by the War Manpower Commission. Larus and Brother Tobacco, DuPont Chemical Company, and Reynolds Aluminum had lucrative war contracts, but even those industries reflected lower priorities for the WMC's regulation policies. The FEPC spent more time on companies in other cities. Given all the hardships that African American women in Richmond faced, perhaps the fact that they filed any complaints at all was a small victory.

Evidence from those who did file complaints in Richmond, the majority of which were against federal agencies, suggests that they were no less convinced of deserving wartime jobs than women in Detroit. Black women in Richmond seemed to understand that their best chances at defense jobs were with the state rather than with private industries that consistently refused to bow to federal pressures to integrate. Many complainants spoke for hundreds of women attempting to secure wartime jobs and claimed positions as leaders in the working-class community, especially in the effort to desegregate state agencies supposed to be egalitarian as a result of the president's Executive Order 8802. Despite the fact that Richmond women's complaints seemed less successful than Detroit's, African American working-class women in Richmond such as Smith, Branch, and others saw some benefit in trying to use the government to equalize employment opportunities.

Securing the Support of Historically Black Institutions

While many African American women looked to the government for help in securing defense jobs, others turned to traditional private institutions of black and working-class power: the NAACP and the Urban League. In each case, working-class women forced the organizations to be responsive to their needs in the name of wartime necessity and equality. Although many historians have cited the NAACP and the Urban League as bastions of middle-class elite leadership, working-class women began to use the institutions during the war to bolster their positions with respect to the government in negotiations over jobs.[22]

The NAACP and the Urban League offered infrastructures, leaders familiar with state officials, and money for litigation. Working-class women needed their power in order to locate themselves closer to centers of state power, and many used the NAACP and the Urban League as bridges to government institutions. It is clear that the numbers of working-class African American women who expected the NAACP and the Urban League to help them secure better jobs during the war affected the policies of these institutions and made them more responsive to needs.

In Detroit, the NAACP took many complaints from African American women. Jack Burke, an FEPC investigator, maintained that a large majority of the three hundred complaints referred to the agency in three months had been referred by civil rights groups. Gloster Current, president of the NAACP, argued that many of the group's referrals came from women whose husbands were in the army but who still could not secure wartime jobs.[23] The fact that the women called upon the government to compensate them for the sacrifice of their husbands is significant in that they used the gendered language of responsible patriotism in order to demand jobs from the state. Detroit women went to the NAACP in groups to complain about specific industries. They must have understood that more complainants could attract more attention within the black community, and they constructed legal affidavits with the help of the NAACP, using its strength to help them as they filed lawsuits and filled out paperwork for the FEPC.

In 1942 the NAACP helped prosecute two major cases with the help of five women. First, Helen Nuttall, Anna Mae Jones, and Elizabeth Jones asserted that Michigan Bell refused to hire them as telephone operators, despite their qualifications. When the NAACP confronted the company directly, it admitted opening few jobs to black women but added that they could work in the cafeteria or as elevator girls. The NAACP registered complete dissatisfaction with that answer, and the three women became part of a massive public campaign against Bell that lasted for years. They starred in national press releases and local news stories as the NAACP continued to fight their case by engaging the black community in the battle through publicity and lawsuits.[24]

Also in 1942, the NAACP helped Buenos Marie Blocker and Jessie Baskins contribute to the desegregation of Hudson Naval Arsenal, a case that contrasts how state and private institutions handled calls for social justice and suggests the importance of local action in enforcing federal laws. When Baskins received a telegram to report to the company for machine work, she waited in the employment office for nine hours only to find she would not be hired because "no work was available." Blocker also received a telegram. After the arsenal assigned her to a plant, a foreman asked her if she was black. When she told the truth, he admitted that a mistake had been made and she could not start work. Both women went to the NAACP, which helped them to file complaints with the union, company officials, USES, the navy, and the FEPC. After strong pressure from the NAACP and the union, both women received jobs by December 1942.[25] Because it was affiliated with the Armed Forces, the arsenal fell under the auspices of Executive Order 8802. The NAACP was successful because it called on the government to enforce that presidential order, which desegregated war agencies and offices.

After receiving continued complaints from numerous women about hiring practices, the NAACP determined to launch a mass protest against how Detroit industries treated black women. In April 1943, it led a call to action: "Trained Negro women war workers are denied employment in most plants and in many where they are hired they are relegated to jobs of a status inferior to their training and skills, or given work so difficult that it was in direct violation of the labor code."[26] The NAACP planned a mass rally that would start with a parade of several miles down the main street of Detroit and end with a demonstration downtown in Cadillac Square. More than five thousand people demonstrated support of working-class women's fight for jobs.[27]

Apparently, industries failed to respond to the demonstration, which led the NAACP to work even harder. The next month four women tested industries to see if the demonstration had made an impact. Although they had more than 374 total hours of defense training, they could not secure jobs at Ainsworth Manufacturing, the American Lady Corset Company, Detroit

Lubricator, the Eureka Corporation, Chrysler, Detroit Gear and Axle, or Palmer Bee Company.[28] When Gloster Current read a WMC press release asking for seventy-two thousand more women in industry, he became angry and sent a press release to the WMC's director: "We know that you are cognizant of continued discrimination against Negro women. We feel that in the interest of the war effort, as well as carrying out the provisions of Executive Order 8802 and 9436, the War Manpower Commission ought to proceed energetically against discriminating employers who still violate the order and set our war effort in jeopardy. This is a form of treason which is as detrimental to democracy as Nazi spies."[29]

The NAACP began to use the discourse of responsible patriotism as it became engaged in the battle for working-class rights. Working-class African American women expected the organization's help in their fight against discrimination, which indicates growing understanding of their importance in the overall fight for equality. The fact that Current equated the actions of racist employment officials to those of Nazi spies shows how strongly the NAACP believed that working-class black women could advance the cause of racial justice by fighting for equal job opportunities. Moreover, the NAACP's language reinforced the idea that those blocking racial progress were unpatriotic, not those who fought for equality.

Detroit's African American women had the largest NAACP chapter in the country helping them desegregate industry. African American women in Richmond had to rely on a smaller NAACP and Urban League as allies. Three women's complaints to the NAACP went directly to the FEPC for processing—without the kind of preparation NAACP leaders in Detroit gave their cases. Although the complaints were docketed in each case, the NAACP failed to push for a satisfactory resolution, and there is no record of a final disposition report for them.[30]

Many Richmond women worked with the Urban League to ensure being first in line when jobs became available. During the war, as a shrinking worker pool threatened local production output, black women went unemployed rather than take the domestic jobs listed with the Urban League job registry. The Urban League understood the actions of these women to be not only a rejection of domestic labor but also a call for better jobs. It recruited and registered women who had not held industrial jobs and reclassified people who sought domestic work in order to try to transfer them to the industrial jobs that came open. The number of unfilled Urban League–registered jobs for women rose rapidly during the war; in 1940 there were only 289, then 414 during 1941, 1,001 in 1942, and 1,599 by 1943. The numbers suggest that women were indeed finding jobs in Richmond. Many took the industrial or nonproduction work offered by the Urban League job registry while turning down domestic jobs.[31] Like the African American working-class women in Detroit, Richmond women took institutions that had previously answered middle-class concerns and made them respond to working-class labor issues. They forced the Urban League to shift the focus of its job registry activities in order to privilege nondomestic work.

Ultimately, the Urban League and the NAACP both had to respond to the needs of working-class women. As the NAACP found itself equating the actions of employers with Nazis and the Urban League had to refocus its job registry, the organizations became more inclusive and diverse. Working-class African American women helped both institutions reach out to more members of the black community as their demands for equal job opportunities found support within these historically black organizations.

Black Women, Unions, and the Fight for Equal Job Opportunities and Equal Treatment on the Factory Floor

The different union cultures of each city shaped the ways in which African American women used unions to secure their rights. In Detroit, the UAW tended to focus on securing rights for the women. In Richmond, the racially restrictive TWIU locals hampered their ability to seek equality within factories. Indeed, much of the time the African American women in Richmond had to contest the TWIU in order to secure equal representation.

While Detroit's African American working-class women endured hate strikes, worked with the unions for better working conditions and job security, and sometimes dealt with physical violence in the factories, the political consciousness shaped by wartime rhetoric in Richmond helped women justify claiming more space in local industries. Unlike industries in Detroit, Richmond industries refused to put black and white women together in any factory, so contestation of space did not occur. Although Richmond women had fewer opportunities to change the racial climate within factories, they did what they could in order to take advantage of the wartime labor shortage. Local unions were weak and only mildly concerned with the rights of African American workers, so evidence concerning black working women's activities is scant. Enough exists, however, to suggest they dealt with some of the same issues as Detroit women. They asserted their rights as workers by claiming better pay and representation by unions and by fighting for promotions and job security. In one plant, moreover, some took on the powerful TWIU hierarchy and won the right to fair union representation.

Detroit women did not just rely upon the help of the NAACP but went directly to local unions in order to secure rights as workers. Although, technically, the union represented only workers in factories, black women understood that the power of the UAW might be brought to bear against industries in the hiring process. The UAW had consistently reached out to the black community in order to bring workers into the union and strengthen its numbers. During the automotive strikes of the late 1930s and early 1940s, the union worked hard to turn black scabs into union members and then represented those who wanted to be hired permanently. In addition, the UAW worked to integrate local unions and supported the election of black officials at the factory level.[32]

Although some UAW locals were unwilling to support employment opportunities for blacks, the national leaders were committed to integration. The UAW was most successful in fighting for the hiring of black women at Ford's River Rouge and Willow Run plants. African American women received UAW support when two hundred black women stormed the employment office at Willow Run after being refused entry at the hiring gate. The show of force and solidarity, the climax to a year of blatant employment discrimination at Ford, forced the company to start negotiating with the UAW and the NAACP in order to create some sort of program for hiring black women.[33]

After several months of negotiation, however, the UAW realized that it had made no progress and pressed the company even harder in order to maintain legitimacy in negotiations with management. The locals at River Rouge and Willow Run held a three-hour meeting with Ford, which refused to hire black women until "outside pressure" ceased. It was a familiar twist to the "outside agitator" rhetoric management used when blaming unions for entering factories and encouraging dissatisfaction among workers. The personnel director at the meeting, Willis Ward, claimed the union had no right to represent the women because they were not workers. Further, he thumbed his nose at Executive Order 8802 and scoffed at the FEPC's effectiveness. It was his opinion "that the Executive Order probably constituted a law and that possibly it was violated but then who would punish the violators."[34] In a response to the Metropolitan Detroit Fair Employment Practices Committee, Ward further stated that the unions were not to be involved in this problem because they "were cutthroats and liars, communistically controlled, . . . [and] if women were hired at the Bomber Plant, they would hire qualified Negresses as well as white women."[35]

The tension between the union and management became apparent as management accused the UAW of being controlled by communists and black women became beneficiaries of a power struggle between Ford and Locals 50 and 600. The UAW, infuriated that Ford questioned its right to determine hiring practices, sponsored a massive demonstration at the River Rouge plant that blocked the gates of the employment office. In a flyer publicizing the event, the UAW related the fight of black women to secure jobs at Ford. In reality, however, the flyer reasserted union power over the issue by emphasizing the union's support:

> We can no longer tolerate the Ford Motor Company's policy of discrimination against the Negro women. We resent Harry Bennett's assertion that the Ford Motor Company is the only company giving the Negro a chance.
>
> Willis Ward, "the Yes and No Man" of the Ford Motor Company relative to the Negro question, is a traitor to the cause of Better Labor and Race Relations among the Ford Workers. The segregated employment office set-up (all Negroes channeled through Ward's office and all white workers sent elsewhere) is a great demoralizing factor. . . . *Mr. Ford, Negro women and men will and must play their rightful part in helping win this war.*[36]

It is significant that the UAW picked up on the patriotic language of working-class black women and equated work in factories with participation in the war effort.

The pressure tactics worked even though the UAW stated that the demonstration was not a strike; it had signed a no-strike pledge to support the war effort. Ford began to hire a very small number of black women at the end of 1942. In November, a young mother and wife of an enlisted man, a Mrs. Anderson, was one of the first hired at Willow Run. She faced eviction from the Sojourner Truth housing projects because she could not secure a job that paid enough to pay the rent; her meager salary was used to support her toddler, nephew, and sick mother. She had eighty hours of training as an inspector and had applied to Ford five times because her husband had worked there before enlisting in the army.[37]

The UAW did not succeed in making Ford hire large numbers of women in 1942, but it enabled African American women to break into factories and establish a foothold, which led to more black women being hired throughout the war. In cases where the FEPC and NAACP failed to effect a solution for the racist hiring practices in Detroit industries, the struggle for primacy over the auto industry between the UAW and management enabled them to gain union support in their quest for jobs.

In Richmond, African American women workers tried to work with their unions whenever possible to secure equal pay and work opportunities. Sometimes, however, they contested union practices as they fought to be represented fairly. Several attempted to go to their unions to get pay raises at Larus and Brother Tobacco's stemmery plant. Harry Koger, International representative for the CIO's United Cannery, Agriculture, Packing, and Allied Workers of America (UCAPAWA), the black women's bargaining unit, notified the FEPC that unskilled white women received between 20 and 25 cents more per hour than unskilled black women. When Koger represented the women at a meeting with Larus and Brother Vice President Charles Reed, he reported that Reed "became very indignant and threatened to call off all negotiations and also threatened to call the F.B.I. and have them 'take care of me' because I was trying to stir up racial hatred."[38] When the FEPC investigated the situation, Reed told the committee that the company believed fully in integrating blacks into the workforce and in equality as a general rule. The black women Koger represented, however, performed different types of work; they were in the stemmery, whereas the white women were in the main plant. The FEPC failed to challenge this historic pattern of segregation, and the women could not do much to upend factory hierarchies without institutional support.[39]

Although Koger pointed out that the stemmery was almost entirely staffed by African Americans and black women found themselves ineligible to work at the higher pay rates, a clear case of discrimination, the FEPC dropped the case.[40] The case appeared to be a clear-cut situation made for FEPC intervention. The FEPC made the case invalid, however, by stating that Koger's original assertion did not match his reply. In effect, there were two different complaints, both of which needed more evidence from Koger and women in the factory to pursue.[41]

Although the FEPC's failure to encourage the case may seem inexplicable, perhaps it had something to do with the warm relationship between FEPC Executive Secretary George Johnson and Charles Reed. Johnson seemed to appreciate his meeting with Reed and a follow-up "gift": "I was pleasantly surprized [sic] to receive a package containing some of 'America's finest pipe tobacco' and a very attractive pipe. I recall the pleasant conference we had with respect to the employment policies of the Larus and Brothers Co. . . . it is my hope that you will play your part in making democracy work by giving equal employment opportunities to Negroes on the basis of their qualifications."[42]

Apparently, the needs of hundreds of African American women failed to eclipse the appeal of pipe tobacco for George Johnson. The stemmery continued to be completely segregated throughout the war. Two years later, the TWIU Local 219B negotiated directly with the company to secure a pay raise for African American women. In 1944 white women received approximately

64 cents an hour whereas African American women received only 44 cents per hour. The union got the company to agree to raise black inspectors' pay to 51 cents hourly in contrast with white inspectors' 70 cents. Larus and Brother voluntarily raised the women's pay to 59 cents an hour.[43] Although the company continued to maintain unequal pay scales, black women at least got a pay raise from the contract.

Because the TWIU local at Larus and Brother had become organized during the strike of 1941 and because the CIO focused efforts on organizing the black workers in its plants, the company experienced more contention within its factories than other tobacco companies in Richmond. Before 1943 the TWIU-AFL represented all of the white workers and the UCAPAWA-CIO represented the black workers in Larus and Brother factories. At times the situation seemed to work well, as it did in 1941 when white workers struck for better wages. Black workers had refused to cross the picket lines "for fear of getting hurt," and the CIO supported their refusal.[44]

Relations between the two unions broke down, however, until the AFL called for a companywide election to determine which organization could retain its union in the company. Apparently, the AFL claimed it would desegregate the local if the TWIU union won the election and so gained the support of African American workers. Yet as soon as the TWIU won it created Local 219 and Local 219B, a segregated black auxiliary. Although the TWIU had secured the pay raise for women in the stemmery, African Americans believed their rights had been violated and that the union did not adequately represent them to the company.[45] They decided to bring back the CIO and, with ACLU help, filed a lawsuit to try to rescind the certification of Local 219 if it did not remove the color bar immediately. The local responded that there was no cause to justify revoking the certification; two equal units did exist in the plants. In answering the ACLU, the TWIU's lawyers used as a precedent *Plessy v. Ferguson* (1896), the famous streetcar case that established "separate but equal" segregation as law.[46]

Two women testified for the CIO before the National Labor Relations Board in 1945. A tobacco dryer since 1923, Isabelle Manigo maintained that when African Americans found themselves required to join a segregated local they realized that the AFL had cheated them. "We could," she said, "have went on and joined up under that same local group they already had, because they [the whites] already had a charter."[47] She refused to join 219B but had belonged to the CIO since 1941. Manigo was one of the workers who signed the original ACLU affidavit.[48] Sarah Jackson also testified for the CIO. In her statement, she asserted that she had worked at Larus and Brother since 1938, and because she was a clerical worker she belonged to neither union. She had,

however, been a member of the CIO until her promotion.[49] She, too, signed
the affidavit asking to have 219's charter revoked.

Both women experienced heated and antagonistic cross-examinations in
which TWIU lawyers attempted to discredit their testimony by questions
about specific legal terms in the affidavit in order to prove they did not know
what they were signing.[50] The lawyers were unsuccessful, however, and the
NLRB allowed the CIO to return to Larus and Brother. This testimony suggests that African American women were very involved in black workers'
successful bid for unsegregated union representation and understood that
the CIO represented their best chance at negotiating power because it appeared to recognize their desires.

Once African American women secured fair union representation and
gained entrance into production and nonproduction work, their struggles
continued on factory and shop floors, particularly in Detroit. There as well
as in Richmond, working-class women fought for better working conditions
and pay as well as for promotions. Because black women in Detroit entered
factories in much larger numbers than black women in Richmond, they faced
especially severe problems with white women workers. In Detroit, they sought
to retain employment gains in the face of wildcat hate strikes, unfair job
demotions, and firings. In Richmond, they demanded promotions and better pay based on seniority.

Detroit's working-class women fought to claim space on the factory floor
as white women tried to maintain segregation on assembly lines and in restrooms and cafeterias. They often feared working in close proximity to black
women, whom they defined as dirty and dangerous. They also wanted to
distance themselves from black women and often walked out in protest when
African Americans were introduced into previously "white" space.[51]

The UAW found itself in a tenuous position over this issue. It had to represent the interests of black as well as white employees and often negotiated
deals enabling black women to continue their work. In 1943 a series of work
stoppages wracked the Chrysler and Packard plants until unions stepped in
to support the black women's right to work. On February 12 at Chrysler's
Highland Park plant, Vera Sutton, Bernice Kirksey, and Pauline Justice joined
the production line as drill press operators, making $1 an hour. White wom-
en walked off the line immediately in a wildcat strike, and the company pulled
the three off the line and returned them to training school. When they took
their case to the union, it called the FEPC, plant security, management, and
an army representative to the plant.[52] Ironically, when faced with opposition
from the union and the state, the company that had been reluctant to hire
black women in the first place decided it would support them. As the FEPC

At work at stamping machine, 1943. (Courtesy of the Walter P. Reuther Library, Wayne State University)

reported, "Management was going to stand firm on the issue of the Negro girls . . . under no circumstances would they be taken away from their machines . . . as that would be a licking for the company."[53] With the company and the unions supporting the African Americans, the white women had no choice but to return to work.

The Highland Park Packard plant erupted several weeks later when four African American women joined the production line. Although the factory went through a series of stoppages, the black women continued to work at their machines. The UAW and Packard determined to solve the problem by increasing the number of black women on the lines, giving white women a more difficult target. Six weeks after the strike Packard had fifty black women on its assembly line, and the FEPC lauded the company's progressive policy.[54]

The series of stoppages at Chrysler and Packard lasted through several shifts and caused the loss of hundreds of production hours. Black leaders attempted to blame the incidents on the actions of radical racists within the plant, and the *Michigan Chronicle* accused a strong Ku Klux Klan element. The FEPC, the union, and other officials, however, viewed the ethnicity of the white women as the cause, in addition to race and space. Both plants were located in Highland Park, an almost entirely Polish ethnic enclave in Detroit. The Polish American women had fought for places in the factories and remained wary of black women who came from outside their neighborhoods to work. The FEPC went so far as to ask the unions to bring in priests to explain equity and democracy with respect to Executive Order 8802 to the women.[55] Tensions among ethnic whites who lived in the neighborhoods surrounding the two plants reveal the fears of other white working-class women. Black women would, they thought, first encroach upon their neighborhood space and then threaten their economic security by taking good jobs from other white women.

Strikes occurred throughout the city during 1943 and 1944 as African American women joined production lines. In every case, they continued working and secured both company and union support in the name of democracy. Strikes occurred at Consolidated Brass, Gemmer Manufacturing, Briggs Manufacturing, and Chicago Pneumatic Tool. The strike at Chicago Pneumatic Tool was especially vicious because the target was one black woman who had been transferred to an inspection job, a job upgrade. When the union ordered workers back to the line, enraged white women threw banana skins at the inspector. She kept working.[56]

In each case the union's local leaders, including shop stewards and other officials, not only supported black women but also chastised white women for being undemocratic and hindering war progress. UAW Local 157 charged the ringleaders of the banana incident with conduct unbecoming a CIO member.[57] In addition, Jess Ferrazza, president of Local 212 (Briggs), refused to give in to the prejudice of those who demanded removal of the African American newcomers. When the women struck, Ferrazza told the shop steward, "Go ahead and tell each one of the girls who refuses to work that they can come in here and get their clearance because they are through. The company is going to fire them and we are not going to take up their grievances. As far as we are concerned, they are out, too."[58] Often, however, situations did not resolve themselves neatly when white women went back to work. Ferrazza admitted that many refused to speak to either union leaders or black workers, and tensions emerged in various ways in many other companies.

African American women had to remain on guard against hostile workers in one-on-one situations and when dealing with segregated facilities and often involved themselves in physical confrontations resulting from built-up tensions created by poor work environments and unfriendly co-workers. Although all workers were responsible for the altercations, only the black women were fired in most instances. Their treatment suggests they were labeled as provocateurs and blamed for white retaliation in confrontations. In this way, companies made African American women responsible for maintaining amicable race relations. In 1943, for example, Lillian Garner found a white co-worker at Murray Body Corporation eating her lunch. The co-worker, "Virginia," apologized and offered her 10 cents. Garner was offended because the lunch was worth much more than that, and she refused Virginia's offer. Georgiaphene Buford, Floysell Jones, and Effie Greer, all African American co-workers, witnessed the exchange and went back to the assembly line with Garner. Although Garner thought that the situation was resolved, Virginia went to get the shop steward to "straighten out" matters. She told the steward that she had offered Garner 50 cents for the lunch, at which point Garner called her a liar. Infuriated by the accusation, Virginia slapped Garner in the face. Garner did not retaliate physically. Virginia received only a four-day lay-off because the company faced a shortage of riveters. Garner, Buford, Jones, and Greer, however, were fired two weeks later for "unsatisfactory work" although they had never received unsatisfactory reports from their foremen.[59]

The women refused to let the company treat them unfairly. They had fought hard for their jobs and were determined to stage a pitched battle over the terms of their labor and the policies of the company. Buford and Jones wrote to Eleanor Roosevelt, and all four went to the NAACP, the FEPC, and UAW Local 2 to file grievances. In the subsequent investigation the FEPC and the UAW found that although the women had training as riveters, and despite the company's riveter shortage, for four and a half weeks they had been dusting and painting. They often had nothing to do because the company refused to move them to all-white production lines. The UAW noted that the company had laid off two other black women for "unsatisfactory work," and the local suspected that the company had fired all of the women before their six-week probationary period was up so they had no protection of seniority under the union agreement.

After the women made their case to the NAACP, the FEPC, and the UAW, each group pressured Murray Body to reinstate them. All were back at the plant by late March.[60] In this case, the women found success when the local union, a local civil rights group, and a state agency converged and pressured a company to give back their jobs. The incident reveals the ways in which working-class women worked with every available institution in order to achieve success in their battle for equality.

Lillian Garner was not the only woman involved in a physical altercation in a Detroit plant. Several women fought back when faced with the threat of injury, and all contested their subsequent punishments but with varying degrees of success. Jewel Henderson accused a plant guard of tearing her sleeve after the police charged her with disturbing the peace at the Chrysler plant in 1944. In court, however, two officers testified that she had been drinking, exhibited clear signs of hostility, refused to show her identification badge, and struck a security guard in the jaw. Not only did Henderson lose her job, but the judge also did not buy her claim of self-defense. She received six months' probation and a $25 fine.[61] Mamie Hawkins complained about the result of an altercation to the FEPC with little success. While leaving an unnamed plant she had accidentally bumped into Frank Kidwell, a white worker. He deliberately bumped her back, and she slapped him in the face. At this point, according to witnesses, three black men became involved, and the plant supervisor claimed they held Kidwell down while Hawkins attacked him. She received a week's layoff, and all the men were fired. The FEPC considered Hawkins lucky to get away with such a light punishment and closed her case.[62]

With white and black workers in such close proximity, working ten or more hours a day, often under inferior working conditions, it was understandable that physical violence erupted as a result of the built-up tensions released over contestations of space. The fact that several African American women fought to overturn their punishments suggests they believed they had as many rights as white workers and knew exactly where to go in order to appeal unfair decisions.

Tensions between black and white women gave employers an excuse to segregate bathrooms, lunchrooms, and even assembly lines, yet some African American women worked hard for equal facilities in Detroit factories in an attempt to enforce the Diggs Civil Rights Law. Because the law banned segregation in public areas, they knew they had legal right to equal treatment in factories and enlisted the aid of the FEPC and the unions. Many protested against inequalities in plants, and often their focus was on segregated bathrooms. While a hate strike at Packard waged by white women protesting the addition of black women onto the assembly lines was in full swing, for example, the black women secured the help of their union local and pressed the FEPC to help them abolish segregated bathrooms. The company allowed them to use only those toilets "formerly condemned as unsanitary and fitted only for the use of males."[63] Although local FEPC officials considered this to be a social problem and not one it should investigate, the union disagreed. After negotiating with the company, it managed to have the separate facilities abolished.[64]

Given that the FEPC's job was to examine all inequalities that affected employment, it is interesting that local FEPC agents turned a blind eye to segregated facilities at Packard. Their failure to look beyond hiring practices and into factory space threatened to stifle black women's activism, but the UAW stepped up to support them and helped change the segregation policy.

The local FEPC's failure to respond highlights the constant roadblocks black women faced when trying to have national policies enforced at a local level. As late as 1945 they complained about segregated facilities, and, as a result of a black woman complaining to a local civil rights commission, an incident occurred at the Chrysler-Highland Park plant that changed the way both white and black inspectors ate lunch.

Gladys Brown told the Detroit Commission on Community Relations (DCCR) that she and her friend faced continued discrimination at the plant. When the women, both government inspectors, tried to enter the cafeteria behind four white inspectors, the guard told all six that the cafeteria was for office workers, not inspectors, and barred their entry. Brown knew, however, that the four white women ate there regularly. The next day, when the white women went alone to the cafeteria, a guard told them they could eat after the regular lunch shift ended. When Brown and her friend asked their government representative, a Lieutenant Waters, why they, too, could not eat in the cafeteria, he replied that their race kept them out. They asked Waters whether he thought that was fair, especially because Brown's friend's husband was overseas and it hurt their feelings to see the white women laughing when the two had to get lunch from an outdoor catering cart. Again, working-class women drew upon the Double V discourse and equated their understanding of female sacrifice—a husband at war—with their right to be treated as citizens. The DCCR notified the War Department, which told Waters to let Chrysler know that all inspectors were to be served or denied service in the cafeteria, regardless of their race. Chrysler denied service to all of the government inspectors rather than serve the black women.[65]

Some factories appeared determined to maintain segregated facilities despite Michigan's civil rights law, which suggests the pervasiveness of de facto segregation despite the best efforts of black women, civil rights groups, and union locals to enforce state law. Nevertheless, black women managed to secure equal facilities within some Detroit factories by using local and national organizations to back their claims for social justice.

African American women also fought for the right to work. They again looked to unions and government agencies to help secure upgrades and promotions and reinstate them after demotions or layoffs. In several cases, the women enlisted the aid of black men to strike for job upgrades and job se-

curity. Their experiences suggest that they viewed their tenure in war factories as long-term commitments and expected to be treated fairly and according to seniority rights, just like any white worker. Many of the problems with
job upgrading surfaced when black women sought to move from nonproduction jobs in factories to assembly-line jobs. When the women failed to
get promotions they often called upon the FEPC and the unions to intervene
and negotiate with the companies.

African American women in Detroit targeted Vickers, Inc., for its unfair
upgrade practices. Vickers had 2,300 women employees but hired only thirty-
five black women, and those as matrons or bathroom attendants. The wom-
en got the FEPC to negotiate with Vickers, which agreed to hire qualified
women as production workers and allow the matrons to attend training
school. The FEPC was astounded, however, that not one of the thirty-five
women agreed to the schooling. It may have been a case of economic necessity superseding job equity goals. Many of the women would have lost as
much as 30 cents an hour by attending the training school for an undeter-
mined number of weeks, and most, no doubt, most could not afford such a
drop in wages.[66] Women in seven other cases complained about various
Detroit companies, and two succeeded in acquiring requested job upgrades.[67]
The small number of women who won demands for performance-based
promotions suggests that the FEPC and the union were not nearly as concerned about the types of jobs black women held once they had broken the
barriers to employment. In the case of Vickers, Inc., they appeared to fight
without much support from the state.

In some cases, Detroit's working-class African American women fought
desperately to retain war production jobs and fought downgrading and layoffs when war production shifted in 1944. In that year, Velum Smith wrote a
poignant letter to FDR, whom she believed was her last hope after the union
disregarded her plea for help:

> I am a Deafence worker trying to help win the war Buying Bond and stamps. I
> am trying to Hold out faithful to the end. I Been employed for Crysler Co, . . . we
> got a Bad Break and a Bad One I work 17 mos. In Side 501 and did not mind it
> But now out side exposure to rain and ice and loading and unloading car bot-
> ies on the Rail Road. Nothing but colored wimon while white wimon wont Do
> it we got to get 8 feet in the air and push Boties to the ones on the Grown and
> the Men looking out the windows loughing saying helo I am telling the truth
> so help me the mens got good jobs in side. . . . The reason I am telling you
> Because I believe you can do something about Please I am Disgusted and sick
> . . . answer as soon please . . . voted for you.[68]

Smith equated her right to a safe job with compensation for participating in the war effort. Although she spoke in a language that reflected working-class concerns, familiarity with the discourse of responsible patriotism is apparent in her demand for help based on participation in the war, which included buying stamps and voting for the president. Moreover, she drew upon the discourse of respectability. She, as a woman, should not have to work outdoors while men worked indoors; gender conventions necessitated that women, defined as more delicate than men, should be protected from the Detroit elements. She claimed the rights to citizenship as a voter and an active participant in the war effort. In this case, Mary Anderson, director of the Women's Bureau, wrote back almost immediately and directed Smith to call upon the local Women's Bureau representative, Kathleen Lowry. At this point, Smith dropped out of the historical record.[69]

At least five other African American women complained directly to the FEPC in order to get their old jobs back. In most cases, companies rebutted by claiming that the women's work records merited demotions or being fired. In one instance, however, a woman at Detroit Axle Company returned to work after an FEPC investigation. Although they continued to call upon state agencies to help them retain lucrative war jobs, it is clear that the FEPC was losing power toward the end of the war and could not help most women who demanded assistance.[70]

Like women in Detroit, black working women in Richmond fought hard to secure job upgrades and better pay whenever they could. Gladys Ross's run-in with the Quartermaster Depot began in 1942 but remained unresolved until 1945. She worked as a checker at the depot until personnel officers found out she was black, although light-skinned, and demoted her to a janitor's position. Finding her salary reduced by $200 a year, she took the case to the FEPC. After many negotiations the depot agreed to promote her to a clerk at an annual salary of $1,440. It took the FEPC three years of pressure, however, to have Ross rehired at a position for which she was qualified.[71] Other women pressured the depot for promotions and job upgrades, and the *Richmond Afro-American* reported that ninety-two received promotions that would raise their combined salaries by more than $13,000 a year in 1944.[72]

Some African American women in Detroit chose to involve their unions when contesting unfair demotions or firings. Given the success rate of the unions over the FEPC, it is noteworthy that more failed to ask for help. It may suggest that several locals continued to be unfriendly toward black women's issues, despite the UAW policy of no tolerance toward discrimination within the union. Gertrude Turner wrote to FDR to complain about being demoted from drill press operator to burr remover at Ternstedt Manufacturing. She also filed a grievance with UAW Local 174, demanding her old job back. By the time the FEPC got around to responding to her complaint, the union had helped her to reverse the demotion.[73]

Eight African American women complained to Local 3 about their forced transfers at the Dodge Main plant. They found themselves transferred from the wire room to less desirable jobs in the foundry, although white women with less seniority received better jobs. The union asked the company to remove five white women from their current jobs, workers who had less seniority than the eight black women. Management replied that it always returned women to their previous departments, and, in fact, the eight black women received $1.12 an hour, 10 cents more than women in the wire room. Because of the pay rates, the UAW president refused Local 3's appeal, and the women had to stay in their current jobs or be laid off.[74] It is important to note, however, that even though the women lost their case on appeal, the union backed their seniority rights. Seniority, however, meant less to the women than having the right to avoid certain kinds of work. Moreover, seniority was racialized because of blacks' relatively late entry into defense jobs. It did not count for much when the women found themselves well behind white women as companies began rehiring laid-off workers.

Sometimes African American women in Detroit refused to rely on government or labor institutions to help secure their jobs. Rather, they called on male colleagues to support their fight for equality in an attempt to rally more broad-based support from within their community. In several instances black men walked off their jobs to support the women. As the site of many race problems during the war, Hudson Naval Arsenal experienced one such walkout in early 1943. Sixteen busboys and porters left their jobs after the personnel manager refused to rehire two black women he had dismissed two days earlier. According to the company, Mabel Freeman and Janella Banks had distracted the cafeteria porters and busboys. When the strikers questioned the personnel manager about his decision, he told them that the women had asked to be fired because the work was too hard for them. Freeman and Banks countered that they were the first black women hired in the cafeteria, and white women employees threatened to quit over the issue. Rather than lose the white women, the company fired the Freeman and Banks.[75] Unfortunately, the newspaper that originally carried the story failed to follow up on it, and what happened to the women is unknown. It is likely, however, that they did not regain their jobs. Had they done so the newspaper would have printed the story. In this situation the union failed to step in and stop what was essentially a hate strike. The women, left on their own without institutional support, did not succeed in retaining their jobs.

Another serious situation erupted in 1943 at Chrysler's Jefferson Avenue plant over the kinds of jobs African American women received. Those who found employment at the plant discovered they were either to be attendants in men's bathrooms or required to haul barrels of metal shavings that weighed up to 250 pounds. In most cases, the women had more than two hundred hours of defense training and did not know what kind of work they would have to do when they accepted the jobs. They contested the assignments based on gendered concepts of work. Heavy work in the factory, they believed, should be assigned to men. When the women quit, they told male janitors at the plants what had occurred.[76] In response, six hundred men walked off their jobs at the Jefferson Avenue plant.

Although the UAW outlawed the strike, the women who quit tried to explain why the janitors were striking.[77] "We are not given the same opportunity for promotions that white women are given," one stated. "We have GOT TO do the hard work, such as pulling steel, running jitneys, and heavy mopping. Many of us were hired as elevator operators but have never run an elevator at the plant because the men on the elevators refuse to transfer to the work we are doing. . . . We have taken our complaints to the union, . . . but there has been no action." It is significant that the women used gender as a rationale for avoiding heavy work. Moreover, their complaint suggests that union leadership was not always responsive to their problems. As another complained about plant conditions, "We are constantly being intimidated because we insist on eating in the regular places. When we first went to the plant they gave us separate toilets—far from our work—and we were told that we would have to eat our lunch in these restrooms. There is nothing but two benches and a low table in there."[78]

Although the fight erupted over gendered definitions of work, it segued into a contestation over inadequate and segregated facilities, a controversy that drew on concepts of equality beyond the work detail and into factory culture. Nine men were laid off as a result of their actions, but Chrysler relented and rehired the women, who received lighter duties as a result of the strike.[79]

All in all, at least five other strikes occurred over the demotion or poor working conditions of African American women in factories.[80] In one instance, nonproduction workers successfully threatened a strike that resulted in much better pay. At Hudson's Department Store, black elevator operators scheduled a strike when the company refused a pay raise. When the union wholeheartedly supported the women, Hudson's agreed not only to raise their salaries, which ranged from $16 to $25 a week, but also to furnish the black stockings that were part of their uniforms.[81]

In some cases strikes were a successful negotiating tool in that they halted production and forced companies to deal with the problems Detroit's African American women faced. The fact that black men supported them during the strikes reveals that class unity among the black community provided strength in numbers for women trying to negotiate for better jobs or better pay.

Progress in Employment

By 1943 African American working-class women in Detroit and Richmond had managed to secure jobs in various war production and nonessential industries with the help of the FEPC, civil rights organizations, and the UAW. In Detroit, the number of black women employed jumped from 14,451 in March 1940 to 46,750 in June 1944. In June 1942 fewer than thirty black women worked in war industries, a number that rose to fourteen thousand by November 1943.[82] Fewer took traditional domestic service jobs, an indication that

Making shells during World War II. (Courtesy of the Walter P. Reuther Library, Wayne State University)

they received better pay in other industries. The Detroit Urban League observed that although the bulk of black women held jobs in nonessential industries, they refused to return to domestic work "despite wages of $5.00 a day, carfare, meals, etc. . . . much to the consternation of former employers."[83] The Women's Advisory Committee of the War Manpower Commission found that Detroit laundries suffered a 40 percent loss in labor, resulting from low wages and a 100 percent turnover every two months because female workers found better pay elsewhere.[84]

By early 1943 the UAW surveyed its plants and found that the increase in employment of black women was significant in some war plants. In most, however, African American women failed to gain strong footholds (table 1). Given this evidence, it seems likely that as white women vacated service jobs and other low-paying employment in factories such as HyGrade Foods for more lucrative war industry work, black women took over their positions, which were a step above traditional domestic employment.

Richmond has no statistics from which to draw conclusions, but contemporary observations of the city suggest that African American women made progress in their fight for employment. In 1943 the *Richmond Afro-American* reported that black women had "invaded" several important industries in the city. They worked at Russell Well Distributor Company, where they made 54 cents an hour repairing auto distributors for the army. They also found jobs at David M. Lea Company, working the nailing and boring machines for shell boxes at 46 cents an hour. Bottling companies hired them for $20 to $25 per week, and they were employed as elevator operators and needle workers in various companies and stores for $12 to $20 per week. Winslow and Company, a feed manufacturer, hired black women to sew bags for 50 cents an hour, and Miller Manufacturing hired them to sand shell boxes for 35 cents an hour. Other black women worked at the R.F.&P. Railway Station as cleaners, oilers, and window washers or found jobs at soda fountains and restaurants, waiting counters and tables. Grant's Drug Store hired black women as night clerks and cashiers, and major department stores hired them as billing clerks and customer service clerks for $15 to $25 per week.[85]

African American women in Richmond had some success obtaining nonproduction work in service industries such as waitressing and elevator operation. The largest department store in the city, Thalhimer's, had to promote African American women to better jobs when white women left to enter defense industries. Blacks applied to the store as maids in order to position themselves for jobs as clerks, elevator girls, and waitresses. The company's newsletters wrote about three women who worked hard to be promoted. Hazel Harris and Grace Bradley moved from maids to elevator girls, and

Table 1. Women Employed in Detroit Factories, April 1943

Corporation	Black Women	Total
Aeronautical Products	65	600
Bohn Aluminum and Brass	125	1,200
Bower Roller Bearing	0	450
Briggs-Connor Aircraft	2,600[a]	6,500
Briggs Manufacturing	—[b]	4,393
Budd Wheel Manufacturing	0	345
Burroughs	0	1,800
Chrysler–De Soto	75	700
Chrysler–Dodge Main	50	1,500
Chrysler–Highland Park	140	600
Chrysler–Jefferson Avenue	40	650
Dodge Truck	202	663
Essex Wire	0	900
Ex-Cell-O	100	3,500
F. L. Jacobs	20	400
Farmcrest Bakeries	0	600
Fisher Body Fleetwood Division	140	900
Fisher Body Plant #23	0	260
Fisher Body Plant #37	25	136
Ford–Highland Park	10	4,500
Ford–River Rouge	600	5,000
Ford–Willow Run	290	15,000
GM-Cadillac	260	5,160
GMC-Ternstedt	4[c]	2,000
GMC–Detroit Diesel	0	2,000
Holley Carburetor	0	1,100
Hudson	50	3,200
HyGrade Food Products	500	800
Kelsey Hayes	40	1,700
Lyon, Inc.	0	325
Murray Corporation	325	2,800
National Auto Fibres	50	1,900
Square D	5	275
U.S. Rubber	4	1,500
Woodall	0	500

Sources: Information taken from UAW Research Department, April 1943 chart, Detroit Urban League Records, box 5, general file, March–May 1943, Bentley Historical Library, University of Michigan; Questionnaire on Employment in UAW-CIO Plants, 1943, UAW Research Department Collection, box 11, file 8, Archives of Labor and Urban Affairs, Wayne State University.

  a. Includes men.
  b. "Small but increasing."
  c. All maids.

Mary Johnson moved from maid to hospital attendant. Pictures from the newsletter also reveal that by 1944 all Thalhimer's waitstaff in its tearoom and all its elevator girls were African Americans. Moreover, many African American women worked as stockroom clerks. One managed to be promoted from the soda fountain to the receiving and marking warehouse.[86]

The sheer number of women working as elevator operators at Thalhimer's Department Store in late 1945 attests to the fact that African American women found jobs in many nonindustrial sectors during the war. (*TBI Talks* 5 [Nov. 1945]: 7; courtesy of the Virginia Historical Society)

As in Detroit, Richmond's black women refused to take domestic jobs with low pay, which caused quite a stir among the white community. As early as 1942 a Richmond newspaper reported that many young black women had been able to find higher wages outside service work and had thus "abandoned domestic work completely." The shorter hours and freedom gained in elevator operator and restaurant jobs was likely a major cause of the drop in domestic workers.[87]

Richmond's Urban League reported problems in filling domestic jobs listed with its job registry. In 1941, 414 domestic service jobs went unfilled—1,772 by 1943. The number dropped to 1,518 in 1944, still many more than left wanting before World War II.[88] That year, as white women found that they could not obtain decent help in the home, Anne Folkes wrote an article in the *Richmond News-Leader* about the distressing situation:

> Few problems have been more discussed in recent months than that of domestic help. The PT-A meetings, the Red Cross production rooms have become merely the places where Mrs. Brown bemoans the fact that Susie has left the kitchen to take up welding or Mrs. Smith discusses the high wages she is forced to pay Clara. . . . Before the war Mrs. Apple had a part-time maid who came at noon and stayed until after dinner at night every day of the week except

Sundays, . . . for that work she was paid $5 a week and was the recipient of any discarded or outgrown clothing that was not used by the Apple family. She has recently taken a new job and left without notice.[89]

Some white women could not understand why their "generous" terms of work, including allowing maids to work only thirty-six hours a week and giving them used clothing, went unanswered during the war. Mrs. Apple had to settle with women just to do the laundry and ironing once a week for 40 cents an hour, and they just did not do a very good job, she said.

White women in Richmond shared stories about how they suffered because of having to take on the burden of housework. Myrtle, a former maid interviewed for the article, had left her job of $10 a week to take a war production job at 35 cents an hour. She warned white women that $15 a week for a 7 A.M. to 5 P.M. day was fair; moreover, white women could likely not get black women to work for them after the war.[90]

Just before the war ended, Richmond's YWCA held an interracial international celebration of National Industrial Progress. On that occasion, two African American women who represented the gains their community had made recounted their contributions as patriotic citizens during the war. If their speeches reflect what the majority of black working-class women felt and did during that period, it can be surmised that those in Richmond were aware of what the war meant both politically and economically; moreover, they used their potential as workers for defense to claim political and social rights.

> I am Lucille Harris. I am twenty-four years old, and I work as an elevator operator at the C. & P. Telephone Co. You want to know what four years of war and war preparation have meant to me? Well, after finishing high school, I entered college for a year. Conditions being so I couldn't continue, I came to Richmond with the idea of working in order to continue my education. I soon discovered that with one year's college and no particular training it can be awfully hard. After trying with no luck, I finally took a job as a nurse maid at $7.00 per week. I worked at this for one year. Not being able to save any money I figured I'd get no where working for such a meager salary and gave it up.
>
> After a few weeks without work I applied for a job at the Telephone Co. The pay was a little more than the former[,] $18.00 a week. This job was formerly held by a white boy, who was called to the armed forces. I work on the midnight shift. . . . At present my salary is $25.00 per week. I can't say I am satisfied, far be it; but I have been able to save some money and I have purchased five $25.00 War Bonds.[91]

Harris represented the thousands of African American women in Richmond who had to take domestic service jobs because of limited opportunities. Although she desired a middle-class career and lifestyle, finances halted her aspirations for a college career. Her job as a nursemaid paid poorly and suggested that few career avenues for Richmond's African American women existed, even for those who possessed high school educations.

By tying her job opportunity directly to the war effort, Harris made it clear that she understood the connection between World War II and the labor shortage. In addition, she had taken advantage of that shortage to find a better-paying job. She aspired to be more than an elevator operator and had traded one unregulated and poorly paid service job for another that offered union representation and a set wage-hour schedule. "The increase in my salary," Harris concluded, "I am sure was due to my belonging to the Union. . . . The war has caused me to act and think more soberly. I feel that we as a minority group need not fear as to the future because we are citizens, who do our jobs well on the home fronts, and a people whose citizens try to do everything well need have no worry about its place in the world, or its own ability to survive. . . . I pay my poll taxes and vote in every election. . . . I am preparing myself for a better job now, as well as in the post-war world."

Sarah Jackson, a tobacco worker, also spoke at the meeting. Whether she had also spoken against the AFL at the NLRB meeting is unclear. That is possible, however, given Jackson's position and tenure with the company. She represented the other type of employment generally available to working-class women in Richmond. As a seasonal stemmer in a tobacco plant, Jackson received the lowest pay and the dirtiest and most difficult work. Like Harris, she realized that the war had altered her career:

> Four crowded years have meant a lot of things to me. I began work in the local tobacco industry about seven years ago. My first two jobs were temporary [seasonal] ones in two leaf processing plants, . . . Eventually, I secured a permanent job in a local cigarette and pipe tobacco manufacturing plant. My job has been different since the war. Due to the manpower situation, the Management of my plant has formulated a policy to replace men with women, wherever practical and possible. This new policy along with my qualifications gained a promotion for me from that of a laborer to the timekeeper in my respective department. I am doubtful whether this position will remain open for me in the post-war world. Personally, I believe that being a member of a minority group may have some effect on the decision made by management.[92]

Jackson was alluding to the structural racism that was rampant in the tobacco industry. She understood that her status as an African American woman could hurt her job seniority, and she was not optimistic about the possibility of her keeping the promotion once men returned from the war.

Nevertheless, she, like Harris, pledged to promote equality: "Three years ago I paid my poll taxes and met all other voting requirements. I voted in the presidential election and met all other voting requirements, . . . I have tried to influence others to become first-class American citizens. I believe that legislation, coupled with education and determination will make our today's racial problem a thing of the past."

Speaking to an interracial audience, Lucille Harris and Sarah Jackson claimed power within the state as active proponents of the war. Their language converged with the discourse of responsible patriotism as they related their efforts to buy stamps and bonds, their labor for the state in a time of war, and their participation in electoral politics. They recognized that the state should compensate their labor with some sort of support for their job seniority. Moreover, both recognized that they could, by voting, create new policies within the state that would give equality to the African American community.

Harris's and Jackson's powerful speeches related the importance of work to patriotic war efforts and the importance of the black vote to society in general. The women had been hand-picked by the middle-class board that planned the event, indicating a convergence not only between white and black women workers who attended the meeting but also the white and black middle-class women who chose the speakers. Because the YWCA considered the women representative of their working-class counterparts, undoubtedly they echoed the sentiments of many African American women in Richmond who struggled for better jobs and better economic futures.

In both Detroit and Richmond, working-class women fought hard to obtain the better jobs that wartime changes brought to white women. In some cases they were successful. African American women in both cities used every organization available to them in order to pursue equality in factory work, and the FEPC, UAW, NAACP, and Urban League helped them obtain better jobs. Most black women did not find work in essential war industries, but they did change the terms of employment in both cities by finding jobs outside the home that had more freedom, better hours, and better wages. African American working women had opportunity to leave constricting domestic work, and their experience with wage work changed the way they would negotiate with private employers, as Myrtle explained in the *News-Leader* article.

In Richmond, African American women could not fight for equality within factories because the hierarchy of the Jim Crow South extended far into industry. The women remained segregated from white women, and city law determined that they had no legal precedent for desegregating either factories or facilities, as black women had in Detroit. Still, in Richmond they claimed power where they could, including in demands for better pay and better union representation. In several cases they created a language that focused on the patriotic nature of their wartime labor in order to place themselves inside the wartime state and gain a stronger position from which to negotiate for rights.

Fighting for Day Care

Working-class African American women's struggles did not end in the workplace. They endeavored to receive services from the state and the community in order to piece together benefits for their families. Nowhere was that more apparent than in the contest for day care. Across the country, women of all races faced problems with child care during the war. Because the Lanham Act, established in 1943 to provide money for communities to set up nurseries for working mothers, failed to determine how much should be set aside for black children, African American women often had to scramble to find safe places for their children.

Severe housing shortages in both Detroit and Richmond forced many into substandard housing, and people fought for community facilities so their children would not be left all day in tenements. In both Detroit and Richmond they tried to create support systems for themselves and their communities so they would have decent places to leave their children. In Detroit, Peter Pan Nursery, originally designed as a place where middle-class black children could come weekly to socialize, opened its doors six days a week (at a suggested $3.50 a week per child) after receiving repeated requests from working-class women to do so. Nursery officials based the weekly charge on an amount the working mothers had requested and could afford. Also at the urging of working women, churches, and private clubs, the Detroit Board of Education operated twenty-nine nurseries for African American children during the war years, accommodating those from three to six. One community nursery was open from noon to 8 p.m. and charged 5 cents an hour for child care, with 25 cents for meals. The centers helped women who had been leaving children home alone or with relatives.[93]

The importance of day care to Detroit's working-class African American women was poignantly expressed when the Urban League's Chestnut Center Day Nursery closed. Although it was in the poorest section of Detroit and the next-closest facility was ten blocks away, the Urban League failed to secure Lanham Act funds and needed at least $500 to continue operating.[94] Working women enlisted the aid of middle-class women to intercede for them in discussions with the Urban League, and Ann Chapman, president of the Capron Women's Activity Club, wrote:

> The mothers feel a great loss in losing the Nursery School. . . . A mother came to us worried and discouraged because she had no one to help her with her small child. With no support, whatever, she was forced to make a living for her child, who was left to run the streets daily without any care. She resigned her job—a sacrifice for her child—a stranger in our community with no income—she had come to her battle's end, but, not defeated because this is our problem too. Some may not agree, but this is how much delinquency starts.[95]

Thirty-nine members of the Capron Women's Activity Club signed the letter. Public outcry was significant enough for the Detroit Urban League to take notice and try to secure funds elsewhere in order to continue the program, which it did, albeit on a limited scale.[96] The board of education also responded to the working-class women's economic needs and in 1944 lowered nursery school fees to 50 cents a day in order to make the Chestnut Center Day Nursery more affordable.[97]

Richmond's African American working women also succeeded in securing child-care centers, although not nearly as many as in Detroit. By 1943 African American women in Richmond could send their children to three day-care centers and one nursery school. At each site the children received three meals daily, and the charge was $2 a week for day care and $2.50 for the nursery. Many African American women, however, could not afford those amounts. The Richmond Board of Education went $325 in arrears in order to care for the children rather than turn them away. Given the board's response to equalizing the pay of black teachers, it was an unusual move for a governing body to make. It is likely that working-class women spoke out for the need for day care in Richmond and that the Office of Community War Services concurred. Each center remained open twelve hours a day, and 179 children attended the four centers.[98] Richmond desperately needed more nursery schools, however, and by 1945, again at the request of working women, the city opened three more for black children.[99]

Although it seemed as if demand always outstripped supply, African American women in both Detroit and Richmond asked for and used neighborhood day-care centers in order to provide their children with safe, supervised, and healthy places to stay while they were at work. The women used all means necessary, including negotiating with private and public institutions for child-care benefits, to provide services for their families and to maintain their jobs.

* * *

Working-class African American women worked hard to secure employment and create better work environments for themselves and play environments for their children. During the war, Geraldine Bledsoe, chief of the Minorities Section of the War Manpower Commission in Detroit, noted:

> Negro women have shown a very intelligent understanding of the handicaps they have had to overcome to obtain employment, and have approached the preliminary hurdles with good spirits and without bitterness. Negro males have often refused to go to a plant unless they were sure they would be hired. Negro girls who were high school graduates and who had between seven and eight hundred hours of training often went to as many as twenty-nine or thirty plants before they were finally hired. . . . Negro women, it seems, have been more willing than Negro men to break down the barriers to Negro employment.[100]

The wife of a prominent lawyer and director of the Michigan Unemployment Commission, Bledsoe recognized the role of working-class women in the fight for social justice. As a middle-class woman, her speech revealed the convergence between the classes on issues of employment equality. That convergence was made possible by the fact that working-class women demanded state and private institutions' support in their battles for jobs. Most likely, African American women's willingness to fight for jobs and workplace respect stemmed from their experience of two kinds of prejudice, racism and sexism. Evidence suggests that because they had seen white women and African American men hired, they wanted the same opportunities as those groups. In any case, black women led the charge to equalize hiring practices, working conditions, and seniority rights; they also demanded services such as child care for their families.

Working-class African American women provided a strong voice to the new, modern civil rights movement. When Louise Thomas exclaimed that "we, too, are Americans," she repeated a claim made on the state by Mary McLeod Bethune in a *Pittsburgh Courier* editorial in February 1941. Bethune had stated: "'WE, TOO, ARE AMERICANS'" in the context of calling on African Americans to demand a place in the new wartime society.[101]

Although it is impossible to know whether Thomas had read that editorial, it is clear that she was representing thousands of African American women who wanted to enter the wartime state as equal players in the struggle for victory. She and the other working-class African American women who fought for job opportunities, equality within factories, and services normally provided to white women expanded the meaning of citizenship within the

new wartime civil rights movement to include the needs of the majority of
the black community. By emphasizing that they were patriotic citizens, deserved the right to work for the war effort, and needed services provided to
working white women, working-class African American women forced government and unions, as well as middle-class African American leaders, to
respond to their needs. In confrontations with employers and state and union
officials, they expanded the issues of equal employment and equal access to
state services to a national level, securing the support of middle-class wom-
en and other leaders in the struggle.

3. Looking Ahead: Middle-Class Women's Activities in the Postwar World

On September 2, 1945, the Japanese government signed the articles of surrender that ended World War II. Although the Allies had cause for celebration as they claimed victory over tyranny abroad, African American women could not assert victory over racism at home. Although they made gains in employment, bought homes in some segregated neighborhoods, acquired political power where they could, and gained moderate recognition from the government, the women still understood that their efforts had not changed race relations in the country as a whole.

Middle-class African American women realized that they stood at an important crossroads. They had fought to be recognized by the government as responsible patriots fighting for victory, but how could they maintain their demands to citizenship in the peacetime state? Nannie Black, president of the Housewives League of Detroit, observed, "Now that the war is over, and many young men who fought for freedom have returned to civilian life broken in body and spirit, others have made the supreme sacrifice that we may live in a country that offers true democracy." Moreover, she queried, "What have we done that the democracy they fought for may become a reality? What is our task ahead?"[1]

African American clubwomen needed to reposition themselves in a postwar world in order to continue making claims on the state and society. They took advantage of the cold war to create opportunities in which to extend the logic of the Double V campaign by asserting that equality and democracy at home could create a united front in the face of outside communist threats. Yet the women also had to work within restricted parameters of cold war society in order to gain legitimacy for their cause.

From 1945 to 1954 the women continued their struggle for equality by continuing activities for the state and their communities. They promoted the discourse of responsible patriotism by constructing themselves as citizens based on their contributions to the state as volunteers helping to secure cold war defense systems. In addition, they employed maternalist discourse in order to define themselves as important players in the domestic containment of communism through activities that helped children. They promoted equality, but they also walked a fine line between contesting the state and claiming legitimacy for their cause. Because definitions of loyalty to the state rested with hostile whites, some black women felt obligated to acquiesce to state demands for conformity by backing off their most militant demands for equality. The state kept African American women's clubs off-guard by threatening to surveil them for un-American activities. The women struggled over deciding how best to maintain credibility while making claims to equality within a dominant order that could judge the claims to be outside societal norms and therefore "subversive."

Middle-class women continued to use the discourse of responsible patriotism after World War II but shaped it to fit cold war politics. Their impact on the postwar civil rights movement was significant, but they tempered critique of the state with anticommunist rhetoric and acceptance of a patriarchal nuclear family structure that did not fit with the reality of most wage-earning African American women. Within a cold war context, middle-class women reemphasized traditional concepts of respectability, but they shored up these notions with "scientific" understandings of social work and community uplift. As they had during World War II, the women actively promoted equality as they supported the NAACP, supported political candidates with civil rights platforms, and sponsored forums on race relations. Moreover, they continued to seek ways to help working-class women maintain jobs they had gained as a result of manpower shortages during the war.

Middle-class African American women believed that their contributions to the war made them participants within the state and gave them the right to criticize problems with the government. Although responsible patriotism had started with abstract demands for equality during and after the war, national organizations moved to make demands on the state concrete. They called upon America's new place as leader of the free world in order to rectify the problems with internal segregation. For example, Beulah Whitby, an Alpha Kappa Alpha (AKA) and member of the new Human Rights Council created by several black fraternal organizations, called for the government to pass an antilynching law, enact a permanent Fair Employment Practices Committee (FEPC) bill, overturn southern Jim Crow laws, and desegregate the army. She also pointed out the problems democracy faced when the nation's capital maintained strict legal segregation. She asked fellow AKA members at their annual convention, "What sadder commentary could there be on American Democracy than that in our Nation's capital, often called the capital of the world, Negro citizens are Jim-Crowed and discriminated against more like than unlike the pattern of the Deep South?" Whitby supported Harry S. Truman, despite his reluctance to desegregate Washington, because of his plans to desegregate the army and his civil rights bill of 1947. She called his election "a public endorsement of the federal civil rights program."[2]

The National Council of Negro Women (NCNW) joined AKA in its support of President Truman's civil rights initiatives, and in 1949 it called upon all of its members to "continue to work with all the resources at our command for full citizenship for all citizens . . . we continue to alert Negroes to their potential strength in the use of the ballot."[3] The following year, Dorothy Boulding Ferebee, former president of AKA and current president of the NCNW, urged clubwomen to do their part to promote equality. "Women of today," she observed, "must use their every means to achieve the higher ideals of democracy and the greatest achievement of personal rights, freedom, and brotherhood."[4]

In 1948 the NCNW created a ten-point plan that outlined clubwomen's demands for concrete changes in the country. The plan urged removing all voting restrictions, outlawing all restrictive covenants, enacting a federal antilynching bill, creating a permanent FEPC, giving federal aid to education with strict safeguards against discriminatory spending, securing Social Security safeguards for agricultural and domestic workers, and addressing the problems of youth and delinquency. The plan was similar to overall civil rights goals of the postwar period. The NAACP's strategies, for example, were to pressure the FBI to look into lynchings, create a permanent presidential Civil Rights Committee, and promote voting and suffrage.[5] The focus on youth and delinquency, however, placed the NCNW's plan squarely within the discourse of maternalism. The plan listed all major changes clubwomen wanted and would work to create from 1945 to 1954. In order to achieve these goals, they maintained claims on the state based on their postwar patriotic efforts.

As they did during the war, national black women's groups led the fight for equality by couching demands within the context of the period. Because cold war society required conformity, clubwomen faced the dilemma of how to make claims on the state from a marginal position when the state judged the loyalty of its citizens based on adherence to dominant societal standards. Although national leaders often drew upon the discourse of the cold war to point out inequitable race relations within the country, they had to police their actions and statements in order to maintain legitimacy within a state that demanded social conformity. Sorority women, for example, shifted the discourse of responsible patriotism from contributing to the war to fighting communism at home and strove to preserve their homes and communities in the uncertain "nuclear age." National organizations asserted that the state could prevail against the threat of outside forces by guaranteeing democracy for all in America. Then, American citizens could show the world a united front in the fight for the free world. AKA's Non-Partisan Council legal representative Thomasina Johnson explained the importance of democracy to America's security in the nuclear age when she observed, "The unleashing of the atomic bomb left us with the choice of one world or no world at all. . . . Unless there is justice and first-class citizenship for every American citizen, America too will probably suffer the fate of the destructive use of the atomic bomb. . . . because America has not yet learned to live with minority groups let alone with other nations. . . . Whether Americans can learn to live with the rest of the world depends on whether they can live with Negroes and other minority groups."[6] Johnson equated the danger of social inequality to the danger of nuclear bombs. Left unchecked, both created dangerous problems that could destroy the country either from within, in a domestic battle over the fate of segregation, or from an international threat by a country that realized the United States could not effect world peace because of problems at home.

The NCNW also focused on the importance of equality to national security. Leaders pointed out the discrepancy between America's place as defender of democracy and its continued denial of equality at home, much as they had during World War II. At their 1948 conference the NCNW's top attorney, Sadie Alexander, noted that American people were "mentally ill" because they refused to budge on perceptions about race. "America must act quickly," she maintained, "and prove herself willing to make her domestic policy coincide with her foreign policy if she is to lead the world to eternal peace. . . . All children are of one God and entitled to equality of all opportunities. America believes in democracy but she does not always practice what she believes, but she must wake up fast as belief in democracy is being destroyed in children who see discrimination practiced daily."[7]

Ostensibly, the women used patriotic language to support their claims for democracy, but they included veiled threats in doing that. They attempted to place the blame for social conflicts, regarded as dangerous to American unity, on those who discriminated rather than on those who protested unequal treatment. In essence, they tried to upend the definition of subversive by characterizing dominant society's behavior as threatening to the social order. They played upon cold war fears by threatening that racism could contribute to a generation open to communism as the only way to advance democracy. They also noted that the United States could face considerable problems in the international context by continuing to discriminate. Considering the climate of the cold war state, these speeches were quite subversive.

African American clubwomen walked a fine line when criticizing the state in order to evade the red-baiting tactics of government leaders. Often, they had to embrace strong anticommunist stances so their organizations would not face scrutiny and denunciation by anticommunist government forces that used a larger new infrastructure to determine "dangerous" and "un-American" activities. In the new repressive climate, state agents suspected any issues or ideas that would undermine dominant social values, including unionism, homosexuality, and all civil rights efforts. In order to keep civil rights activists in line, the state used surveillance and the threat of repression to force marginalized groups to police their own members. The FBI and other state agents inhibited free speech in order to protect national security, and many groups came under fire for harboring "communistic" tendencies.[8]

The women may have been genuinely concerned with fighting communism on the home front. In fact, other civil rights organizations and unions had focused on eradicating communism within their ranks. The NAACP, for example, purged leftist members and focused on nationalizing policies rather than allowing renegade local chapters to move to the left. Given the era's overall climate of fear, it is entirely possible the clubwomen were determined to support government attempts to eradicate communism. It is important to note, however, that, within the context of the time, so many organizations, including the Southern Council for Human Welfare and the Council of African Affairs, found themselves targets of anticommunist efforts that it made sense for the clubwomen to support anticommunist efforts, whatever their personal feelings on the subject.[9]

The NCNW urged members to fight for the country's survival by promoting civil rights on the domestic front. African American women's groups, however, were wary of coming down too hard on the American system, because they feared being branded communists. In fact, several distanced themselves publicly from any hints of communism in order to preserve legitimacy as being democracy-supporting but still activist. When the noted black singer and entertainer Paul Robeson spoke to communists at the Paris Peace Conference and allegedly claimed that African Americans would not fight Russians in a war because they would not help a country that refused to grant them basic rights, Mary McLeod Bethune denounced Robeson on behalf of the eight hundred thousand African American women whom she claimed to represent. Bethune's concern about the NCNW being associated with Robeson is reflected in her press statement, which shows how cold war fears could stifle protest: "Negroes have always stood by America in any emergency, and Negroes will always stand by America in any emergency. . . . Whatever our differences may be here, we stand as one against whatever intrusion might come upon us as a nation. We feel that we are Americans. We have always defended and will always defend the American ideals."[10] The statement downplayed the NCNW's criticisms of American society in order to stress the organization's loyalty to the state.

The National Association of Colored Women (NACW) also fell victim to threats of censorship during the period and had to censor itself and its members in order to exist without being denounced as a communist organization. Ella P. Stewart, president of the group, claimed it was necessary to intercede with the FBI in order to be kept off the government's list of subversive organizations, drawn up by the FBI, House Un-American Activities Committee, and Justice Department. Backlash against civil rights activities occurred during this period, and organizations such as the Council of African Affairs found their ranks decimated by the fact that it was engaged in a battle over whether it had to register as a "subversive organization." Likely aware of the situation other civil rights groups faced, Stewart warned other NACW members to monitor groups to which they gave money or in which they had memberships. "I hope, ladies," she cautioned, "that you will think seriously about joining organizations and consider what organization you are joining. It was quite an ordeal for this President to confer with various people in high places in Washington to keep us from being placed on the U.S. Subversive list."[11]

Stewart's statement reveals the fears of black women, who, after working hard for democracy, had to suppress the speech of their own members in order to maintain some legitimacy within a state that coerced conformity on political and social issues. While African American women's national organizations worked hard to promote democracy, they faced constricted parameters because they continued to work from within the state to effect change. When the state changed and stopped accommodating certain types of protest, the discourse of responsible patriotism had to reflect that change. Although fighting for democracy still meant fighting for equality in order to secure America's place as the free world's champion, adherents to the discourse of responsible patriotism had to be careful not to embrace ideologies that could seem subversive so they would not undermine their efforts to obtain civil rights. In a way, clubwomen placed much hope in a state that continued to disappoint them by failing to make any substantive changes in racial policies in the immediate postwar period.

Maternalism in the Cold War State

Because the state kept a close eye on civil rights activities, middle-class African American women redefined their activism in terms that the state could accept. They couched the discourse of responsible patriotism in terms of responsible motherhood in the postwar period in order to legitimize their activities by claiming power within a traditional gendered sphere. In effect, the women drew upon their power as mothers as they tried to change the state and take charge of community welfare issues.

Although many historians equate the term *maternalism* with white middle-class women's reform movements, others argue that black women also claimed the term and used it for their own reform efforts. These scholars, however, focus primarily on the early half of the twentieth century as the height of the maternalist movement. They note that maternalist discourse enabled white women to create space in the state in order to gain public authority and enact policies that focused on the welfare of the poor. The maternalists' status as middle-class clubwomen allowed them to engage with the state. They secured several reforms in the Progressive and New Deal eras, but their reforms reflected class and race prejudice. They created a welfare system that reinforced class and race inequalities with the morality clauses in Aid to Dependent Children programs and a system of distribution that allowed local welfare boards to refuse to disperse funds to minorities.[12]

African American clubwomen also embraced maternalism during this period. Those who were progressives linked motherhood and uplift to civil rights as they provided the fund-raising and networking skills in order to finance community institutions and assist the poor blacks whom maternalist state policies forgot. In the period before World War I, African American clubwomen practiced a "social motherhood" that provided the community with services denied them by the state, which blurred the lines between state and community institutions.[13] Although the height of maternalist rhetoric occurred during the first half of the century, black women chose to privilege this discourse in the 1950s in order to engage with the state in traditional gendered terms, a maternalist discourse that proved especially valuable after the war. Because the state privileged women's domesticity as part of its plan to fight communism, African American clubwomen could use their power as mothers to enact social change.

Middle-class African American women's maternalist responses to the cold war state were often problematic. Because the discourse necessitated that they accept the state, flawed as it was, in order to locate themselves closer to the center of power and make changes inside the state, women had to maneuver within the changes and restrictions wrought by the international cold war dialogue that followed postwar peace conferences. Americans created a family-centered culture after the war that reflected their fears and hopes for the future and acted as a buffer against the threat of internal communism. Reflected by a patriarchal nuclear family that contented itself with promoting American values through consumerism and patriotism, domesticity was at the forefront of cold war American culture.[14]

Of course, a major part of the family as defense called for mothers to be in their homes, protecting their families against outside threats of nonconformity. Because often even middle-class African American women had to work outside the home, albeit in professions such as teaching and social work, they had to adapt to the new cultural landscape. They often defined themselves as mothers working in the home and community to help future generations experience democracy, the American way of life. Such language recalled the much earlier discourse of respectability and uplift, but it was prominent in this era of conformity.

Local organizations in Richmond and Detroit often projected language concerning traditional respectability and domestic womanhood into discussions of citizenship. As Zeta Phi Betas in Richmond concluded, "An ideal woman molds her life so that it will fit in with the life [sic] of others . . . home is the best place to do our work, ... Women should live so that their lives may be the proper example to follow."[15] When addressing the Michigan Association of Colored Women's Clubs, Detroit attorney Jean Campus claimed that women, in building a world for tomorrow, must set an example for the entire community in order to secure "the betterment of the future generation."[16] Although wartime discourse of responsible patriotism was gendered in that it called upon women as volunteer and waged workers to give service to the state, postwar discourse called upon black women as mothers to provide state services and claim rights based on their position as domestic guardians.

Many middle-class women set out to politicize motherhood and become guardians of the world at large. They did not intend to remain at home and raise their children, turning their backs on their communities. Like many white and black reformers in the Progressive Era, they used the language of domesticity without making it a goal. Instead, they placed themselves in the tenuous position of supporting a lifestyle to which they did not necessarily adhere—one that revolved around a patriarchal family. To many clubwom-en, using this discourse was a matter of expediency; it enabled them to achieve their goals without the interference of hostile government agents.[17] AKAs discussed the fact that they, as Christian women and mothers, could appeal to women across the country and around the world in order to eliminate misunderstandings and mistrust as well as end conflict in general.[18]

African American women also understood that although their race made them vulnerable at home it made them powerful abroad. They could appeal to women in the global community as "sisters of color" who had experienced violence firsthand. At a regional institute held by the Richmond YWCA, Nancy Wooldrich of Hampton Institute noted, "'Our suffering has made us sisters under the skin, . . . we [must] view the path over which we have trod and strive to establish peace on earth, and good will to all men.'"[19] Wooldrich and others linked pan-African and anticolonialist ideologies to efforts for world peace in that they identified with sisters of color worldwide who strug-gled for equality and freedom. By focusing on them as agents of world peace, she claimed power in womanhood.

Middle-class women's language reflected optimism in being able to change the world and bring peace to all nations, again recalling the maternalist pol-icies of earlier twentieth-century peace movements. While earlier reformers had focused on the power of women as mothers to fight both for nonvio-lence and world equality for women, they suggested that peace was neces-sary in order to further justice for women. Middle-class white women formed groups such as the Women's International League for Peace and Freedom and the Women's Peace Union in order to take the lead in establishing world peace and gaining a voice in world politics.[20] Although they failed in their bid to outlaw war, their rhetoric for advancing the cause of peace and social justice influenced African American clubwomen after the war. Bethune placed the NCNW squarely in the midst of the world peace movement by claiming, "'The peoples of the world are looking largely to the women in the building of lasting peace. Therefore, it is vitally important that an organization such as the National Council create that kind of organization structure which shall strengthen the fulfillment of the principles on which it was founded.'"[21] Rosa Gragg, president of the Detroit Association of Women's Clubs and a mem-ber of Sigma Gamma Rho, the NAACP, the NACW, and the USO, decided that because men had thrown America into wars it was up to women to keep America out of them. In speaking to the women of the Second Baptist Church, she observed that world peace started with how children were edu-cated at home, "'It is the job of women to rebuild a war-torn world because men have not been able to build a world of peace and goodwill.'"[22]

The language Gragg used was not new, but it is significant that African American women employed it to reflect belief in being able to effect world harmony and international democracy for women of color around the globe. Through maternalist peace discourse, clubwomen claimed power as mothers and reformers working for social justice. They believed that working to achieve these goals at home would jump-start the international peace process and that the interracial programs and awareness conferences that linked middle-class white and black women would affect global politics.[23]

Maternalism, Citizenship, and Social Work

Middle-class African American women did not just look to facilitating international relations as part of their maternalist program. As self-described guardians of their community, they also sought to continue providing local community institutions and poor mothers with desperately needed services that were not forthcoming from the state. Moreover, they provided a service to the government by stepping in and running programs for underprivileged children in order to ensure they would grow up patriotic and less susceptible to communist ideology. During this period many government officials feared that children who grew up outside a normative family tradition (one with a mother at home and a father earning money) were at risk for delinquency and extremely impressionable. As a result, they were considered open to communist infiltrators seeking vulnerable citizens to co-opt into the movement. Because so many African American women, of necessity, worked, their households fell outside the normative definition of family and, therefore, were thought to put children at risk of betraying their country. Young women's sexuality in particular became a focal point of anxiety during this period because women's deviant behavior, including sex before marriage, could undermine the traditional nuclear family.[24]

When middle-class women taught responsibility, respectability, and civic values to children in day-care centers and youth programs, and when they surveilled the activities of young women deemed deviant, they provided an extremely important service to the cold war state by ensuring that the values necessary to perpetuate the normative family and uphold the country were being taught. Throughout such efforts the women continued to focus on merging the tenets of respectability with citizenship.

They recognized the importance of their gendered contributions to the state and claimed as a prerogative for their services the right to reform those who received their maternalist efforts. Clubwomen in particular understood that for their efforts to achieve equality (and their discourse of responsible patriotism to survive beyond World War II) they had to make sure that the next generation played its part by supporting civil rights and being upstanding citizens. Their desire to raise children to be participants in the state, coupled by their desire to keep them from becoming delinquent and casting a shadow of disrespect on the entire black community, led African American women to continue sponsorships of nurseries and play schools for children of working mothers as well as canteens and programming for teenagers. That significant combination of goals and ideologies suggests they still defined their citizenship status as being reciprocal rather than inherent. The services they provided to the cold war state created responsible and patriotic youths. As a result of such services, however, women expected to be compensated through official recognition that their contributions were important.

In much of their programming, middle-class women maintained a class bias made evident in the form of critiques against the mothering efforts of working-class and poor women. Unlike many middle-class white women, middle-class black women understood that African American women needed to work because they were segregated into low-wage jobs. As a result, although clubwomen did not focus as much on workplace issues, neither did they always construct working mothers as unworthy. Instead, they often helped them with various programs for children.[25] In some projects created to help the children of working women, however, middle-class women exhibited bias against working-poor mothers, not so much because they had to work but because their parenting skills were suspect, especially in the raising of teen-aged girls.[26]

In both Richmond and Detroit, clubwomen tried to keep nursery schools open for preschool children because they recognized that many women had to continue working in order to support their families. The mothers of 95 percent of the children at Richmond's only remaining postwar black nursery school worked outside their homes, for example, and the facility had opened so "adequate care, supervision, and protection [could] be available to all children, especially those who are deprived of a mother's care primarily because of economic reasons."[27] When its director revealed the necessity of imminent closure because of a lack of funds, AKA and Richmond community leaders swung into action. The local AKA chapter donated $100 and held a very successful barn dance that netted $500.56 for the school, funds that allowed the school to remain open. Other groups volunteered their services in order to make the school's future secure.[28]

Detroit clubwomen focused on continued sponsorship of Peter Pan Nursery, which maintained its mission to help working-class families' children. By 1950, fifteen of those who attended were from broken homes, only three lived in homes where the father worked, fourteen had their mothers as their sole support, three had mothers who received welfare, and twenty-eight had both parents in their households, working low-wage jobs.[29] The clubwomen worked to provide financial support through fund-raisers and materials drives. In 1947, when the nursery lost funding from the War Chest, its all-female board of directors requested support from "city churches, organizations, and clubs." The board held fund-raisers like a "subscription tea" as well as cabaret parties to sell $1 memberships in order to contribute to the general operations fund.[30] Fund-raising for Peter Pan turned into an annual gala affair; in 1954 the Peter Pan Auxiliary Club was created to sponsor bridge fund-raisers and charity balls.[31] Such efforts provided desperately needed services, otherwise threatened by state cutbacks, to working-class women.

Clubwomen sponsored programs for school-aged children in Richmond and Detroit in order to make sure the youngsters learned responsibility, healthy living, and citizenship. The programs' goals reflected a middle-class bias. Essentially, the women were stepping in to teach respectability to the children of working-class mothers in order to make them responsible citizens. Their activities suggest they believed working-class women to be inadequate for that task. In Richmond, Phi Delta Kappa continued to sponsor a recreation room where boys and girls learned art and drama and took part in social activities after school. Chi Eta Phi, the national nursing sorority, sponsored a film at the Booker T. Washington Movie Theater to raise money for convalescent children who had rheumatic fever and to teach the importance of maintaining healthy habits. More than a thousand children and parents attended. AKAs donated $1,500 to Detroit Parks and Recreation in order to buy playground equipment in black neighborhoods, which vastly improved the quality of the children's recreation areas. In addition, the YWCA of Detroit also sponsored several camps for girls in elementary and junior high schools, as well as scholarships so underprivileged children could attend its sleepaway camp in northern Michigan. One twelve-year-old won a scholarship as a result of her efforts to clean up the projects in which she lived. Another, eleven, won because she cared for her five siblings and sick father every day while her mother went to work. The YWCA also held parties for poor children, often receiving help from other clubs. In 1953, for example, AKA, the Premier Homemakers, the Detroit Study Club, and the Excelsior Homemakers helped sponsor a Christmas party for 150 children at the YWCA.[32] Such activities revealed clubwomen's efforts to provide wholesome, health-oriented programs designed to take children out of the socially, psychologically, and physically unhealthy ghetto environments.

Although clubwomen's activities for children in Richmond and Detroit helped working mothers make sure their children had safe activities in which to participate, the focus on parenting reveals a class bias. They believed that poor behavior resulted from poor parenting and was a pathology that needed to be corrected before it cast shame on the entire African American community. A middle-class belief in working-class pathology was not a new phenomenon, but postwar clubwomen focused on the "scientific" causes of children's problems and attempted to control the behavior of the youngsters. Social workers, for example, concluded that family poverty, the squalor of ghettos, and the hours poor women spent working outside their homes all contributed to malnutrition, disease, and "poorly behaved" children. While nursery schools worked to incorporate the tenets of good nutrition, good education, and good social skills, programs for older children focused on the benefits of camps far from neighborhood confines. Middle-class clubwomen recognized the structural causes of poverty, including poor living conditions.

Nowhere was class bias more prevalent, however, than in clubwomen's programs for teenaged girls. As they had been during the war, the women were concerned over the behavior of daughters of working-class women. In a direct attempt to stem problems of sexuality and delinquency, clubwomen in Richmond and Detroit used a three-step process to eliminate trouble. First, they provided wholesome entertainment as alternatives to delinquency; second, they sponsored personality clinics in order to teach young women how to develop into respectable and responsible citizens; and, third, in Detroit, members of Delta Sigma Theta recognized delinquent behavior and tried to correct it through the Delta Home program. The programs did not appear to move far beyond earlier efforts that promulgated tenets of respectability. The fact, however, that social workers ran the programs and, in a scientific bent, called them "clinics" suggests that middle-class women embraced new methods of psychoanalysis and clinical studies in order to "prove" their ability to solve young people's problems resulting from working-class lifestyles.

The YWCAs in Richmond and Detroit were instrumental in planning recreational and learning activities for young women. Richmond's Phillis Wheatley branch held fashion shows and music and dance classes and sponsored service projects and dances. Detroit's Lucy Thurman branch sponsored youth canteens with the YMCA for eighteen- to twenty-five-year-olds and gave them charge of the facilities.[33]

The YWCAs also focused on changing young women's behavior in order to create future responsible patriots. The Richmond Y-Teen group held clinics on health, work, social problems, religion, the arts, and personal relations in addition to personality contests. The directors had a specific plan in mind:

One of numerous dances the YWCA sponsored for the young people of Richmond during the 1950s. (YWCA Collection, box 47, Blue Scrapbook, "November
1952 Dance for the Y-Teens"; courtesy of Special Collections and Archives, James
Branch Cabell Library, Virginia Commonwealth University)

"Y Teens try to prepare for their roles as adult citizens."[34] Detroit sponsored
a statewide Girl Reserves meeting, where "equal opportunities in education,
adequate recreation, full employment with jobs for all who need work, and
happy married and home life" took center stage in discussion workshops.[35]
Later, the YWCA revealed how it "quietly" fought delinquency. The directors stated that the organization was "devoted to character building and to
creating, by [its] programs and facilities, an atmosphere in which . . . members may grow and develop, morally and physically, into worthwhile citizens."[36]

Both the Richmond and Detroit YWCAs made it clear that respectable
women made good citizens, a message carried to all young women who
joined. The ideology of respectability was a pervasive one, and clubwomen
were unable to drop it from the discourse of responsible patriotism. Respectability was, in fact, integral to discourse on responsible patriotism in the
postwar world.

In no other place was the attempt to stop delinquency more apparent than

Detroit's Delta Sigma Theta Home for Girls. The home was the pinnacle of clubwomen's social work and scientific efforts at reform in the Detroit community, and it remained a linchpin in their efforts to stop the effects of poor mothering and urban pathology, to which they ascribed girls' delinquent behavior. After raising money for the home, Deltas opened the institution in 1947. The house, licensed as a social agency and run by Delta social workers, provided accommodations for ten girls. Caseworkers analyzed their problems and tried to prescribe solutions based upon normative gender roles, for example, teaching the girls to cook and sew. The sorority and United Community Services paid for the facility's general expenses, which included salaries for a resident director, two assistant directors, and a cook.

Deltas used Wayne State social work majors to evaluate the effectiveness of the home in a clinical study that promoted scientific sampling methods. The students considered ninety-eight young women who lived in the home from 1947 to 1954, eighty-two of them between the ages of thirteen and fifteen. Of these, 59 percent had lived in their own homes although few had both parents present, and 41 percent had resided with relatives or friends. Half of the residents had lived in the home for fewer than six months. The majority came from poor neighborhoods and had grown up in families deemed substandard by the Deltas. They were "poor economically, morally, and socially" and came from homes broken by "divorce, desertion, death, or incarceration." The Deltas believed the families had allowed the young women to become delinquent: "Lack of parental interest or control, cruel punishments, neglect, all combined to create distrustful, starved, personalities."[37]

Because the Deltas thought the parents had failed to provide adequate care, they petitioned the court to take cases welfare agencies presented to them. Most of the girls had been charged with delinquency in the courts in acts ranging from sexual promiscuity and "general immorality" to truancy, theft, aggression, and vandalism.[38] Social workers sought to change such behavior by setting rules and standards to which the girls had to adhere, including school attendance, and by teaching them homemaking skills.

However high the hopes were for the Delta Home, the sorority members themselves admitted a less-than-stellar success rate despite their best attempts to teach the young women responsibility and domestic skills. Although half of those studied changed dramatically during their stay at the Delta Home, a large percentage reverted to their previous behaviors after leaving. Deltas blamed this on continued poor parenting by the girls' families.[39]

The Deltas' stress on mother-blaming shows that middle-class values were often at odds with working-class ones. The sorority women's refusal to recognize that the young women's behavior had an economic basis suggests they were not cognizant of problems the working class faced. Still, it is important that the Deltas tried to prepare young women for futures as mothers and workers in the new postwar world; the state refused to provide such structural support for poor black girls.

The Delta Home is significant not necessarily because of the changes it accomplished in its clients but because of what it revealed about clubwomen's attitudes toward delinquency and the methods of rehabilitation that were to lead young women to become responsible, respectable citizens who would further the movement for equality. Deltas thought that a structured home environment would enable girls to "build character, to build morals, good citizenship, and lasting friendships."[40] Those who had been rehabilitated would become wives and mothers and could, in a domesticity-oriented state, make claims as citizens themselves. To that end, committee caseworkers created group life-therapy sessions intended to develop "personality, character, and intelligence."[41] In addition, they helped residents create their own rules— for example, setting schedules for laundry, kitchen, and cleaning duties— which were all set forth in a pamphlet entitled *Fitting In*.[42]

Such programs mirrored those that white, middle-class women sponsored for unwed mothers. White clubwomen, however, created homes in order to rehabilitate young women and enable them to rejoin society, whereas the Deltas created a home for "unruly" teenaged girls in order to rehabilitate them and make them respectable citizens.[43] The sorority refused to allow entrance to those who were pregnant; they would be, the clubwomen considered, a poor influence on the others. As the pamphlet's title shows, Deltas believed that conformity with certain behaviors would enable the girls to advance morally and socially and become successful in life. In 1954, and despite figures that spoke to the contrary, the Deltas held a dinner in celebration of the several hundred girls who "had another chance to 'make good.'" Many had "developed into fine women and [were] living highly useful lives."[44] The Deltas believed in the project and maintained the home for several years following 1954.

Unpaid Service to the State

In addition to maintaining maternalist programs with which to make claims on the state as mothers and guardians of home and community, middle-class African American women continued to promote their discourse of responsible patriotism through volunteer work, both in the cold war preparedness campaign and during the Korean War. Their work for the Red Cross and USO kept the discourse of citizenship alive as they agreed to support the state on a new home front—the cold war.

By volunteering for cold war defense projects, middle-class women continued to make claims on the state for equal citizenship based on contributions to the postwar environment. In order to downplay the seriousness of a potential attack, the government called upon them to "sanitize" nuclear war by likening preparedness to homemaking skills. The state actively developed the concept of homemaking as a profession in order to ready women in case foreign aggression brought on dire emergency. State agents likened stockpiling foods to "grandma's cupboard"—always full in the event of unexpected company—and showed women how to cook and keep house with makeshift utensils and appliances. Above all, the state sought to maintain gender roles as a form of stability in the face of nuclear attack.[45] By supporting the Red Cross and the USO throughout the cold war and the Korean War, middle-class African American women located themselves within the state as providers of important domestic services that provided a link to cold war preparedness.

Many middle-class women spent much of their time participating in Red Cross activities. Under threat of immediate and disastrous nuclear strikes, Richmond and Detroit homemakers took preparedness classes as part of postwar efforts to give substance to the discourse of responsible patriotism. As domestic guardians, homemakers were critical to the preparedness effort and were to plan and learn first aid and sickness prevention, detection, and cures in order to help out, freeing doctors and other medical personnel in the event of nuclear crises. The women believed they were performing an essential function for the state by learning how to keep their families in perfect health. As Richmond's state health commissioner noted, "'It is very important for every woman in the home to know how to care for sick members of her family'" in an emergency.[46]

Like the courses offered during the war, preparedness classes were intensive and costly in that they took many hours to complete and books were expensive. Many African American homemakers participated in order to prepare for potential disasters.[47] Richmond's Red Cross home nursing director, for example, praised twelve black women who completed twenty-four hours of nursing classes in 1949 without missing any. Their attendance set a local record; never before had a class, black or white, achieved perfect attendance.[48]

With the outbreak of the Korean War in 1950, Richmond women stepped in to fill the needs caused by shortages of medical personnel. Eight trained for the Civilian Defense Corps, and seven took twenty-nine hours of theory and forty hours of practicum to become Volunteer Nurses' Aides (VNAs). The VNAs essentially performed the same duties as Certified Nurses' Aides but without pay, contributing hours of labor to the state.[49]

Detroit's middle-class women also volunteered to help the Red Cross after the outbreak of the war. In one case, sixteen graduated from VNA training and planned to spend three weeks in hospitals gaining practical experience.[50] In 1954 Mrs. M. R. Rhonenee, a homemaker and member of Detroit's United Council of Church Women, exhorted other women to take home nursing courses to promote home-front defense and make their households safer: "'Learn how to discharge this part of [your] mother job. . . . It is one of the privileges as well as one of the duties of mothers to care for their families when they are ill.'" She praised the work of the Red Cross volunteers as patriotic mothers who kept home and country safe through preparedness.[51]

In addition to maintaining preparedness through Red Cross activities, middle-class women continued to provide care for those who returned from European fronts between 1945 and 1947 or had participated in the Korean War from 1950 to 1953. Their continuous support for the USO signified continuous support of the state. As they fed and entertained men who fought for the state, they implicitly demonstrated willingness to sacrifice sons and husbands for security. In both Richmond and Detroit, African American women supported USOs, despite a serious cut in funding and major cutbacks in programming, in order to maintain troop morale.

Richmond women also provided essential work in obtaining financial support for the USO after the government reduced support for local facilities. Providing labor and funds to keep the USO afloat furthered their connection to the state. As they did when supporting private institutions, the women pooled their money and worked through club networks to maintain facilities for black soldiers, continuing the work on behalf of the state through private groups. When personnel cutbacks affected the camps surrounding Richmond, the national USO council cut funding and forced the closure of the black and the white USOs several months after the black facility's six-year anniversary celebration. The Traveller's Aid Society also closed its Transit Lounge in the train station.[52]

African American women scrambled to rally the community around the soldiers and create programs for them. The USO and senior hostesses began a new group, the Girls' Service Organization, to provide entertainment for hospitalized veterans and soldiers in camps. Determined to continue their work, the group went to fraternal organizations and black businesses in Richmond in order to find sponsorships.[53] Starting in 1948 and continuing through the Korean War, GSO members took more than 120 Easter baskets and 150 Christmas stockings to McGuire Hospital for wounded soldiers. They also raised money by selling Christmas cards and collected presents and food from sponsoring businesses. During the Korean War, the GSOs worked with the Phillis Wheatley YWCA to sponsor dances and parties for Fort Lee and Cheatham Annex Naval Station soldiers. Everyone always enjoyed a "wonderful time" the YWCA director maintained.[54] Despite a serious lack of state support, African American women labored throughout this period to maintain an institution that had become important for black soldiers and the black community at large.

Detroit's USO volunteers remained lucky enough to keep the support of the national USO council. Not only did they continue their work, but they also expanded it to fulfill the needs of soldiers during the Korean War. Moreover, USO leaders merged black and white USOs into one desegregated unit, something Richmond's USO Council would never have considered. Because more men shipped out from the West Coast, midwestern bases were important in the transport of soldiers, and bases that surrounded Detroit continued to need places for soldiers to spend furloughs. In 1946 hostesses served more than two thousand soldiers a day while also providing facilities for the wounded and convalescent who were on leave.[55]

While the Richmond USOs fought for their existence, the black USO in Detroit expanded during the Korean War. Clubwomen sponsored a snack bar, and the Sympathizers Charity Club and Women's Council of the Second Baptist Church volunteered to cook and serve food there.[56] The women labored for the state. Their work for the desegregation of USOs had began during World War II, and it finally paid off.

By 1954, in a stunning example of the changing racial climate in the city, black USOs merged with white ones into an integrated "Downtown Club." Because President Truman had integrated the Armed Forces several years before, Detroit's USO council decided to follow suit and save on money and volunteer needs. A problem emerged, however, in that many African American women stopped volunteering when the USOs merged despite the council's pleas for hostesses. The USO called for a general enlistment of volunteers to help soldiers at the center: "There is at the moment a particular need for Negro girls. The USO program is an integrated one, as are the armed forces, but the number of colored girls who have signed up and who carry out their assignments faithfully is under par."[57]

Although no evidence exists to explain why the number of black women volunteers fell, enough racial tension may have existed within the center to cause the drop. In pictures of USO events, black and white women play games with mixed groups of soldiers. If the center needed more black women, however, then mixing between black men and white women was probably negligible if not nonexistent, even though the center was interracial. It is also probable that young black women were reluctant to work in a climate fraught with hostility. Nevertheless, those who did volunteer as junior hostesses served alongside white women, dancing and playing card games every night and visiting bases for weekly dances.[58]

Throughout the period, senior hostesses continued to vouch for the respectability of junior ones, who had to endure a three-month trial or training period once being "carefully selected for personality, graciousness, and understanding of youth activity." Moreover, the girls were said to "radiate charm and personality."[59] Undoubtedly, the respectability of black women was important in a desegregated context because black and white women observed each others' behavior on a daily basis. Again, middle-class women supported their gendered service to the state with respectability and worked to provide decent entertainment for the troops.

Middle-class African American women continued to provide support to the state by participating in traditional gendered volunteer efforts as they had during World War II. They expected their contributions to locate them within the state in order to negotiate for equality. That expectation became clear as they emphasized civil rights activism after the war and called upon the state to enact laws guaranteeing equality.

Civil Rights Activism

At the same time that local African American middle-class women maintained voluntary efforts for the state and their communities, they also continued to promote equality by using activist strategies to establish a permanent FEPC, support NAACP desegregation attempts, and gain a strong voice in government by voting and becoming partisan supporters of politicians who proved friendly to civil rights issues.

National organizations clarified the issues important to the women, as they had during World War II. From 1945 to 1954, when prominent national women's groups went on record to support civil rights, they focused on urging concrete changes. They demanded that the federal government enact laws and policies that would change segregationist policies across the country. The NACW, for example, resolved to support Truman's policies to secure full and equal employment opportunities, a democratic housing program, and Department of Justice investigations into voting rights violations. Moreover, "In order to accord the Negro full citizenship status, Be it resolved that we urge the American people generally accept the principles and application of no segregation—no discrimination until every racial distinction shall have been removed in America."[60] By means of legislation and litigation, African American women focused on enacting change within the system in order to make legitimate their message of equality. By using state systems such as the court and electoral politics to demand the change, they did not threaten the general state structure. As a result, their claims for equality did not appear to be subversive.

When middle-class women used the altered language of responsible patriotism to equate their service to the cold war state with citizenship, they mobilized networks and proved themselves activists for civil rights. As during World War II, members of national organizations moved quickly to fight for equality by demanding support for the FEPC. In Richmond, for example, Senora Lawson, a member of Alpha Phi Omega sorority, the Delver Women's Club, and the NACW and an executive board member of the YWCA, chaired the Richmond Chapter for a Permanent FEPC. She also secured eleven women to canvass their communities to raise $2,750 for lobbying efforts. The committee sponsored an FEPC fund rally at which a prominent singer from New York provided the headliner attraction. Nine women made up the event's organization committee.[61]

Middle-class women in Detroit also proved very active in supporting the FEPC, and the local Panhellenic Council sponsored a talk by the Detroit NAACP president about the aggressive effort to do so.[62] In addition, "those popular little debbies" the Co-Ettes held a mother-daughter tea and raised $30 for the Committee to Establish a State FEPC.[63] Although the Senate killed two separate bills to establish the FEPC and the national council to establish a permanent FEPC collapsed in 1950, middle-class women's activism in support of the committee suggests an understanding of how important economic opportunity was to establishing full equality. Club networks enabled women to support continuation of the FEPC as a part of efforts to achieve full economic opportunities for all African Americans.

After the war, when overt and militant actions often appeared subversive, women's efforts at fund-raising for NAACP litigation proved even more important because the litigation effected the greatest change during this period, especially in the advancement of equality in education. In 1949 Martha Powell, a member of Richmond's First Union Baptist Church women's auxiliary, a Girl Scout troop leader, and an official on the executive board of the NAACP, single-handedly raised $100 selling NAACP memberships that ranged from $1 to $5. Later that year thirty-five women from a group at the Sixth Mount Zion Baptist Church pledged to lead a membership drive among their congregation.[64] Richmond teachers involved themselves in the NAACP fund drive of 1951. Those at the Navy Hill School, for example, became the first group in the city to achieve 100 percent enrollment of $5 memberships.[65]

Detroit women also raised money for the NAACP as they chaired and led fund-raising drives. In 1946 division leaders of the yearly drive met to hear Ella Baker, director of NAACP branches, praise the chapter for being the largest in the country. At that meeting, sixty-one women received merit certificates for selling memberships.[66] Detroit clubwomen again found it difficult to separate traditional gender norms from responsible patriotism. Five "beauties," all "charming," for example, wrote memberships for the NAACP at the 1950 Booker T. Washington Trade Association exhibit.[67] The NAACP must have decided that beauty and charm could raise money, because in 1954 it worked with Detroit's society women to sponsor a "Fight for Freedom" fashion show at the Arts Institute. Funds raised supported nationwide desegregation cases.[68] Once again, women in both cities were critical to NAACP fundraising. They used their social connections to galvanize support for the civil rights organization, work that enabled the NAACP to fight desegregation battles across the country.

In addition to supporting the NAACP by raising funds, Richmond clubwomen worked with the organization to mobilize against a racist judicial system that continuously oppressed African American men. Florence F. Wood and Madeline Smith called upon three hundred Richmond women to raise funds to help the "Martinsville Seven." In 1947 seven men in rural Martinsville, Virginia, had received the death penalty for allegedly raping a white woman. When, after the trial, they sought NAACP assistance, lawyers discovered that their original defense attorney's trial record was so poor that immediate grounds for appeal existed. The appellate court refused to hear the case, however, and the NAACP could not obtain clemency for the men. The money the women raised did not save them.[69]

Richmond women also raised money for the NAACP's defense of Mabel Crews's son, who had been charged with assault with a deadly weapon when defending his home against white vandals. Crews had just bought a house in an all-white neighborhood and her son had moved in with her when white neighbors immediately began to throw objects at the house and threaten the family. One night, when the crowd got out of hand and stormed the home, Crews fired a pistol to deter the mob from tearing it down. The clubwomen asserted that women had to defend men, because "'if this type of destruction is permitted to continue without a legal fight, none of us will be safe in our homes regardless of where we may live.'"[70]

In defending the Martinsville Seven and Mabel Crews's son, women were promoting the construction of men as providers and women as nurturers, a concept that reflected the dominant middle-class ideology of the time. Moreover, they proved themselves caretakers of the black community beyond Richmond by fighting for the rights of people in the country town of Martinsville. The women spoke in terms of fatherless children and destitute mothers or widows who remained behind to carry on as best they could without a source of income. The fact that they failed to effect a successful outcome in either case—the state executed the seven men and convicted Crews of assault—reveals the continuing problems black women faced when dealing with an entrenched system of racial domination defined and upheld by the state. This class-laden discourse did, however, enable the women to call upon the NAACP to help families of persecuted men and point a finger at injustices resulting from the inequality in Virginia's court systems.

Middle-class African American women in Richmond and Detroit believed that helping the NAACP would further equality but worked even harder for their voices to be heard in government, becoming activists in the electoral process. Not only did they work to support political candidates who would embrace civil rights, but in some cases they also ran for political offices themselves.

As with the defense and uplift projects, national organizations provided impetus to partisan political action, and grass-roots volunteers carried out national programs. In 1946 NACW members sponsored a last-minute drive to protest lynching and back an anti-poll tax bill under discussion in Congress. Five hundred clubwomen stormed Washington, demanding to see their senators. According to NACW members, Wall Doxey, the senator from Mississippi and sergeant at arms, panicked, however, when he saw them advancing up the steps of the building. Fearing they would stage a long protest, he ordered that guards not let them sit. The women stood for two hours, waiting to see their senators. Only those from California and Kentucky came out to greet them and assure them of their support for the anti-poll tax bill.[71]

Two years later, a nonpartisan political forum at the NACW's national conference quickly became partisan when several members questioned the relevance of the Republican Party to African Americans. Mildred Younger, representative of the party, was caught off-guard and had to recover quickly. Younger "said she believes that there are tremendous Negro problems which the Party has gone on blindly ignoring but which she believes will no longer be ignored under the wise, far-seeing leadership of Thomas E. Dewey."[72]

The NCNW also focused on political parties when it called upon members to educate themselves about each party's platforms: "The Democratic and Republican parties are committed by their platforms to support FEPC,

ANTILYNCHING, ANTI POLLTAX, HOUSING, and FEDERAL AID TO EDUCATION Bills. if [sic] they *are* sincere, you want to know it NOW! If they *are not* sincere, you want to know it NOW!"[73] The call to arms proved important because it placed the responsibility of reforming the political system squarely on the shoulders of black clubwomen. It remained up to them to learn their representatives' positions and then vote in a way that would reshape the state.

In addition to exhorting members to keep abreast of the platforms of each dominant party, the NCNW also urged them to vote in a way that would strengthen the position of blacks in America: "Strengthen your relationship with your government by participating actively in the selection of its leadership. . . . Be sure that you are registered and be sure to influence council members who have not registered to do so as quickly as possible. After you register, vote in the November national elections!"[74] Both the NACW and the NCNW, the umbrella groups that represented myriad black women's clubs across the United States, understood the importance of becoming political activists for change during the postwar era. In addition, both organizations incorporated political party support into a strategy to exert power within the state.

Although alerting fellow clubwomen to support specific platforms and candidates actively remained an important goal, the women also encouraged other citizens to vote for those who had the interests of the black community at heart. Some African American women believed they would be the best candidates and ran campaigns for local and state elections. Lula Patterson, social editor of the *Richmond Afro-American,* discovered an important change taking place in the postwar world: Both the Democratic and the Republican parties had begun courting black women for their votes. Thomasina Johnson and Jeanetta Welch Brown, for example, were being considered for a key position as National Democratic Committee Women's section leaders (which Brown eventually secured). Moreover, Patterson recognized that other black women worked as lobbyists in Washington and had gained important positions nationwide; Pauli Murray, for example, was the newly nominated deputy attorney general of California.[75]

Middle-class women in Richmond involved themselves in political campaigns as African American men began to run for local and state offices. Oliver Hill, president of the local NAACP, ran for city council. Because his wife was a Delta, he gained the support of the sorority, which gave him $200 for the campaign.[76] Efforts to register voters and politicize the black community paid off when Hill won. He became the first black councilman in Richmond since the nineteenth century, although he lost the seat two years later in a close election.[77]

Hill's victory encouraged women in their efforts to place black politicians in power. In 1949 a group of prominent women gathered to support Dr. W. L. Ransome in his race for the House of Delegates. Under the auspices of Senora Lawson, at least twenty-four formed radio, block, and finance committees in order to campaign for Ransome. The race proved competitive, but Ransome lost in the primary by 440 votes. The women decided that the close vote meant that change could be accomplished in Richmond with enough organized effort. They formed a new group, the Women's Voters League, that affiliated itself with the Civic Council and determined to help in future civic ventures.[78] Although the racial structure in Richmond hurt black political representatives' abilities to gain positions within government, clubwomen's support suggests they understood that the interests of their race lay with black politicians and mobilized the community in partisan battles in order to effect changes through the electoral process.

Detroit clubwomen claimed a major victory as a result of supporting Charles Diggs for the U.S. House of Representatives. Thirteen chaired Diggs's campaign, holding teas, meetings, and forums to highlight his platform and raise money for the popular candidate. With the support of women's clubs and the UAW, Diggs won the election in a landslide, becoming the first African American from Michigan and the fifth in the United States to hold a seat in Congress since Reconstruction.[79]

The efforts of black women proved critical to Diggs's victory and demonstrate how women's formal community networks could mobilize effectively in order to galvanize the black community around a candidate and create change from within the state. Diggs secured victory only when the UAW, representing working-class African Americans and whites, and clubwomen, representing the black middle class, converged to support him.

Two women, Senora Lawson in Richmond and Jeanetta Welch Brown in Detroit, refused to remain behind the scenes and support male politicians, and their willingness to campaign marked a change in the methods of middle-class women's activism. When the women believed they did not have fair representation in the state, they determined to become political players and represent their communities. Lawson and Brown both ran unsuccessfully for state representative positions, although they placed African American clubwomen squarely at the center of political action.

After supporting other politicians' unsuccessful bids for office, Lawson decided to run for the Virginia House of Delegates as a Progressive in 1950. She created a platform that reflected the concerns of the state's African Americans and drew upon the legacy of Virginians, who stood up to unfair government practices during the American Revolution and took the discourse of responsible patriotism to new historic lengths. In one speech she said, "I feel it my duty to enter this crusade for representation because I believe, with the great patriots of Virginia, that 'taxation without representation is tyranny.' . . . To win this crusade for first class citizenship, however, we must have unity within our ranks regardless of party affiliation. The time has come for us to judge candidates not on the basis of party labels alone but on the basis of issues."[80] Lawson supported an immediate end to the poll tax so all African Americans could be represented by government. She also supported abolition of segregation, establishment of a state FEPC, and creation of better welfare assistance and unemployment benefits programs. Although she lost, her campaign gave a prominent voice to Richmond's African Americans and provided an alternative to the traditional white male political power structure.

Jeanetta Welch Brown campaigned unsuccessfully for the Michigan senate. She did manage, however, to mobilize large groups of women in her campaign and involve many from Detroit directly in the politics of that city. She spoke at a women's neighborhood voter meeting and discussed methods to get voters to the polls. On another occasion, Eugenia Brayboy, resident of the Boston-Edison neighborhood, sponsored a tea to raise money for Brown.[81] It is important to note that Boston-Edison was a wealthy and integrated area of Detroit. It is likely that white women attended the fund-raiser, which would bring class interests across racial lines. Brown effectively organized sorority and clubwomen in her campaign and brought them even closer to the center of state power by enabling them to engage in the arena of electoral politics.

While women in Richmond and Detroit worked hard to support candidates and in two cases ran for political office themselves, they also appealed to all-black as well as interracial audiences in forums that discussed human rights. In this way they tried to educate whites about problems African Americans faced; they also exhorted African Americans to work hard for equality. In Richmond, the Daughters of the Elks sponsored a talk by Theresa Robinson, director of the Grand Temple of the Elks's civil rights program, who discussed various methods to attain equality. The Delta chapter held an open chapel service at Virginia Union, "Freedom! What Does It Mean to You?" The audience was told about the importance of supporting the NAACP and the Freedom Train program, and music composed by African Americans was performed. In addition, the NCNW held a forum to discuss ways of desegregating public carriers in Virginia.[82] The women who sponsored these campaigns suggested their belief that voting for change would not be enough. Gaining the white community's support for civil rights efforts, however, could be a substantial part of reversing discrimination in the city.

After the war, interracial coalitions formed between women's groups in Richmond and Detroit in order to promote civil rights, highlight progress in race relations, and point out inequality in each city's social structure. Richmond's white Women's Missionary Union, the black Educational Association, and Good Wives Baptist Convention sponsored a two-day interracial rally that featured speakers from the National Baptist Convention. The YWCA in Richmond was also instrumental in leading interracial meetings after 1946, when the integrated Business and Professional Girls' Clubs held an interracial dinner to celebrate the World Wide Y Observance Day. Although Y leaders hoped to increase the number of meetings held jointly, rumors of communism in the group surfaced as a result of the interracial meetings. Talks that focused on civil rights were tabled; to many whites, interracialism itself seemed suspect.[83] Once again, cold war fears had stifled open talk about equality by threatening a prominent community organization that dared speak about civil rights to interracial audiences.

Detroit also sponsored forums that focused on civil rights, but the most important advance among black and white clubwomen were friendship tours. After a hundred black and white women's clubs had gathered successfully to discuss policymaking, several decided to continue annually and promote friendly race relations. Led by the Beulah Whitby, the assistant director of the Mayor's Interracial Committee and an AKA, friendship tours took groups of women to each other's communities to tour businesses and private homes. The Women's Council of the Second Baptist Church attended the first tour, and the annual event became a venue where clubwomen of both races could talk and socialize. Apparently, the meetings led to much better understandings among black and white clubwomen.[84]

Interracial coalitions joined women along class lines, and those who participated in such meetings had a common economic status in their respective communities. In reality, class-oriented organizing limited African American women's abilities to create change on a broad social scale because they did not encourage cross-class mingling. It is possible that class status within the cold war climate remained an obstacle to structural civil rights changes. The clubwomen seemed to focus more on socializing, and they failed to address serious problems of structural racism for fear of receiving state and community scrutiny, as in the case of the Richmond YWCA.

Working-Class Advocacy

Often, middle-class African American women failed to connect with working-class black women, especially over children's issues and during interracial, class-oriented meetings. Although their social functions remained ex-

clusive and their beliefs in urban pathology often stigmatized poor mothers, middle-class women were concerned for working-class women's issues
because such issues contributed to the overall development of civil rights in
the country. It is important to note, however, that even though they often
failed to sympathize personally with working-class women, middle-class
women fought for their economic rights and became effective spokespeople
for them.

As they had during World War II, clubwomen continued to advocate working-class issues in an attempt to stop economic discrimination. Although they
continued to be biased against the behavior of some working-class women,
local women's groups, led by their national organizations, held vocational
opportunity campaigns and clinics on job performance, charm, and personality. Several programs held in Detroit, for example, showed a definite shift
away from respectability-oriented programs and promoted real alliances with
working-class women.

National organizations took the lead in identifying the problems African
American women workers faced, as they had during the war. The NCNW
continued support of economic measures to help workers as it lobbied to have
those employed in agriculture and domestic service covered under Social
Security in 1946. Testifying before the Senate Ways and Means Committee,
Bethune talked about the precarious position of African American workers
that resulted from societal discrimination: "Realizing as we do that the majority of Negro workers . . . because of discrimination and lack of economic opportunity are unfortunately relegated to the lowest level of employment
and their need for insurance against instability is greatest, the NCNW is
particularly concerned [about Social Security benefits]."[85]

The NCNW also called on members to help working-class African American women survive the postwar shift back to less-lucrative jobs. Ida Coker
Clark, a former USO secretary for workers in Pennsylvania, told the NCNW,
"Again the Negro woman worker is faced with problems similar to those
encountered after World War I, when she had to return to low-bracket jobs,
to unemployment, and to suffering."[86] Clark urged the group to coordinate
new programs of study, enabling middle-class women to better coordinate
lobbying efforts that would effectively gain working-class blacks some legislation that could ensure at least some permanent employment and job security.[87] Increasingly, clubwomen understood the structural racism that kept
working-class blacks at the lowest economic levels, and national organizations turned toward supporting legislation that would create equal economic
opportunities for all African Americans.

Clubwomen also tied support of equal employment opportunities to a general support for civil rights. Even when the national FEPC bill failed, national organizations kept trying to secure some sort of equal opportunity bill or at least the passage of state FEPC bills. Bethune addressed the House of Representatives Committee on Education and Labor in 1949 in order to support legislation to prohibit employment discrimination. She spoke on behalf of mothers who had to work in order to support their families, thus giving workers' rights discourse a decidedly gendered spin:

> Discrimination in employment because of race, color, and religion that exists in this country today has a devastating effect upon the morale of the human family. For the one who is discriminated against, and I take that Negro woman as a case in point, this evil in our national life undermines the building and keeping together of good, strong American families. When a large number of mothers have to leave their homes to seek work in order that their husbands' pay can be supplemented, they cannot maintain a good standard of living adequate for the health and well being of themselves or of their families. Thus, we find the lives of thousands and thousands of children being neglected, the homes of thousands and thousands of families being destroyed just because we have lacked the courage and vision to extend to all the opportunity to share equally the bounties of this rich country.[88]

In this speech, Bethune appeared to completely reverse her original stand to protect domestic workers under Social Security. In denouncing the conditions "forcing" women to work, she seemed to nod toward domestic defense cold war strategies. She appeared to be calling for the abolition of employment bias so men could earn better wages—indeed, a family wage—so women could stay at home and take better care of their children.

Although she acknowledged that women had to work because of economic necessity, Bethune's judgment of working women's families as neglected and unhealthy reflected a very middle-class standard of domesticity. Clubwomen still believed that if working-class men could find jobs that could help them maintain a decent standard of living, then working-class women could raise their children properly and create the next generation of respectable citizens. To that end, the NCNW continued to press members to telephone U.S. senators and lobby for the passage of an FEPC or equal employment bill. It also called upon members to send telegrams to President Truman in support of his stand on employment opportunity. The clubwomen's move away from supporting working women's rights reveals, in this case, the tension between domestic ideologies and the needs of working-class women. By focusing on the rights of working men, Bethune placed herself and her organization squarely within the cold war state. They became domestic guardians who wanted to protect the nuclear patriarchal family.

While national organizations created the policies that focused on helping workers, local groups sponsored programs that directly affected working-class women in their cities. In both Richmond and Detroit, middle-class women supported African American workers by sponsoring vocational opportunity campaigns, as they did during the war. They also attempted to keep working-class jobs secure by providing performance-enhancement classes. Moreover, middle-class women sometimes aligned themselves directly with working-class women over such issues as strikes and slum clearance.

In Richmond, Delta Sigma Thetas, teachers, and Sigma Gamma Rhos sponsored vocational opportunity campaigns from 1945 to 1954.[89] Deltas worked with high school representatives, for example, teachers, to hold programs in schools and make students aware of opportunities available upon graduation. In addition, teachers also worked to provide students with planning for future vocations. Grace Matthews and several other teachers established a distributive education program in local black high schools to train students for jobs in retail sales and service establishments. The teachers found results placing graduates as stock clerks and in part-time work as delivery boys and receptionists. They even enabled a few girls to graduate and obtain positions in sales.[90] Sigma Gamma Rho held its own opportunity clinics in 1952 and focused on jobs in broadcasting and drama—perhaps not the most realistic way to present potential job opportunities to Richmond youngsters. In addition, three teachers chaired a very successful Urban League job campaign in 1954 that not only described jobs but also considered the importance of equal opportunity. The vocational campaign's theme centered on "the equalization of opportunities for education and vocational training; full opportunities for job placement for all who are trained and qualified, and the complete elimination of discriminatory practices from all American industry."[91]

In Detroit, Deltas and teachers gained prominent roles in Urban League vocational opportunity campaigns and in their own guidance clinics. As part of their 1947 May Week celebration, Deltas took a hundred children on tours of local businesses and industries, showing them opportunities for employment and highlighting black-owned businesses. Then, in 1948, 1949, and 1950, Delta cosponsored the Vocational Opportunity Campaign with the Urban League. In these campaigns, members chaired seminars on opportunities in industry, and Ford Motor Company representatives were featured. In 1949 they held tours of hospitals. Deltas also supported unions by allowing the UAW-CIO to hold forums on wage-earning. Their eagerness to engage with the UAW suggests middle-class women's continued acceptance of unions as legitimate vehicles for fighting workplace inequality despite the state's distrust of unions after the war. Each year more than eight hundred people participated in the tours, and more than 1,300 attended clinics and presentations.[92]

Teachers also helped students prepare for careers. Those at Detroit's Sherrard Intermediate School, for example, held a career clinic in order to show graduates "various job opportunities and possibilities that are open to them when they become ready to assume their responsibilities in our democratic society," including dressmaking, nursing, skilled mechanical trades, and food service. Two teachers refused to stop with bringing career clinics into schools—they took their children to the careers. Katherine Routt and Georgia Adams of Wingert School took sixty-two students to the A. W. Curtis Laboratories plant and sales office to highlight job opportunities available to high school graduates.[93]

It is important to note that in both Detroit and Richmond many job clinics focused on traditional blue-collar and service work rather than employment requiring a college education. Perhaps those who sponsored the campaigns wished to reach a broader audience, yet such a focus might suggest that clubwomen sponsors and teachers believed a vast majority of students could do no better than secure employment in a field requiring no higher education.

Middle-class women in Richmond and Detroit also tried to encourage their working-class counterparts to attend classes and improve their skills in order to secure jobs. The YWCA was a leader in trying to standardize the work of Richmond's domestics. In 1946 it discussed holding domestic-service clubs for factory workers laid off after the war. If the domestics would attend courses to learn about household standards, then the YWCA could institute benefits for them, such as a fifty-hour work week, paid vacation, and sick leaves as well as written contracts.[94] In 1947 and 1948 the YWCA and the Urban League sponsored a household course focusing on child care, cooking, and use of modern equipment. The 120-hour course remained open to "housewives, mothers, and others interested in the field of household employment," but sponsors clearly wanted domestic workers to attend and offered placement upon graduation through Virginia's United States Employment Services office.[95]

The YWCA wanted to set standards in domestic work similar to those of factory work. Program directors were perplexed by the turnout in 1948, when only seven registered for the course. In 1947 thirty-five women had attended the class, although only seven had received their certificates. The directors decided to go house to house in order to secure enough students to run the course.[96]

The facts that so few women received certificates and few matriculated the following year suggest that working-class women in Richmond resisted a standardization of domestic work, the lowest-paid and least popular job option after the war, even though layoffs forced many back into their homes in 1946. It seems, however, that many domestics refused to spend their free time learning how to become better at their skills for no extra pay—and no guarantee of extra pay after the end of the course. Once again, middle-class women made assumptions about the needs of working-class women without realizing that better jobs, not more qualifications for the worst jobs available, were what concerned them.

In Detroit, middle-class women moved beyond domestic work to help found a school for vocational trades. They also focused on how to enhance the job status of working women after postwar layoffs. As in Richmond, the YWCA sponsored a program for domestics that included a three month-course on home management, cooking, child care, and "personal development."[97] The greatest development in terms of advancing workers' opportunities, however, proved to be the school founded by Rosa Gragg.[98]

Gragg began the Slade-Gragg Academy for vocational arts when she noticed that "World War II had left a considerable excess of displaced and unskilled persons" in the Detroit area.[99] She received financial support from numerous clubs in the Detroit Association of Women's Clubs (DAWC) and mortgaged her own house to start the institution, which offered courses in tailoring, dressmaking, food production and service, home service, and waitressing.[100] Gragg then opened a dormitory for women of low income, not only to provide them with a place to live but also to "improve the habits of work, and raise economic standards of living by creating and maintaining an invironment [sic] where these values will be normally developed."[101] A self-proclaimed Bookerite, Gragg believed strongly in the uplift of the race through skilled labor, thrift, and respectability. Although she held vocational courses for the women students, they also received counsel in "music, charm, grooming, and personal hygiene."[102]

While other clubwomen moved away from sponsoring specific courses in respectability, Gragg believed that working-class women needed charm school in order to be good workers. Many employers expected secretaries to be charming in that they were dealing with the public, but that could be dangerous for black women who worked for white men, given dominant society's constructions of those women as less than virtuous and a misconception that charm and affability meant sexual availability. Gragg continued the program of previous middle-class reformers by merging the tenets of respectability with attempts to help women gain economic equality. By 1952 her efforts on behalf of working-class women, combined with her work with the DAWC, earned her the presidency of the NACW.

Although Gragg, the Deltas, and several other groups continued to focus on the disparity between working-class women and respectable behavior, several Detroit groups sought to align themselves socially and politically with working-class women after World War II. In a stunning reversal of tradition, for example, the Zeta Phi Betas nominated Mary Clark, a Detroit Street and Railways employee, "Miss Charming" of 1950 at the end of their charm school week. Moreover, two years later they named Lillian Hatcher, the UAW-CIO Fair Practices and Anti-Discrimination Department representative who had worked her way up from the factory floor but "first and foremost [was] a wife and mother," as woman of the year.[103]

In the interests of building cross-class coalitions, middle-class women chose to ascribe qualities of their own social definitions of respectability to working-class women, perhaps to make the work of those women more palatable to elite socialites. Deltas also sought to become more socially conscious about the lives and labors of working-class women. Although no evidence suggests they followed through on the ban, the Deltas' national leadership ordered a boycott of tobacco products in order to aid strikers at the American Tobacco Company who wanted 65 cents an hour minimum wage and a nondiscrimination clause in their employment contract. As former Delta president Elsie Austin commented, "All organized groups should recognize their opportunity and responsibility in the abolition of hatred, bigotry, and prejudice."[104] Deltas in Detroit also heard the City Planning Commission describe plans to fix blighted ghetto areas, including creating large playgrounds, modern schools, and libraries.[105]

Middle-class women failed to disengage their postwar program of responsible patriotism from respectability altogether, but they slowly moved away from regarding respectability as a major way of solving working-class women's problems. Doing so involved a hesitant detachment from their analysis of working-class problems as "urban pathology" to interpreting problems resulting from structural racism in both the industrial and nonproduction sectors of the economy.

* * *

Middle-class African American women's efforts to help children, service the state, and promote voting rights and the needs of working-class women continued to be a strong influence on the modern civil rights movement in the wake of World War II. Institutions like the NAACP turned to building membership in the South, litigation, and negotiation with state officials on all levels of government. Middle-class African American women supported the NAACP by raising money and soliciting membership, and they counted on the NCNW and the NACW to step in and work for change at the highest levels of government as they worked for equality in their communities. The women supported the fight for equality by participating directly in electoral politics, whether supporting candidates or running for office. They modified their discourse and continued their civil rights activism in order to make responsible patriotism relevant to the new cold war world. As a result, they secured themselves a prominent place within the national civil rights movement of the period.

4. Trying to Hold On: Working-Class Women's Activities in the Postwar Era

In 1945 the *Michigan Chronicle* ran a story that investigated the plans of working-class African American women in the postwar period. Mae Coleman and Bessie Smith, both of whom had worked for Aeronautical Products Corporation and received pink slips in 1945 along with hundreds of other Detroit workers, did not seem bothered by unemployment. As they planned a vacation together, they told the reporter that "'just keeping house'" would satisfy them, because "the war is over and they have done their patriotic duty." Mrs. Wayne Maddox, a riveter at Briggs Manufacturing plant since 1943, began a dressmaking business after she was laid off. She looked forward to remaining at home with her children.[1] Coleman, Smith, and Maddox constructed their postwar lives in a way that supported traditional domestic roles, just as the government wanted, but they were among a minority of workers in the postwar struggle to retain jobs.

In a much more typical case, Minnie Wilson was laid off from her riveting job at Dodge Main plant on V-J Day and discovered that although other workers had been rehired soon after the layoffs, she could not get her job back. The company claimed it could not reemploy Wilson because she had high blood pressure. Suspecting the reason for her continued layoff was a matter of race rather than health, she called on her union local to look into the seniority system. Officials of Local 3 discovered that those few black women who returned to work at all worked in the Heat Treat and Foundry positions, the worst jobs at the plant, even though they had seniority and qualified for much better positions. Wilson did not get her job back, but the union sponsored antidiscrimination workshops at the plant.[2]

African American working-class women faced serious problems after the war. Their relatively late entry into factories placed them low on seniority lists, and they found it hard to find skilled mechanical work after they had been laid off. All women were laid off before male workers, and industries often overlooked seniority to hire men in fields that had hired men before the war. Moreover, some UAW locals refused to support women's grievances about seniority and unfair hiring practices. African American women were left with very few options in order to regain some of the jobs they had claimed during the wartime boom.[3]

In addition to job displacement, working-class African American women faced a more repressive work atmosphere and restricted opportunities as a result of the government's move to the right and its subsequent red-baiting of liberal organizations. The fact that civil rights organizations and unions backpedaled on issues promoting working-class equality hurt the women's chance of gaining institutional support for their efforts to hold on to gains made during the war. With society's shift to the right, they operated in a more difficult context of increased structural impediments to the goals of desegregation. Moreover, city planning policies in Detroit and Richmond put their communities at risk of destruction.

The government's shift toward the right in the form of increased surveillance of liberal groups threatened the existence of civil rights organizations and unions. Although the wartime government had tried to suppress social conflict, cold war tensions heightened government surveillance of agencies perceived to threaten the dominant social order, including civil rights organizations and unions. The government's anticommunist efforts created such fear that people began to guard their thoughts and actions and information about the associations to which they belonged.[4]

Government repression extended to people's private lives as the newly created National Security Administration policed people's "nonconformist" activities, including homosexuality or promoting unionism. Any behavior or activities the state deemed nonconformist were redefined as threatening and subversive. Many liberal organizations found themselves watching membership lists and press releases carefully so as not to come under the watchful eye of state anticommunist agencies.[5]

State repression affected civil rights organizations and industrial unions, two institutions that had supported working-class black women's claims to citizenship during the war. The Fair Employment Practices Commission (FEPC) became an institution of the past, mired in Senate filibusters and then permanently eradicated by 1946. The NAACP and Urban League purged their most radical leaders in order to stay alive. They also turned away from working-class issues in favor of such middle-class concerns as school and neighborhood desegregation. Both groups moved away from radical protest movements like sit-ins and marches, which would have undermined both by showing a dangerous, subversive side of the civil rights movement to the state. Instead, both continued to promote lawsuits against schools and neighborhood racial covenant laws as primary vehicles for change.[6]

Unions also fought for survival within a state that often conflated workers' rights with communist or socialist activities. Communism became the discourse that dominated such union issues as civil rights activism or collective bargaining methods.[7] In order to retain some of the power gained during the prewar and war years, unions struggled to purge socialist members, dropped civil rights programs from a position of prominence, and focused on gaining private welfare benefits, like pensions for members. Walter Reuther, president of the UAW after the war, was especially virulent against communism. He claimed that his union rejected all "outside influence" and worked openly with employers to negotiate worker benefits, which industrial leaders agreed to provide. Employers gave workers private employee benefits that kept the power of the welfare state in check and guaranteed industry control over worker subsidies. The problem with the new union focus on welfare benefits rather than employment and equality issues was that women and minorities remained outside such negotiations because they lacked the seniority or job levels to have access to private welfare benefits.[8]

Not only did working-class women lose the support of civil rights organizations and unions as a result of the government's shift to the right, but they also faced the destruction of their communities as a result of "urban redevelopment" plans. Both in Detroit and Richmond, thousands of African Americans lost their communities when slum clearance projects and freeways rolled through historically black neighborhoods during the late 1940s. Because poor African American women depended on their neighbors for survival, they faced real danger and also saw their community networks at risk of destruction in the face of city projects.

In Detroit, tens of thousands of blacks lost their homes to expressway projects and slum clearance. Some moved into new public housing high-rises, but many could not afford even subsidized housing. Still more found themselves on waitlists for entry. Detroit maintained segregated projects and refused to allow blacks into white housing, which usually went unfilled. Richmond's black community faced the same problems. In 1946 and as part of a plan to revitalize the downtown area, the city council planned a street-widening project through Jackson Ward and an expressway through Fulton, two black districts. The city did not see the need for public housing, so the seven thousand African Americans who found themselves homeless in the wake of the construction projects had to make do and find adequate housing without government help.[9]

Within the more restricted parameters of the postwar era, the women worked to retain their claims to citizenship, which they defined as equal access to employment, welfare benefits, and housing—even as the state tried to keep those rights from people of color. In Detroit and Richmond, working-class black women refused to give up their rights to decent employment without a battle, despite the hostility of employers and some unions. They fought for seniority rights, the right to be rehired after layoffs, and better working conditions in factories. Moreover, they pushed for welfare benefits, housing rights, and help from the state and private organizations when they could not stretch their budgets enough to support their families. The women drew upon their rights as workers and contributors to industry in order to receive benefits from employers, unions, the state, and private philanthropic concerns. And as they struggled to support themselves they became activists for equality in employment and entitlement benefits. In this way they continued at the forefront of the modern civil rights movement.

The massive layoffs that began in 1944 in both Detroit and Richmond affected African Americans and women who had managed to break into industries during manpower shortages. The Detroit Urban League found that three hundred thousand jobs had been eliminated in 1944 and 1945; eighty thousand workers would remain in reconverted industries, and a hundred thousand would remain in aircraft plants. In 1946 the *Richmond Afro-American* determined that, nationwide, twenty million white and black women had either left the labor market or dropped out of it. In Richmond, and nationwide, there were "forgotten" black women who faced problems getting jobs.

While Richmond had problems with reconversion as the War Manpower Commission downgraded the importance of its industries, Detroit struggled with a real economic crisis. As late as 1949, sixty-three thousand workers remained idle and wages dropped. Even with increased production for the Korean War in 1950, several hundred African American women were refused jobs at the Cadillac plant although white women had been hired. The plant claimed that white women had seniority and experience, whereas the black women were recent migrants. That was not true according to the *Michigan Chronicle*, which found that all the potential hires had experience in factory work.[10]

Using State and Private Institutions to Continue the Fight for Equal Employment

Not only did working-class African American women in Detroit and Richmond lose jobs, but they also continued to face barriers to employment in various industries. Without an FEPC to support them, they turned to various other agencies to gain support against discriminatory hiring practices. In Detroit, women turned to state institutions like the Detroit Commission on Community Relations (DCCR) and the Mayor's Interracial Commission (and even to the mayor himself) and to the UAW, Urban League, and NAACP. Because state equal-opportunity agencies, historically black institutions, and unions found themselves weakened by the state's move to the right, many African American women called upon all three simultaneously in order to maximize support.

Many working-class women revealed their understanding of local power structures when they called upon state leaders to help in bids for equal employment. They politicized their working-class status in order to claim the same benefits white women received. In Detroit, Sweetie Hall did not complain about a specific employment problem. Instead, she wrote to Mayor Albert Cobo about her problems securing any decent employment:

> I am a citizen of the United States. . . . I have always worked and I feel that I did my part to help win World War II, but as soon as V.J. came, it seem as if my family and I have been put on the forgotten list. I don't feel that we have had justice in regards of employment. I am a widow, forty-eight years old but able to work. . . . I have had to go hungry sometime and I didn't have the proper clothing, trying to keep a place for us to live. . . . We go to the employment service and the ones they have in charge are hiring by choice not qualifications. My daughter went to one of the employment offices, . . . After she had waited almost a half-day, they told her that she had been called by mistake, but upon further investigation it was found the position was for white. . . . the Draft Boards and the War Department are not using the word "white only." I am not white but I would appreciate and I think I deserve a fair chance to do the work of my choice, whether it is common labor or professional.[11]

Hall employed several different strategies in her letter to Cobo. First, she based the demand for a job on her previous performance as a war worker, thus couching her citizenship in terms of her value to the state in wartime. She then contrasted discrimination in industry with the race-blind drafting of soldiers during the Korean War, pointing out the hypocrisy of the state allowing black men to die for the country but not supporting black women's "fair chance" to work. She understood that the black community's sacrifices to the wartime state, both during World War II and in Korea, went unappreciated by the military-industrial complex, as evinced by the fact that she, her daughter, and, of course, other black women found no jobs at all.

Hall saw equal, state-guaranteed opportunity as the appropriate reward for wartime support of the state, and her sophisticated use of patriotic discourse got the mayor's attention. Cobo forwarded the letter to the DCCR, but after opening the case the committee failed to follow up on her complaints, and the matter died.[12] Hall may have failed to receive justice, but her use of a discourse that incorporated the themes of social justice, wartime sacrifice, and equal employment opportunity suggests her understanding that World War II rhetoric had shifted after the war and she could use that language to support claims for work.

Working-class women's use of state systems in Detroit suggests that they felt empowered enough at least to attract attention when they complained about unfair hiring practices. Bonita Blair, a member of the Congress of Racial Equality (CORE), complained to the DCCR that Sam's Cut Rate Store refused to hire her and other black women. She threatened to involve CORE in a massive boycott of the store, but the DCCR stepped in to negotiate the problem with the personnel department of Sam's. The DCCR suggested that Sam's hire fifteen black saleswomen in three months or it would wholeheartedly support—and even help organize—CORE's boycott.[13] After a continued battle in which the Urban League and CORE as well as the DCCR participated, Sam's Cut Rate hired its first black saleswoman in 1952. Eva Pruitt was promoted from a stock position, which she had held for five years, to hosiery sales.[14] Several other women attempted to use the DCCR to investigate their complaints about employment discrimination in Detroit, and others looked to the Urban League to help them gain equality. At least three different groups of African American women made complaints against Household Finance Corporation, Ford, Murray Body Company, and J. L. Hudson between 1945 and 1954.[15]

The League generally forwarded complaints against automakers to the UAW, but it tried to meet employment discrimination at J. L. Hudson head-on in a battle over department store job placement. After hearing angry African American women complain repeatedly about Hudson's hiring practices, the Urban League sent four to answer an advertisement for packers and wrappers. Employment officers told each woman that the positions had been filled. Then, over a period of ten months, several African American women responded to other advertisements at the store in order to wear down its reluctance to hire black women in sales and clerical positions. Johnnie Kendrick, Pauline Adkins, Ruth Price, Annie Mae Little, A. J. Moore, and three other women represented the League as they applied for sales and clerical positions. None had any success, and they filed depositions that the Urban League used in the DCCR investigation of Sam's Cut Rate and other department stores in the area.[16]

Moore also went to Lane Bryant to apply for a job and reported her experience both to the manager of Lane Bryant and to the Urban League:

> On November 26 I replied to your ad of November 25 in the Detroit News for cashier and clerk. Upon inquiring about the same, I was told by the switchboard operator, very quickly and curtly, that the job was taken. I was first in line to inquire concerning the job; behind me was a white girl who inquired about the same job. She was told to be seated. In the meantime I shall discuss this experience with Mr. F. A. Korenegay of the Detroit Urban League, who heads the Vocational Services Department. It is my hope that such matters as these concern you and are worthy of your consideration.[17]

Moore recognized that employment officers at Lane Bryant continued to employ racist hiring practices, and she protested both her treatment and the injustice of the system. She had also situated herself within the black institutional power structure by indicating willingness to work with a leaders of the Urban League in order to overturn the company's practices.

The women who fought for the Urban League gained success for others. Although J. L. Hudson remained adamant about hiring black women, Lane Bryant employed several black saleswomen, Crowley-Milner was training three, and Gutman's Department Store used at least four.[18] In addition, Sears-Roebuck, in what the black community considered a major event in the advancement of civil rights, hired its first black saleswoman. Minnie Roberts moved from maintenance to bird and plant department sales after working in the store for only six months. A high school graduate, she was chosen from among several candidates, black as well as white, for her "amiable character, her industry and sincerity."[19] The saleswomen formed part of the vanguard of what would become a large nationwide movement of African American women into new employment fields.[20]

Perhaps the greatest battle won in Detroit during this period was the desegregation of Michigan Bell by the Urban League and its women members. After a campaign that began in 1943, four black women finally secured jobs as switchboard operators in 1946. The company hired Lillian Campbell, Jacquelin Oliver, Wilhelmina Irvin, and Josephine Taylor because they had high school educations and were young, healthy, and tall enough to reach all the switchboard lines. Several years later, many more black women worked as operators; Bernice Ford, Hattie Anderson, and Joynal Muthleib, for example, gave out the correct time and weather reports as part of their jobs. As successful as the NAACP was in desegregating the industry, women still had to continue pressing the company for employment. Michigan Bell continued to be reluctant to raise the number of black women in its offices. A year later, when two women found themselves initially turned down for jobs as operators, they went to the Urban League for help. Both Doris Burney and Irma Robinson received jobs from Michigan Bell after the League questioned the company's refusal to hire them.[21]

In Richmond, working-class African American women had neither a city race relations committee nor a strong Urban League. They even lacked powerful unions that would support their bids to gain entry into postwar jobs. They did, however, have the War Manpower Commission, at least for a time, and the Quality Services Employment Agency supported by the director of Richmond's Associated Agencies (which included the YWCA) to help them.

Even in Richmond, where legal impediments to racism constrained their abilities to obtain jobs in fields dominated by white women, African American women continued to press for jobs in production and in unproductive work but with varying degrees of success. In 1944, as they were being laid off at various Richmond plants, the DuPont Chemical Company needed more workers. When the women brought this to the attention of the War Manpower Priorities Committee (WMPC), it asked DuPont why the factory could not use black women. The employment manager argued that he could not afford to pay black women the high wage rates needed for the job because doing so would offend white workers. After pressure from the WMPC, however, DuPont hired forty black women in the shipping department, paid them from 83 to 93 cents an hour, rates equal to those of white women, and agreed to hire more in the near future.[22]

Richmond's working-class African American women also tried to break into pink-collar jobs, whether clerical, receptionist, or stenographic work. They found resistance at many white-owned businesses until Horace Gillison, a black businessman and civil rights activist, created Quality Services, Inc., to place African American women in such jobs across Richmond. During the late 1940s Gillison circulated a flyer to white-owned firms, trying to appeal to employers' senses of justice:

> Our colored Girls find it difficult to secure jobs in the stenographic field, even though they have been fully trained for this work. Therefore, we are trying to make opportunities for them by offering you a complete and efficient STENO-

GRAPHIC SERVICE outside of your office. . . . We feel that this approach . . . is better than asking you to employ them in your office. We understand your position in not being able to employ eligible Colored Girls in your Offices. We also understand the social pattern that forbids them employment in many fields. However, we are hoping that the plan of service we are presenting you will enable these ambitious Girls to be of service to you. We want them to live decently and respectably and sometimes it becomes very discouraging when doors of most real opportunities are closed in their faces. . . . We are not going to let them live a life of bitterness; we are trying to do something ourselves about the matter in this way. We hope you understand and take no offense.[23]

Gillison appealed to employers who believed they could advance social justice by farming out work to stenographers rather than hiring them in their offices. In so doing, employers could maintain the boundaries and fictions of racial segregation by maintaining a constructed space for whites—even when black women did the work. The employment agency did not challenge the strict social segregation of Richmond but called upon the beliefs of paternalistic employers. They were reminded of their responsibility toward the black race and the need to help in some small way so women would not need to lose respectability.

The flyer's language was fraught with concerns about middle-class respectability, and the fact the YWCA supported the program wholeheartedly reveals its top-down organizational structure. Nevertheless, working-class African American women signed on with the agency and gained work. In 1947 Quality Services managed to place Edna Hall in clerical work at Neuman's Clothing Shop. She became the first black woman in Richmond to obtain clerical work in an all-white firm.[24]

Activism and Unions: Strikes and the Fights for Seniority and Equality

As they did during the war years, African American women refused to accept excuses for racism in industrial hiring practices. In both Detroit and Richmond they continued to claim rights based on their position as American citizens and as workers who supported democracy. From 1945 to 1954 several groups of African American women workers were able to clarify the meanings of citizenship by engaging with their unions and constructing new definitions of labor unionism and patriotism. Laborers have equated the right to control their own labor with the rights of citizenship since the first inception of worker insurgency movements during the late eighteenth century, when white men tried to oppose losing status as skilled laborers. This language evolved into pro-unionism in the late nineteenth century as they fought for collective bargaining and the right to be recognized by the state.[25]

African American women drew upon this history as they juxtaposed the right of equal access to work with citizenship and recognized unions as primary vehicles for ensuring those rights. The women worked to secure the benefits unions provided, employing union power not only to claim jobs in industries that now turned them away but also to reinforce their seniority rights. They often turned to unions to support their campaigns for equality on factory floors. Moreover, they struck for better wages and benefits, often with the support of the unions. Often, unions also provided support necessary for gaining or retaining jobs in industries that had hired black women during the war. Many filed grievances with UAW locals in order to change hiring practices at the factory gates.

Although some women proved successful in finding jobs in auto plants, others found indifference in many UAW locals. For example, Beatrice Woodruff wrote to Guy Nunn, a vice president of the UAW, about her repeated failure to secure employment and asked for help: "I am very much in need for a good job. I am a sewing machine operator 'power sewing machine, that is.' I worked in a factory during the war. The main thing I want in a good job is I want it to be a union shop! I am working in a small cleaners now, inspecting and doing the minor sewing, working around seven hours a day and underpaid! I am colored; which is a handicap. I dont look for special favors, but I do want to live!"[26] Nunn forwarded the letter to the president of Local 400 at Chrysler's Highland Park plant because he had heard that sewing operators were needed there.[27] Woodruff did not bother to file grievances with various locals but went straight to the top in order to secure help from UAW officials. It appears that her direct appeal and praise of unionism may have helped her to find employment in one of the few fields still open to women after the war, machine sewing in factories.

Other women who had problems gaining employment in factories filed grievances with the Fair Practices and Anti-Discrimination Department of the UAW and with the locals. They lodged complaints against Champion Spark Plug, the L. A. Young Company, Murray Body, Ford's Willow Run, Dearborn, Hamtramck, and Highland Park plants, Dodge's Main plant, and Drapper Motors.[28] Their letters about discrimination in the plants compelled the UAW to launch a massive assault on Detroit auto companies, based on President Harry S. Truman's Executive Order 10210 of 1951 that banned bias in plants with defense contracts during that year. The UAW claimed that the "'basis for this attack against Detroit auto firms originated from a series of reports from local unions of auto firms refusing to permit Negro women applicants to file applications—as well as outright by-passing of Negro women on employment lines.'" Initially, this move resulted in twenty-five black women being hired at the Cadillac plant; overall, however, very few were hired because of it. The union did not have the time or inclination to investigate all hiring offenses.[29]

Still, women's willingness to use unions as resources for advancing civil rights, even when the women were not members of those unions, suggests they understood how to manipulate power structures in Detroit in order to maximize success in gaining employment. Their actions reveal that a working-class consciousness was central to their politics.

In postwar Detroit and Richmond, African American women faced not only problems securing employment but also problems with layoffs. In many cases they fought to retain seniority rights in order to be recalled when rehiring began. They faced an uphill battle, however. Companies were reluctant to rehire any women at all, black or white. In one instance at a Ford plant, women members of Local 600 were so distressed that men found employment at the River Rouge plant before those who were on the seniority list that they considered a picket line to protest the practice. After intense negotiations with the UAW, Ford began to recall women and promised to furnish a complete recall list so the union could oversee the rehiring process.[30]

When working-class African American women in Detroit faced unfair firings and seniority violations, they took their grievances to the UAW or to other unions. In some instances they managed to retain their jobs. In late 1945, for example, Lonnie Mae Arrington and Aline Perkins engaged in a fight while working at the Great Lakes Steel Company. When the company fired them, the women claimed that the punishment was unfair and racially motivated. It was, in essence, an excuse to get rid of them as workers. They filed a grievance with their Local 1209 of the United Steelworkers of America (AFL), claiming that white employees had always received shorter layoffs after fights. After more than five months' arbitration the union negotiated a deal— the women were reinstated and won about $2,000 in back pay and lost vacation time.[31]

The UAW also had some success in reinstating African American women who had been unfairly fired. In 1946 Louise Hamilton transferred to a new job at Ford's River Rouge plant after working there for two and a half years and clocking 1,440 hours of defense work training. After an hour on the new job, Hamilton was fired for failing to keep up with the production line. She filed grievance with Local 600, but when it failed to respond quickly she wrote to William Oliver, head of the Fair Practices and Anti-Discrimination

Department: "My work during that time [of employment] was satisfactory, because there was never a complaint that was serious enough for me to have been sent to labor relations or to have been laid off. After V.J. Day I was laid off and was called back in January 46. I worked two weeks and was fired because I was not able to keep up with production in an hours' time. An hour time is not enough time to justify whether a person is qualified for a job."[32] Apparently, Oliver agreed with her and called upon Richard Leonard to order that Local 600 conduct a thorough investigation of the incident. Almost a year later, Hamilton went back to work and received proper training in the new job.[33] From 1947 to 1953 at least three other women petitioned the UAW, trying to get jobs back after unfair firings. In two of those cases the women were successful after filing grievances with their locals.[34]

Other women in Detroit fought to retain seniority and tried to be reinstated after being laid off when whites returned to work. Several took complaints to the DCCR and in each case could not get anywhere in their own, AFL-affiliated, unions. Five laid off after the termination of war contracts from Auto City Plating Company, for example, complained that the company had reinstated white female employees who had less seniority. The DCCR suspected that the AFL metal polishers' union discriminated against black employees, especially because the women had been accused of being "CIO-Minded." As with most cases investigated by the DCCR, the committee made suggestions but failed to follow up on them. All in all, six black women appealed to the DCCR for help when their AFL-affiliated unions refused to support their grievances. In each case, the DCCR failed to secure enough information and in the end closed the matter.[35]

The refusal of AFL locals to act in such cases suggests that some of Detroit's AFL locals maintained hostility toward black workers just as Richmond locals did in tobacco factories. It also suggests the power of local unions to help or hinder African American women who looked for equality, because in one situation the women found an ally—Steelworkers 1209. The reluctance of AFL metal polishers' locals to support the rights of black workers suggests hostility on the part of its leadership, a fact that constrained women who sought to use the locals as vehicles of change.

UAW members often fared much better when they contested the auto industry's violation of seniority rights. As early as 1945, Gladys Dixon, Julia Turner, Bertha Robinson, Mable Thompson, and Earline Anderson fought layoffs from Ford's Highland Park plant aluminum foundry. When the five women discovered that workers who had less seniority remained on the job because they were white, the women filed a grievance. Ford admitted its fault and found them all employment in its River Rouge plant.[36] A year later, Fannie Brown, a light-punch press operator at River Rouge, found herself transferred to a heavy-punch press despite having four year's seniority. She developed stomach and back pains from trying to operate the heavy press and filed a grievance when she discovered that white workers who had less seniority remained on a light press. As a result of pressure from Local 600 and the UAW Fair Practices and Anti-Discrimination Department (and a doctor's note describing her health difficulties), Brown was transferred to an easier job several months later. She enjoyed the new work, although, she complained, her new supervisor seemed prejudiced because he checked up on her when she took quick breaks.[37]

Chrysler also faced a battle with its local union at the Dodge Main plant when it laid off thirty-one women, both black and white, unfairly. Silretha Love, an African American who had worked for the company during the war, filed the grievance that won the other thirty their old jobs as auto body wipers as well as $55,000 in back pay and penalties. Love had originally been laid off when the war ended, a violation of her seniority agreement. Upon being rehired, however, she faced extreme opposition from the assistant superintendent of the plant, who followed her as she worked and streaked the auto panels with his fingers. At the end of five days the superintendent had made enough fingerprints to claim that her work was shoddy, and he fired her. Love filed a grievance with the union and also tried to make money selling aprons and dresses door to door. During the hearing the company claimed that she and other women in the wiping division had failed to perform their duties. "'Its [*sic*] funny' Love replied. 'I was all right during the war. What's wrong with my work now?'" The union found that she had been a good employee who was not given a fair chance to work after being rehired. The grievance enabled her to receive $1,684 in back pay and her job back, as well as those of the other women who had been unfairly laid off, rehired, and then fired.[38]

From 1946 to 1954 many other African American women brought suit against several companies for seniority violations, including Murray Body, Freuhauf Corporation, the C. M. Hall Lamp Company, Fleetwood Auto Body, Briggs Manufacturing, Packard, DeSoto, and the new American Motors Corporation, a product of the Hudson/Nash–Kelvinator merger. The UAW managed to get the women's seniority back at Murray Body and won back pay for them at Freuhauf, C. M. Hall, and Fleetwood.[39] In most cases, several women at each company went in groups to file grievances in order to show strength in numbers. Unlike immediately after the war, however, unions appeared unresponsive to most of the complaints. The UAW was becoming more concerned with its negotiating power among the big industrialists to secure pensions than with helping women regain jobs.

Black women faced gender and race discrimination, as evidenced by the fact that black men fared better than they did in securing jobs in postwar industrial plants.[40] Moreover, Reuther's decision to promote benefits for union employees hurt blacks and women, whose seniority levels and overall position within factories usually made them ineligible for such benefits.[41] Given the UAW's ambivalence toward all women after the war, it is significant that any African American women won grievances.

Women workers in Richmond failed to receive the same level of support as those in Detroit in opposing seniority-based issues such as pay increases and forced layoffs from AFL-TWIU unions. In some cases, however, CIO locals that functioned as unions for black workers in tobacco factories gained victories for them. Unlike in Detroit, most Richmond protests operated within the limitations that company segregation policies imposed, forcing the women to maneuver within more constricted parameters than those in Detroit. Sometimes the CIO-sponsored Food, Tobacco, and Agricultural Workers unions gained wage increases for its members. In addition, local AFL chapters heard their grievances in some cases.

As a result, the women were accorded some small victories in tobacco factories. For example, 280 workers, both male and female, at the Larus and Brother Stemmery won $25,000 in pay raises after their CIO Local 45 determined that being paid 7.5 cents an hour violated seniority rights, as promotion levels appeared minuscule. The CIO also secured eighty-eight hours in annual paid vacations for them.[42]

African American women were involved in the union at the stemmery. Two, Evetta Hampton and Emma Howard, also leaders in Local 45, were chosen to be among five operatives throughout the South in the CIO-sponsored Operation Dixie, intended to organize unions in tobacco plants. Hampton and Howard were assigned to plants in South Richmond, including the Carrington-Michaux Stemmery.[43] The fact that the CIO placed them in positions of leadership to advance its causes suggests the differences between the AFL and the CIO in terms of racial policy.

The AFL American Tobacco Company union, Local 216, seemed to be the most receptive to women's grievances about seniority because, in this case, black workers created a local strong enough to effect change. Six leaders, three men and three women, made progress in securing factory wage increases for the entire union, as well as two weeks' paid vacation and 1,300 members enrolled in 1946. The leaders then turned their attention to two women's seniority cases in 1949 and 1950. In 1949 Pauline Christianson found herself transferred to part-time work when employees who had less seniority were working the entire day. After she complained to the TWIU local she received $156.80 in back pay and reinstatement as a full-time worker. The same year, Hattie Hubbard and four or five hundred other employees at the plant found themselves laid off when the company converted to seasonal employment. The following summer, Hubbard was not recalled at all. She complained that although people with seasonal-worker status were being recalled, she, a full-time employee, deserved to be the first. The union agreed and negotiated with the company to reinstate her and provide back pay.[44] Although the AFL often exhibited hostility toward integrating and promoting black workers, black leaders in Local 216 took control of the union's leadership and effected changes for black women.

The major difference between Detroit and Richmond factories at this time was that jobs in Richmond were entirely segregated, and, therefore, union locals and seniority lists remained segregated as well. In order to racialize space, separate plants and factories were constructed for white workers and for black workers. Although members of AFL 219B had won the right to be represented by the CIO, it was still an entirely black union, as were Locals 45 and 216. Therefore, black women who contested seniority issues had not been replaced by white women workers but by other blacks.

African American women in Richmond did not have the right to challenge employers to promote them to jobs done by white women in tobacco factories, and it is likely that unions would have refused to support such a measure. Filing grievances may have politicized individual black women, yet all of African American women's gains in Richmond factories failed to change the racial status quo within those factories. In Detroit, black women observed the UAW's increasing reluctance to support union seniority rights but continued to file grievances in the hope that locals would back their battles to retain jobs. As their grievances filed against seniority violations demonstrate, women in Richmond and Detroit remained active participants in union politics despite demobilization.

In both cities, working-class African American women refused to stop trying to break into industries or to fight for seniority rights. Often, they appealed to unions for support in their battles. In several incidents they contested their treatment within factories by challenging segregated facilities and prejudiced employers, just as they had during the war. Incidents of segregation decreased in Detroit, but some individual companies still practiced segregation within factories. Several individual locals chose to look the other way instead of addressing the problem. In Richmond, where the entrenched system of segregation in the tobacco industry disallowed white and black women contact with each other let alone the ability to deal with the issue of facilities, black women still worked for fair treatment, albeit within the confines of segregation.

In Detroit, Margaret Sammons took her case against Local 36 of Consolidated Brass all the way to the UAW-CIO national appeals board in 1946. Sammons, a shop steward who took grievances for other union members, had originally reported a grievance: The company kept Jim Crow bathrooms, which 1944 union factory rules outlawed. The Fair Practices Division managed to desegregate the bathrooms, but company officials branded Sammons a troublemaker. She next complained about not being upgraded from the foundry into a better job because the company did not want her or any other black women working with white women. In response, Consolidated Brass charged her with seeking to create dissension among workers and trying to slow work rates to protest the bathroom situation. The union local president proved unsympathetic. Sammons was, he claimed, slow, absent, and late on many occasions; moreover, she loitered in the bathroom. She then went to the Fair Practices Division and charged the union local with misconduct when it refused to enter her grievance about unfair firing. She claimed that the company and the union were engaged in a conspiracy to get rid of her. Sammons received a fair hearing in that the UAW reprimanded the local for not supporting desegregation of the bathroom, but company records indicated that she was absent on many occasions. The UAW refused to support her reinstatement at Consolidated Brass.[45] Sammons won the battle over desegregation by bringing in national leaders to support her, but she lost the war because the local raised the issue of her conduct, for which she was fired. Perhaps the local was punishing her for trying to institute a change that national leaders and local union law did not support.

In Richmond, African American women failed to contest formal segregation, but they did protest inhumane treatment at the hands of whites. Susie Reed, for example, filed a $10,000 lawsuit against the British-American Tobacco Company, claiming a foreman had beaten her with her own umbrella. Reed, who had worked at the company for three years, had endured vulgar language from the foreman before finally speaking up. In so doing, however, she broke a racial code—speaking against a white man's actions—and the foreman retaliated by brutally beating her with the umbrella she had been holding. Rosa Williams, a co-worker, asserted that Reed had not provoked his violent rage, but the AFL local's president testified that she had struck first. She did not win the lawsuit.[46]

On at least two other occasions, once in Detroit and once in Richmond, African American women workers filed grievances or lawsuits against their treatment in factories or businesses.[47] Only Margaret Sammons managed to win a battle over segregation, but in the end she lost her job and her influence at Consolidated Brass. In Detroit, grievances filed both during and after the war had an impact on the way the UAW's leadership promoted race relations.

After the war, conditions in plants improved as the UAW promoted better race relations and workers began to socialize at union-sponsored events. In 1947 the sister-in-law of a Ford employee, Bertima Guillony, who was black, was named Miss Ford Local 600 at the annual picnic attended by five thousand. She beat forty other candidates, most of whom were white. The next year, the UAW banned segregation in its very prominent bowling leagues.[48] African American women's attempts to effect change in working conditions in both Detroit and Richmond suggest they believed strongly that they had the right to decent and equal working conditions despite company policies that sought to restrict the space in which they operated.

When the women failed to resolve problems in the workplace through the usual grievance process, they readily struck, often with the support of their union locals. Sometimes they struck because their employers refused to allow union organization in the workplace. In Detroit and Richmond, they picketed for better wages and better working conditions among a diverse range of businesses and industries. In a vast majority of cases, both in Detroit and Richmond, industries were so race- and gender-segregated that black women composed the majority of the picket lines. Although the few men who worked in hospitals and laundries did join strikes in those establishments, it was women in each instance who dominated the industries.

In Detroit, the antagonism that still existed among social classes in the black community exploded when women employed as clerical workers at Great Lakes Mutual Life Insurance, a black-owned business, struck for better pay. The women, members of Local 26 of the CIO–United Office and Professional Workers of America (UOPWA) struck for a $5 weekly raise; their $25 a week was well below the amount earned by other industrial workers in the area. When the twenty clerical and pink-collar workers struck in November 1948, the company management's wives came in as scabs for the duration. In doing so, middle-class women were helping undermine working-class women's campaign for better pay. Violence sometimes erupted. In one of three major incidents, for example, Dycella Nicholson struck Nettie Cherry, a scab, with a picket sign. The strikers gained the support of policyholders, two hundred of whom attended a rally and canceled their policies in support of the women.

The Great Lakes Mutual strike went on for five months until local authorities branded the CIO-UOPWA a communist stronghold, weakening its bargaining position. The company refused to recognize the local, and internal dissension among the twenty workers led to a breakdown of the strike. In the end, all the women returned to work with no raise.[49] For all their programming that sought to bridge the gap between classes and advocate for the working class, middle-class black women were among those who oppressed the workers in this situation. When faced with having to support better wages for women or bolster the authority of husbands who employed the women, they sided with the latter.

Women employees of Harper Hospital in Detroit fared better than the clerical workers of Great Lakes Mutual. Their strike shut the hospital down as they picketed for a closed shop in order to negotiate wages. The hospital maids and laundry workers struck at about the same time that women at Great Lakes did. Like some at Great Lakes Mutual, moreover, several hospital workers were violent; one tried to knife a scab who attempted to cross the line. The strike lasted about a month, until the hospital finally allowed the AFL Laundry Workers' union to organize workers after no longer being able to admit patients.[50] The successful action suggests that even the lowest-paid and least-powerful African American women workers could mobilize co-workers and shut down a hospital. They could also force employers to recognize the importance of their work and win the right to bargain collectively.

Working-class African American women also struck for better wages and working conditions in several Richmond businesses. In 1946, 115 Sunlight Laundry workers, predominantly African American women, struck for two months for better wages. There is no record of the strike's outcome, but less than a year later the workers struck again after several were almost killed in a plant cave-in. This time they demanded the right to unionize, have safe working conditions, and receive decent wages. Estelle Ewell and Evelyn Stokes, who had worked thirty and fifteen years, respectively, at Sunlight, told the *Richmond Afro-American* that, for all their seniority, they were still paid only $23 a week. The strike occurred in several Sunlight Laundry factories and involved more than four hundred workers by the time it ended in late 1947. As in the first strike, there is no record of an outcome or whether the workers were successful.[51]

Apparently, no Richmond business was too small to be a strike target. In 1951 four African American women, members of the AFL Baker's Union Local 358, struck against Mrs. Chamberlain's Pie Shop for a 10 cent an hour raise. The strike's outcome is again unknown. Even those employed at a small shop, however, found union support in a notoriously anti-union town.[52] The strikers in each case apparently failed, yet the fact that African American women worked through AFL-affiliated unions to effect change is significant because they made the city recognize their political activism as workers.

In Detroit and Richmond, African American women workers in many diverse fields were willing to risk losing their jobs permanently by striking against poor wages and working conditions. Both with and without union support, they challenged employers en masse and made their work problems public by becoming active picketers—activists for change in their respective industries.

Progress in the Nonproduction and Light-Industrial Sectors

Despite the fact that African American women in Detroit and Richmond fought a generally losing battle to maintain wartime industry gains, they worked hard to take every advantage—other than live-in domestic work—open to them after the war. While those in Richmond and Detroit lost ground in factories as they saw their seniority rights trampled, they took advantage of openings in service, clerical, and smaller industrial operative fields. Nationwide, even though 40 percent of black women were employed in domestic labor by 1950, progress had occurred in the apparel industry and in other occupational categories, including, in both Detroit and Richmond, waitressing and pink-collar work.[53]

One of the most significant signs that African American women were finding more job opportunities than before the war was the fact that many refused live-in domestic work. Detroit's Urban League Vocational Services Department reported in 1948 that "a large number of the unfulfilled job orders result from the requests for domestic help to live on the premises. This type of job order is extremely difficult to service."[54] The vocational services department in Detroit continued to have problems filling such job orders throughout the 1950s because the work paid too little and required a lifestyle that was too demanding and confining.[55] The number of domestics placed through Urban League job services declined rapidly from 1947 to 1951, until the League decided to refer domestic service requests to the Michigan Unemployment Commission.

Richmond's Urban League reported that black women did not profit from wartime gains as much as it would have liked, although, it noted, "it is now next to impossible to find full-time domestic workers. Those who are willing to accept full time work are making serious attempts to prescribe the hours of employment, and to a person, practically refuse any work that calls for time on Sunday. This is a significant and revolutionary change in the domestic field."[56] Moreover, the Urban League found that the average educational level of domestic workers dropped from 9.5 to 7.2 years of schooling, suggesting that women who had more education could find more desirable jobs. In addition, the average age of Richmond's domestic workers dropped to twenty-four, a statistic the Urban League took to mean that a new generation of domestic workers, unwilling to work unless they received better wages and significant concessions in hours and duties, would change the way local domestic work was performed.[57] White women employers discovered that workers preferred to take jobs as elevator operators, waitresses, dishwashers, or cooks in restaurants. Of those who had to settle for domestic service, however, 75 to 80 percent insisted on eight-hour workdays and at least one and a half days off per week.[58] Such evidence suggests the impact of waged production and nonproduction work on domestic service and the

African American women in Richmond continued to secure jobs in service industries after World War II, including work in the tearoom of Thalhimer's Department Store. (Courtesy of the Virginia Historical Society)

importance placed on restructuring the contours of the job to make it more like waged work in the public sector.

Whether in Detroit or Richmond, women found jobs in many different fields. Through the Detroit Urban League's Placement File, they worked in retail sales as well as at pink-collar jobs and as nurses, waitresses, survey takers, counter clerks, seamstresses, substitute teachers, and receptionists.[59] In addition, ninety-five women worked as counter girls, box assemblers, and porters at Farmcrest Bakeries; six found employment as clerical workers for Blue Cross Medical services (the first time black women had been hired by the service); and six worked as clerical workers at Michigan Consolidated Gas through the Urban League's pilot placement program.[60]

Women in Richmond who attempted to make gains in nonindustrial work had to do so within the contours of legal segregation, which restricted their ability to claim sales jobs in department stores. The fact that African American consumers frequented Richmond department stores, however, had already challenged strict racial hierarchies within those venues. Department stores offered spaces in which whites and blacks shopped together, and consumer choices expanded racial space and threatened ritualized hierarchies.[61] Although Richmond's middle-class African American women could not use the restaurants or restrooms of department stores, they could spend their money there. Working women after the war attempted to move up the hierarchy of jobs in an atmosphere that often privileged economic status over race, blurring racial bars to jobs. Thalhimer's Department Store, for example, promoted six African American women from maintenance positions to clerking ones. One became supervisor of marking in the receiving warehouse after working at the store for ten years, and another became an embosser of monogrammed paper after being a part-time clerk. By 1949 all of the waitresses in Thalhimer's tearoom were African American women, and eleven black women and five black men worked as elevator operators. Still, Thalhimer's refused to hire African American saleswomen.[62] The Richmond Urban League reported that several "anonymous" department stores had hired black saleswomen, however, and Crawford Manufacturing hired a complete shift of African American women as machine operators. In addition, the Little Mending Shop started breaking racial barriers by hiring a black woman to work as a machine operator. She worked out so well that by 1946 black women staffed the entire shop. B. T. Crump Feed Company was so impressed by the work of the woman at the Little Mending Shop that it decided to hire several black women on as machine operators in its factory.[63]

In these cases it is unclear whether the women actually broke racial barriers. It is entirely possible that employers profited by moving to a labor pool that they could pay less than white women. In addition, the fact that so many women entered service jobs like waitressing suggests that whites accepted the labor of African American women who filled service jobs and were outside the domestic field. Still, those jobs were more desirable than domestic work because the hours and pay were better.

In both Detroit and Richmond, working-class women made progress in nonproduction and light-industrial work as they found opportunities in heavier industrial fields constricted. By fighting to gain entry into those jobs, they took advantage of openings left by white women who had gone into more lucrative work. Their unwillingness to perform domestic labor indicates that wartime opportunities fostered a major change in attitudes toward work. When working-class African American women found access to defense jobs closed, they shifted to postwar activism, drawing upon civil rights groups, unions, and state agencies to desegregate work outside the heavy-industry sector. The women progressed in other fields of employment because they continued to contest racist hiring practices.

Fighting for Entitlements from State and Private Agencies

Working-class African American women worked for equal employment and were active in trying to obtain welfare benefits for themselves and their children. Used to inadequate wages, substandard housing, and unsympathetic welfare officials, they attempted to piece together help from numerous places after the war, whether from public or private institutions or friends, family, and neighbors.[64] The women claimed their citizenship by demanding access to adequate welfare entitlement benefits, which were dispensed more freely to poor white women. Moreover, by directly contesting with the state over amounts of (and conditions of receiving) welfare benefits, entry into public housing projects, and slum clearance issues, poor black women became players trying to control the outcome of decisions made by state welfare officials in Detroit and Richmond.

African American women found themselves at a distinct disadvantage when trying to obtain benefits because of racist welfare policies that dated back to the inception of mothers' pensions in the early 1900s. During the Progressive Era, white middle-class maternalist reformers left black women out of their welfare programs. Many maternalists assumed that private agencies and community networks would take care of African American children, so black women were directed toward work rather than toward pensions.[65] Moreover, mothers could only claim benefits if they maintained households that reflected aspirations toward a normative definition of middle-class domesticity, which tied the benefits to moral standards. Because white women constructed them as laborers rather than mothers, black women had a hard time meeting the criteria of welfare officials.[66]

During the New Deal, black women gained access to some public welfare benefits. State welfare programs, however, privileged white male heads of households, so women and people of color found themselves vying for scant local funds rather than federal funds disbursed by the New Deal administration. Most blacks found themselves outside "entitlement" or the "good" welfare system because New Deal officials constructed social insurance programs based on payroll contributions that specifically excluded domestic work and agricultural labor. Moreover, federal programs such as the Works Projects Administration remained racially stratified and hired many more white men than black men and women. As a result, black women gained access to public welfare rolls, which became stigmatized as "bad" welfare because of being an outright public expenditure and because of the racial makeup of recipients. The women received Aid to Dependent Children benefits and public assistance, but state governments rather than the federal government controlled access to those funds. Women and blacks found themselves negotiating with capricious welfare officials and underfunded state systems in order to claim benefits.[67] In both cities, the presence of black women as caseworkers likely helped other poor African American women win claims. In some cases, however, the caseworkers' class bias perhaps inhibited the poorer women.

During and after World War II, African American women continued to seek welfare benefits. Those benefits, however, continued to be stigmatized and were reduced, especially in the face of government support of union-gained pension and workers' compensation benefits. With the new focus on private welfare doled out by industry, black women found themselves further marginalized as a result of being unable to find jobs because of the structural racism involved in business hiring practices.[68]

In Detroit, African American women often appealed welfare official decisions thought to have resulted in an unfair assessment. In 1949, for example, Abbie Louise Veal complained to the Department of Public Welfare (DPW) when she found her assistance cut off. A widow and on relief since 1948, Veal received approximately $30.84 a week from Social Security and made $10 more by "supervising" young women at the Club Sedan. DPW caseworkers believed that she failed to report her income correctly. Veal's daughter, sixteen, had moved home when she became pregnant and was abandoned by her husband, and mother and daughter fought with the manager of Brewster Projects over Veal's "active political affiliations." DPW agreed to continue her relief if she got rid of her personal telephone, ostensibly so she would not have another bill to pay. Veal told her caseworker, however, that she had enjoyed a telephone for twenty-seven years and was not about to give it up. She used it to campaign for the fall elections. Veal lost her money but appealed the case, claiming it was unfair to keep a widow alone and with no contact to the outside world. Besides, she needed a way to contact her daughter at work in case of an emergency. The appeal board turned her down, noting that she could use the pay telephone on the corner for emergencies.[69]

Although the caseworker did not actually define Veal's "active political affiliations," it is apparent that DPW punished her for being a politically active poor woman. At the very least, it tried to impede her activism by threatening to withhold welfare benefits. Veal lived in the projects, but even though she was poor she considered herself critical to the success of her chosen political party. She dropped out of the historical record after her appeal failed, but it is important to recognize that she considered herself a powerful and important person, which suggests a strong sense of self-worth regardless of the opinions of middle-class welfare officials. She fought the caseworker's assessment, but the bureaucracy was too powerful and she lost her welfare entitlements. Women who received welfare evidently considered themselves empowered and as having authority to work for change within the political system while still receiving benefits due them by the welfare system.

Veal was not the only African American woman turned down by welfare, and she was not the only woman to fight the system. So many black women complained about their treatment by DPW in 1950 that they galvanized community action against the "brutal new policies" of the agency. Residents of Detroit's east side neighborhoods formed a commission to challenge the welfare system's unfair assessments and mobilize the community around the issue of welfare reform. At the first meeting, union members, church members, and community action groups heard Earline Nealy describe DPW's attempts to deport her and her month-old daughter to Texas, where her husband had fled after abandoning them. Minerva Davis told the group that although she received relief, her son helped pay the bills through his job at Chrysler. When Chrysler workers went on strike, however, Davis could not pay her rent. She showed the group the eviction notice she had received when DPW refused to issue an emergency rent check to her. Bernice Fisher added that DPW had dropped her from welfare when she refused to follow her husband to Tennessee, where he resided with relatives after deserting her in Detroit. In each case, women tried to stay in Detroit and make their own decisions about their marriages, despite welfare policies that attempted to reunite them with their husbands. The new community group vowed to help

them, and all others abandoned by the system, by challenging welfare officials' rulings.[70]

When appeals to DPW did not work, African American women took their
complaints public and received the support of neighbors. Like the women
who spoke to east side community groups, Alberta Adams found herself "put
off the welfare rolls some months ago for some unexplained reason." The
widowed mother of twelve relied on neighbors and family for food and other necessities because she housed eight children in two rooms. DPW had
given her only $30, which she used to buy her children secondhand clothes
and pay the rent. She took her story to the newspapers in order to try to secure help from DPW and the community because she had crippling arthri-
tis and could not work.[71]

Other poor working mothers picketed DPW and the board of education
when the board planned to curtail nursery schools and DPW had no plans
to help the mothers with child care. DPW had not taken action until eight
years after the board had decided to reduce the number of schools rather than
discontinue them altogether in order to continue helping working mothers.
When DPW did act, it created a nursery school for children whose mothers
provided the sole or major support to their families.[72] Such evidence suggests
that African American women understood that as citizens of Detroit they
were entitled to certain welfare benefits and sought help to get what they
deserved—and get it on their own terms. Moreover, the women refused to
accept the state's distinction of entitlement versus charity and instead asserted
their right to public welfare benefits.

Richmond's African American women also fought for benefits, which they
sorely needed. The local Urban League studied a random sample of families
in Richmond in 1947 and found that thirty-six earned less than $25 a week,
whereas sixty-seven ranged from $25 to $35 a week. Twenty-three families had
to reduce their milk purchases, and thirty-two could not buy butter. Twenty-
six more reduced spending on various other necessities.[73] Although Richmond's welfare department failed to keep records and did not record the
number who received aid, by studying the notes of the Lumdsen Fund, the
local YWCA's grant-giving foundation, it is still possible to see that African
American women had help.[74]

The fund provided money for everything from school clothes and other
necessities to fees for vocational programs and training courses. Although
the YWCA created the fund in the 1930s, African American women failed to
receive its benefits until the late 1940s. The scholarship-grants program was
entrusted to YWCA officials, and the committee was a middle-class one, although whether it was interracial is unknown. The trustees' economic sta-

tus, however, put working-class women in the position of being supplicants to economically stable ones. For example, Mrs. E.H. "did very well during the war when wages were sufficiently high." Because her husband was injured and her income had dropped, however, her daughter could not afford clothing and other necessities to finish high school. E.H. applied for money through her public social worker, Louise Blane, and received a grant so her daughter could buy clothing and notebooks, finish high school, and find a decent job.[75] M.P.'s daughter needed money to complete her final year at Virginia State University. M.P., a widow, had managed to put the daughter through her junior year in the pre-medical program using ADC and Social Security pensions but could not afford the daughter's final year. Fund trustees debated giving M.P.'s daughter the money and concluded, "The mother [was] probably not very realistic in planning her daughter's future since there are probably only two medical colleges in the South that accept Negroes." They turned her down.[76]

The trustees' response shows class and race bias. The request had been refused not because of the daughter's grades but because most black women could not go to medical school in the South. Moreover, trustees were reluctant to send women for training in anything other than vocational training programs. It was as if they were attempting to police black women's aspirations by denying funds to anyone who wanted more than a vocational education.

Other African American women asked for funds to improve their own lives. For example, in 1948 A.H. asked for money to enroll in St. Phillip's Nursing School's Practical Nursing Program: "I am a Negro girl 18 years old who for the past 9 years has depended on my fraternal relations . . . we had had no contact with my father since August 16, 1943 as he has not only deserated [sic] us but failed to support us. . . . I have been working as a clerk for the Marshall Street Poultry Co., and with the money I have earned have been able to partially support myself. However, I have not been able to save any money towards preparing myself for further study. I have learned you help working girls am therefore asking will you help me." The trustees gave A.H. enough money to enroll, but she did not perform well in class. The year 1949 found her working at Awalt's Ice Cream Company, making $20 a week, but she remained determined to return to nursing school, which she did that same year. No evidence suggests whether she finished, but the Lumsden Fund denied a subsequent application for aid during her junior year at a nursing school in North Carolina, which suggests that she had at least two years after originally leaving school.[77] I.S. also asked the fund's trustees for money for herself. Through her caseworker, Jean Collmus, she requested funds for the delivery and after-care of her baby because the father had abandoned her as soon as he discovered she was pregnant. I.S. was from a broken home, lived in Richmond, had a fifth-grade education, and did part-time domestic work. The trustees found her to be "nice, well-mannered, and a co-operative girl" and decided, albeit reluctantly, to give her what she needed. It was the only case in which Lumdsen trustees faced such a special situation, but they felt compelled to help her because she "came from a broken home in North Carolina [where the] father drinks regularly and the father of the baby would not help financially."[78]

From 1947 to 1952, thirty-nine black women applied for help to the Lumdsen Fund, either for themselves or their daughters. Requests ranged from clothing and money to pay foster families to house their children (in two cases) to money for nursing, beauty, and dental hygienist courses at St. Phillips, Virginia Union, Virginia State, and West Virginia State University. Twenty-two received money. In every situation mothers were either working poor or on disability welfare. Thirteen of the daughters also worked at low-wage jobs—from $8 to $25 a week—in domestic service or as soda jerks, janitors, kitchen helpers, or babysitters. Lumdsen trustees refused requests for a number of reasons, whether having poor grades or being "domineering" mothers with children who were either not "go getters" or else had too much ambition (i.e., they wanted a four-year liberal arts education rather than a two-year vocational degree).[79]

Several of these explanations reflect negative middle-class conceptions of working-class people. The fact that trustees refused to fund women who wanted more than a vocational degree shows they did not believe poor women needed or deserved more than a position in a skilled trade. Although middle-class trustees believed there was nothing wrong with wanting to be a beautician or a nurses' aide, their decisions to not fund women who wanted to go to medical school or become teachers reflected a skewed middle-class value system under which they did not think that such women could succeed at a middle-class job. Black social workers often brought the cases to the trustee board; their actions suggested collusion with white women across class lines to maintain strict job definitions for working-class women.

Moreover, the trustees' decisions reflected the system of white patronage as a component of racial etiquette in the South. Black applicants needed a social worker as a sponsor (a middle-class woman of either race) and had to appear to the board as deserving women who appreciated the generosity of middle-class patrons. I.F.'s letter to the board reflects her subordinate position in the process: "I know you and the Lumsden Fund committee both get tired of me writing and I hate like anything to bother you. . . . I don't have any money as my husband is in Pine Camp [hospital] and I don't have any more than what I get from the Social Services Bureau."[80]

Middle-class trustees maintained the construction of superiority through their decisions. They refused, for example, to pay the living expenses of a woman who was trying to get through nursing school and whom they judged to be incompetent. Trustees believed that her application resulted from the fact that her domineering grandmother was apparently behind her ambition to become a nurse: "Mrs. L.'s own parents, C. and J.B., had seven other children in rapid succession after her. Therefore, with a complete unawareness she allowed Mrs. L. to become completely absorbed by her matriarchal grandmother whose method of control is disguised with honeyed, disarming solicitousness."[81]

In another case, the committee became very "interested in sterilization for A.A.," whose husband did not make enough money to support her and her three children although his job made the family ineligible for social services money. The Lumsden Fund helped A.A.'s family from time to time on an emergency basis, but the trustees' interest in sterilizing her (apparently without the knowledge of A.A., whose opinion was never reflected in the social workers' reports) suggests that middle-class women had more than dispensing money on their agendas. Apparently, they believed that not having more children would enable her to rise above the poverty level, even though her husband continued to make only $32 a week at a paper factory.[82]

Class and race biases permeated the welfare system of Richmond, but working-class and poor women understood how to manipulate the system of middle-class trusteeship and managed to get money to help themselves and their children. They worked for entitlements because they believed they deserved them as citizens. Moreover, they claimed money that had been available only to white women before the postwar period.

Just as they negotiated with welfare officials for entitlements, African American women in Detroit and Richmond also negotiated issues involving housing in order to secure decent living arrangements for themselves and their children. They endeavored to get into publicly funded housing projects, tried to clean up their neighborhoods to make them livable, and attempted to stop slum clearance when such actions left them with nowhere to live. The women maintained that they deserved decent places to live and used the context of motherhood and state citizenship to protest the razing of slum areas and being barred racially from public housing.

In some cases, cleanup efforts and safety projects subsidized the state in that the women provided services given to white communities as a matter of course. In other cases, the state, when neighbors had to organize against highways going through their communities, became an obstacle to the welfare of poor black communities. As such, it compelled women's political participation in order to combat highway encroachment. Throughout the postwar housing battles, working-class African American women continued to claim their right to live in state-funded housing as mothers, citizens, and workers.

In Detroit, the women faced an uphill battle when they tried to enter public housing projects. Because the projects remained segregated as late as 1952 and the city had built many more projects for whites than blacks, African Americans endured long waiting lists to get into those few open to them. In 1952, for example, there were 5,500 vacancies for whites and 1,600 applicants; black projects, however, had 1,470 vacancies and 8,000 applications.[83]

Women trying to get their families into public housing turned to many sources for help. Cleo Benson, a homeless widow who lived in an emergency shelter, took three of her children to city hall, sat on the steps there, and demanded that Mayor Cobo find her and her family of seven a decent place to live. Although there is no record of her after that point, most likely she found herself referred to DPW and being put on a waiting list, along with hundreds of other applicants for public housing.[84] Her actions, however, were a compelling act of protest and an assertion of her rights and needs as a mother.

Another woman who called upon her status as a mother to claim the right to occupy publicly funded housing turned to the Urban League for help after trying for a year to get into the projects. When Willie Mae Johnson found out she might have to wait another two years to get in, she became angry:

> Why is it men with fewer children and work in the factory can get a project so easily. I am a permanent government employee, divorced and doing all I can to care for my 5 children and have to wait and wait, it seems so unfair . . . I get so discouraged, I sometimes think I'd be better off on the welfare like a lot of other women do. The place I'm living is no place for any children. There is no hot water, no bath, and only one entrance and exit . . . it would be a firetrap. . . . I have four girls and one boy and the environment and cleanliness out [in Sojourner Truth projects] would mean a lot to them, if you know what I mean, and if you are a Father you'll understand my concern over the locality I'll be placed in.[85]

The Urban League has no record of a follow-up, but all it could have done was talk with welfare officials or caseworkers and try to move her up the waiting list, something that would have been hard to do.

Willie Mae Johnson addressed the major concerns of many working poor women in Detroit and used the discourse of motherhood to elaborate on her own. Among them was the fact that she needed a safe, healthy environment in which to raise her children. Her language mirrored that which middle-class women used when claiming rights in the postwar world. Johnson also pointed out a gender conflict. Men who worked in factories received housing priority as workers, especially in 1951 during the Korean War; many single mothers, however, could not find the factory work that could get them war-worker priority in the projects. Like middle-class women, Johnson called upon her status as a mother in order to claim entitlements from the state—in this case, for state-funded housing. Many women still remained on waiting lists for the projects, but they did everything they could to move into decent housing with their children.

Although Detroit had several housing projects, Richmond did not. The Richmond city council, like many others in the South, was reluctant to build more public housing after the first project had created a controversy over property values in black neighborhoods and caused fear of black encroachment in white neighborhoods.[86] Until 1952, the city of Richmond had only one public housing project. Most black Richmonders were housed in tenements throughout black neighborhoods. It is significant, however, that when Creighton Court opened in 1952 its first tenant was Francis Jones, a widow with five children ranging from ten years to three months. She received welfare relief and fought hard to get into the projects. Her victory resulted in a two-bedroom apartment in place of the "squalid, two-room shack" she and her children had endured in the heart of Jackson Ward.[87]

Working-Class Women and Social Motherhood

Because so many African American women in Detroit lived in terrible conditions while they waited for vacancies in public housing, they became major participants in block-cleanup programs intended to make existing communities healthier and safer. By filling in the gaps created by state and structural injustice, working-class women performed the activities that paralleled middle-class women's "social motherhood" programs. From 1948 to 1952, for example, the Detroit Visiting Nurses' Association listed such common slum conditions as falling plaster, broken porches, inadequate heat, overcrowding, trash in the streets, and rat infestations.[88] The women could not force landlords to fix heat and other structural problems, but they did work to clean up the outsides of the houses and lessen rats and disease.

The Detroit Urban League set up block clubs in 1945. Among the membership of ten units scheduled for cleanup participation, there were 134 women and only 39 men. The high incidence of women as leaders signifies that they were the primary providers of neighborhood services. One block club secured incinerators for each home in the neighborhood, and another raised money to have the road oiled. Within several years the block clubs had raised enough money to put up streetlights in order to reduce crime and had also built playgrounds, improvements the city undertook as a matter of course in white neighborhoods. In addition, from 1945 to 1951 the *Michigan Chronicle* sponsored block cleanup campaigns, invariably with women as directors. Six won the contest for their blocks in 1945, and the next year Flossie Stapleton, Kellie Cheatham, Julia Carter, and Patricia McKeethan enlisted the participation of children and young adults. The tradition continued until 1951, when Detroit elected a "Clean-Up Queen" at the close of the contest.[89]

Slums remained disease-ridden, overcrowded, and rat-infested, but several African American women in Detroit and Richmond tried to save them because slum clearance would have left them homeless. In 1946 Detroit city officials condemned and scheduled the razing of the Gratoit area of town. Although the mayor called it the worst slum in Detroit, several women protested being evicted, arguing they could not find housing anywhere else. Two complained to the Urban League that the Housing Commission had never offered them alternative placement, and one related that the relocation office had tried to move her from her tenement to one equally as bad. Another women stated that her husband made $27 a week and they paid $39.50 a month in rent. Without help getting into the projects, they would be out on the street. Seven other women told the Urban League that they would not move until the Housing Commission found them better housing. The League secured lawyers and won a three-year continuance to stop the clearance until alternative housing was found.[90]

With help from the Urban League, the seven hundred affected families were moved up the projects' waiting list, although 160 of them moved from the Gratiot area in 1949 were still waiting for housing in 1952.[91] In 1950, two hundred tenants of the Douglass projects faced a similar situation when the city attempted to evict them in order to raze and rebuild the project. With support from the Urban League, eighteen women and twenty-three men filed lawsuits against eviction, and seven women formed a committee to petition the mayor and find an alternative solution. As in the Gratoit battle, the litigants proved successful in their court battle and received a restraining order against the city until the Housing Commission could find other housing for them.[92] Their success suggests that when a large group of activists received institutional support from a prominent organization they could negotiate with the state and gain victories.

African Americans in Richmond faced the same dilemma. In 1951 when Richmond decided to build freeways through Jackson Ward, dividing and destroying that historically black community, three women seeking to fight eviction called the *Afro-American*. They were pictured in front of their homes, caring for their families, again calling on the discourse of motherhood to bring about justice for those facing eviction. Several of the women interviewed, however, seemed ambivalent about the move. Having dealt with Richmond city government before, they thought that whatever they said would make no difference; clearance would go on as planned. They did, however, intend to work so the city would buy their homes at a fair price. If they stayed, and if the homes were not part of the clearance project, their property values would drop as a result of expressway traffic.[93] That determination was also a form of activism in that cities tended to pay as little as possible for property condemned by housing projects. In this instance, city policies had forced working-class African American women into activism in order to save their homes and communities.

In Detroit and Richmond, working-class African American women became activists as they tried to stop slum clearance. Although those in Detroit knew their neighborhoods appeared blighted, they also understood that they had little choice but to live there so long as housing shortages necessitated emergency welfare shelters across the city. Entire neighborhoods in both cities worked unsuccessfully to keep the expressway from cutting through their communities. Property owners then turned to the state to ensure fair treatment when the cities bought their homes.[94] In both cases, working-class women demanded to be recognized by the state as citizens who had rights to housing and fair treatment by housing authorities. In many cases they politicized their status as workers and as mothers who had the right to welfare benefits and decent housing for their children. Working-class African American women became community leaders, claiming benefits for themselves and others in the face of a hostile state reluctant to provide assistance to which they were entitled as citizens.

* * *

The continued activism of working-class black women contributed significantly to expanding the range of interests within the modern civil rights movement. Their discourse and activities reflected the fact that they were, despite the beliefs of African American clubwomen and historically black institutions, the best qualified to speak about what they needed. The women fought for employment rights, welfare benefits, and community services at a time when the federal government exhibited hostility toward radical unionism in addition to any other forms of activism that undermined the constructed consensus of cold war society. In so doing, the women kept alive issues that the majority of the black community faced, and those matters would be addressed by national civil rights leaders in ensuing decades.

5. Claiming Space: African American Women and Public Protests against Inequality, 1940–54

In 1943 Sarah Pettaway and Lavinia Wilder boarded a south Richmond trolley for a Saturday excursion. Although the only two empty seats on the streetcar were located in front of a seated white woman, she ignored Pettaway's request to move to a seat in front of the couple. The black women then sat in front of the white woman, which posed a strong if unintended challenge to Richmond's racial hierarchy. When a police officer spotted them, he exclaimed, "'What are you trying to pull? . . . you know better than this. Get up and move back.'" When Pettaway and Wilder started "mumbling" about their forced move, the officer arrested them. Despite support from sympathetic white passengers who had seen the entire exchange, police court judge Carleton Jewett fined each woman $2.50 for disorderly conduct. Although Jewett claimed that the issue was not racial in nature, the women received the support of NAACP lawyers and planned to appeal the case.[1]

One year later, Detroit playground teacher Gwendolyn Coleman ordered a sandwich at the Western Front Restaurant. When the proprietor gave her the sandwich in a bag and refused to let her eat in the restaurant, Coleman secured witnesses and reported the incident to the NAACP. NAACP officials accompanied her to a police station, and she filed a warrant against the proprietor for violating Michigan's civil rights statute. Detroit's chief prosecutor, who praised Coleman for following the correct steps in trying to desegregate the restaurant, thought he could probably secure a conviction against the establishment.[2]

These cases reveal several obstacles to African American women's efforts to obtain equality. It was necessary to contest a hostile society that wanted to preserve the racial status quo, and various groups attempted in each case to thwart the women. In Richmond, the police officer and the judicial system acted as agents of the state and set up roadblocks to racial equality for Pettaway and Wilder. In Detroit, whites' hostility in the restaurant hampered Coleman's efforts to enforce a state law.

Both cases suggest that racial climates were more forgiving in the South and more oppressive in the North than they appeared at first glance. In Richmond, for example, some sympathetic white passengers tried to uphold informal norms of social etiquette by supporting black women who posed no threat to anyone and had been, in fact, harmed by a white woman who failed to help enforce the status quo. Not all white Richmonders were intensely interested in maintaining racial hierarchies. Many white Detroiters, however, did support and maintain segregation in public facilities despite a state law that made such actions illegal. In both cities African American women worked equally hard to claim public space.

Throughout the war and after it, middle- and working-class women sought public space in the electoral process through voter registration campaigns and in public facilities and transportation through informal sit-ins and court cases. Each group constructed different meanings of citizenship during the war and shifted those definitions after it to try and integrate themselves within cold war society. They confronted racism directly, however, by challenging segregation and fighting for the vote. Women of both classes merged their discourse with activism, and their strategies were similar in the forms of public protest they espoused, including registering their communities to vote, staging sit-ins, filing lawsuits against abuses on public transportation, and desegregating neighborhoods and housing projects.

Confrontations with whites over space coalesced around the public meanings of equality and citizenship. In other words, women of all socioeconomic levels claimed space based on their right to enjoy equal access to the political process and to facilities. After the war, African American women continued to fight for social equality by filing lawsuits against discrimination in public places and contesting hostile whites in the streets. Their actions placed them within the context of a militant civil rights movement, and community members and institutions like the press, the NAACP, and the Detroit Commission on Community Relations (DCCR) often rallied to support their efforts. Although this kind of protest is normally associated with the civil rights movements of the late 1950s and 1960s, it is clear that the women's actions helped to begin those movements.

African American women's claims to citizenship within the wartime state and then after the war translated into direct and immediate challenges to segregation. First, they worked to register their communities to vote so that all African Americans would work within the system to change laws. Then, they tried to desegregate entertainment and recreation sites. In addition, women attempted to reinforce the power of the law or change public opinion by demanding equal treatment in the restaurants of Detroit and the public transportation system of Richmond. Moreover, they pushed residential boundaries in both cities by moving into formerly white-only neighborhoods and in addition protested police brutality and court segregation.

Even though black women failed to secure victories over racial hierarchies in all cases, their actions were significant. Through them, the women had deployed institutional structures of power, including civil rights groups and the judicial system, in order to claim space. In some instances, when racial tension reached breaking points, the women demonstrated on public transportation, in the streets, and, in Detroit, during the massive riot of 1943. As visible forms of protest and litigation captured public attention and grounded the modern civil rights movement between 1940 and 1954, the women's activism forced whites to recognize the black community's discontent with segregation.

Securing the Vote

In order to try to claim space in electoral politics, African American women worked to make sure members of their community qualified to vote. Although women of both classes were active in voter registration and education campaigns, sometimes the campaigns differed within middle-class and working-class communities. Whatever the differences, women of all classes worked toward the same goal—trying to carve out space in the formal political systems of their cities.

Because so many African Americans could not vote, the women worked to get the ballot to the disfranchised and urged those in areas where the vote was possible to register, pay poll taxes, and do whatever else was necessary to ensure their community a voice in government. African American clubwomen took their responsibility seriously and described the right to vote as a patriotic duty. In their opinion, it was women's responsibility to vote and change the country while men were away at war. In 1944 Jeanetta Welch Brown, an Alpha Kappa Alpha and the newly nominated director of Women's Special Activities of the Democratic National Committee, commented, "As wives, mothers, sisters, and sweethearts of men in the armed forces, it is our patriotic duty to fight for democracy with ballots just as they are fighting with bullets."[3]

Brown's remarks rooted African American women squarely in the center of the Double V movement, likening the promotion of democracy to the actions of soldiers in the field. The National Council of Negro Women (NCNW) also concerned itself with ensuring that women got out to vote, and its members used the tropes of patriotic responsibility to define themselves as true citizens exercising their civic right and duty for community good. The NCNW *Telefact* warned all members, "COUNCIL WOMEN MUST ASSUME THEIR FULL RESPONSIBILITY. . . . in helping citizens get into the habit of exercising our democratic rights in ALL elections—city, County, State, Federal, boards of education, dog cathers [*sic*] and all kinds of elections where are [*sic*] future is at stake."[4]

Women in Richmond and Detroit worked hard to get their communities to the ballot box. In Richmond, the Community Junior League advanced loans to members so that they could pay their poll taxes and register to vote. Nine women from Richmond's NAACP chapter chaired a poll tax drive that sponsored meetings and teas to promote payment. Once again supporting her effort to put pressure on government, Mary McLeod Bethune came to Richmond and told a group of women meeting at the Leigh Street Methodist Church that the vote was like a weapon that could be used to equalize salaries and secure more federal jobs and appointments.[5] A Miss Bouldin of the Providence Park Protective League informed fellow members that the vote was critical to change in Richmond: "Whether you are seeking better homes, streets, traffic lights or larger social and economic justice, the vote is the path to these things."[6]

There was no poll tax in Michigan, but Detroit's black community, by all accounts, seemed apathetic in that many eligible voters did not go out of their way to register. In all probability the "apathy" revealed the black community's underlying skepticism about the power of the vote in context of the city's injustice. The mayor wholeheartedly supported segregation in all industries and public housing projects, so the black community knew that the city government supported racist community practices. Jeanetta Welch Brown was disgusted with her community, and in an editorial directed at fellow middle-class women she fumed, "We have a vote. Why can't we use it to see to it that our rights are defended instead of being offended in Congress? The fight for Democracy is Ours, Ladies."[7] Apparently, several women took the admonition to heart. Several months later, Ruth Ellis, Sue Colbert, Helen Buford, and Blanche Smith registered more than 1,400 voters in one day on the Detroit streets as part of an NAACP voting registration drive.[8] The women's campaigns to encourage people to vote and register them to do so showed the government that they supported words with action. They were helping provide a direct political dialog between their communities and the wartime state.

In Detroit and Richmond, the same obstacles existed after the war as during it. Detroit's community could vote in any election but needed to mobilize effectively in order to support candidates, and Richmond's community faced poll taxes as a structural restriction to voting. After the war, Richmond and Detroit's middle-class women remained especially concerned with ensuring that fellow citizens could vote, because it was necessary to pay poll taxes and qualify for registration several months before an election.

Women of Richmond's Fifth Avenue Baptist Church sponsored a voting registration campaign at which Bethune spoke to 2,200 eager listeners. She pleaded with the audience to register to vote in order to gain a voice in government policies. "'No group of white people, no matter how liberal,'" she said, "'can speak for the sixty thousand citizens of Richmond.'"[9] Women canvassers outnumbered male canvassers by two to one. The Richmond Civic Council secured the help of Marian Blackwell and Senora Lawson to register voters and preside over a rally for canvassers. As a result of the committee's work, 6,330 people paid poll taxes and twelve women won 100 percent certificates by registering their entire families.[10] In 1949 Margaret Spurlock, Ethel Furman, and ten other women canvassed their neighborhoods as representatives of the Civic League, looking for unregistered voters.[11]

Detroit women also promoted voter registration, which was particularly important after the war as more liberal candidates such as Richard Frankensteen and George Edwards faced off and lost mayoral elections to Edward Jeffries and Albert Cobo, who both exhibited hostility toward civil rights issues.[12] The Detroit Association of Women's Clubs (DAWC) sponsored voters' institutes in order to educate people on how to register and on issues involved in the elections. Although the DAWC prided itself on helping the community, it revealed its class bias in allowing only clubwomen to attend the institutes. As Millie Hynson, the president of the DAWC, explained, "It is the desire of the Detroit Association to provide an opportunity for the clubwomen of Detroit to be fully informed about the issues of the pending municipal election and to urge this vital segment of the electorate to full exercise of citizen privileges—to actively participate in the selection of the persons who will be charged with the responsibility of administering our city government with the best interests of the citizens of our community."[13] The attitude of the DAWC reflected its belief that privileged women needed power. The clinic kept the clubwomen aware of the importance of registration, reinforcing their ideas about the importance of being at the forefront of civil rights changes. By registering, they could vote in a way that represented the best interests of the entire community.

Working-class women also participated in voter registration and awareness campaigns. When labor unions came under fire by government officials who claimed that they were too left-leaning during the 1940s and 1950s, African American women recognized the necessity of voting for officials sympathetic to labor unions and thus preserving their rights to bargain collectively. Faye Stevenson, head of the CIO Women's Auxiliary, spoke in Detroit of the importance of working women and wives of working-class men using the ballot in order to preserve democracy and the labor movement. She told members of interracial auxiliaries who dined at the Lucy Thurman YWCA, "'Our country is in danger as long as the labor movement is in danger as it is today. . . . It is your responsibility to live up to promises to the world to take the leadership.'"[14]

In Richmond, the black American Tobacco Company local elected four women and four men to a vote-qualifying committee in order to make sure that its 1,400 members became eligible to vote. Nina Langley, member of the committee, observed, "As citizens, we have an interest in the administration of the government of the State, and the only way that we, as citizens, may have a voice in deciding how it will be operated is to become qualified voters. . . . May we remind you that your vote is power. To vote is your constitutional right. The vote is a weapon every citizen should use and use wisely. Our motto is 'Be prepared to vote and use the power vested in you as a citizen.'"[15]

In each case, as they stood up for the working-class communities of Detroit and Richmond the women used language that revealed understanding of the importance that working-class voting efforts could have on democracy and, in Detroit, on the power of unionism in an age of anti-labor and anti-red movements. In this way, they indicated they understood that the vote could protect them against the problems of the postwar world. In promoting voter registration, working-class women joined those of the middle class in advancing their communities' power. African American women of all economic backgrounds contributed greatly toward the ability to claim space in the electoral process.

Battles over Recreational Facilities

In both Detroit and Richmond, cramped living facilities and a shortage of recreational space led to tensions over the segregation of the few recreational facilities in each city. These issues emerged during World War II, when a massive influx of migrants caused overcrowding in residentially segregated black communities. The dangerous and unhealthy situation in which many African Americans lived necessitated escaping, if only for a few hours, to some sort of recreational facility. The poor conditions that housing segregation caused in each city, coupled with whites' refusal to desegregate recreational areas or even provide adequate segregated facilities, led many black women to become activists and seek entry into key recreational venues.

In Detroit, the women concentrated on the Bob-Lo boat company. In 1944 the company refused to take a group of YWCA Girl Reserves on an excursion because two in the thirty-five-member group were black. A company official stated, "'We positively will not accommodate Negro passengers.'"[16] The mothers of the group encouraged the chair of the YWCA to take the matter to Mayor's Interracial Committee to resolve the problem because the boat company's actions constituted a clear violation of the civil rights law. Apparently, the Mayor's Interracial Committee failed to effect a solution, because less than a year later an employee at the Detroit Ordnance Depot, Elizabeth Ray, had a run-in with the same company. She and some white friends had planned a picnic on the island, and she successfully purchased a ticket for the boat ride over. When a company manager saw her on the boat, however, he insisted that she quit the area immediately. When Ray refused, two "tough-looking" employees dragged her off the boat. She secured a warrant and asked the NAACP to represent her in court.[17]

In the ensuing trial, the judge found Bob-Lo guilty of violating the Diggs civil rights law and fined the company $25.[18] The small fine and the guilty verdict made no impact, however. In 1947 Pearl Bruce, a student at Wayne University and counselor at the Pioneer House for Children, complained to the Detroit Commission of Community Relations that Bob-Lo refused her admittance as a chaperone on a field trip because of her color. At this point Bob-Lo had appealed the Elizabeth Ray case to the state supreme court, and it refused to make any further concessions or decisions until that case was over.[19] Although Bruce considered her particular case closed, the supreme court decided that the Bob-Lo excursion company's exclusion of Ray constituted a direct violation of the civil rights law. Therefore, its actions were illegal. The NAACP, which had supported Ray and taken over her fight in the appellate court in 1945, claimed victory over discrimination in Detroit.[20] Evidence suggests that some African American women spent much time and effort on repeated and energetic attempts to create small changes in the racial hierarchy of the city. It took three years, several litigants from various socioeconomic backgrounds, and the actions of two civil rights institutions to change the policies of the company.

In Richmond, African American women focused on desegregating a public theater, the Mosque. In at least two instances they challenged the Jim Crow seating at the public venue, despite the city ordinance that made such seating completely legal. In 1945 Clara Jackson Brown, a teacher at Armstrong High School and wife of a veteran, sought to buy a $100 war bond, which would gain her admittance to a Frank Sinatra concert at the Mosque. When she attempted to buy a bond in her baby's name from a clerk at Thalhimer's Department Store, Brown found she could only purchase one for $25, which would give her a seat in the "colored section." The War Bond Committee had reserved the $100 bonds for whites only. Brown also discovered that children who raised the most money for selling bonds would sit onstage with Sinatra, and black children could never raise as much as white children if they could only sell $25 bonds in their community. "'I was feeling patriotic and wanted to get the baby a bond with our last allotment check,'" she told the *Afro-American,* "'but now . . . [her ellipses] I had a desire to see the show because of Frank Sinatra's fight for decent treatment for colored and other minority groups and I was hoping that a colored child would be on stage with him.'"[21] When her complaint prompted the newspaper to call the War Bond Committee about the problem with the children's sales, that group explained that because of city-imposed seating it could do nothing. Blacks were more than welcome, however, to give more than $25 to children selling the bonds, although they would still sit in the segregated area.[22]

The experience of these African American women suggests that wartime bond sales by blacks failed to create changes in racial status. Still, it is clear that African American women called upon the discourse of responsible patriotism to justify attempts to equalize facilities in order to locate themselves within the state as they negotiated for change.

Two years later, the Delver Woman's Club, a black organization, sponsored a concert at the Mosque in an attempt to challenge the city's seating arrangements. The group, formed in 1945 to promote culture, literacy, and knowledge of current events, only admitted a certain number of members per year. In this case, a middle-class organization spent money to rent the Mosque in an attempt to "privatize" it for an evening and reorder the racial seating structure. Although the club opened admission to all Richmonders, clubwomen refused to maintain segregated seating arrangements. Because the group had rented the entire theater for the night, the seating should have been a private concern. When a janitor, acting, in the words of the newspaper, as a "glorified policeman," saw three black and white women seated together, however, he forced them apart and gave the white women the best seats, although they paid for seats in the back of the theater. The women, unnamed in the newspaper, failed to desegregate seating, even at a private function.[23] Even when they sponsored events, middle-class black women found attempts to create their own seating policies thwarted by the racial system in place—in this case, at the hands of an angry janitor. Despite the fact that no law was in place to help Richmond women desegregate the Mosque, they still used various tactics to oppose segregation.

Because recreational areas were critical to the well-being of all city residents, especially African Americans, who often faced cramped conditions in their own neighborhoods, African American women took the effort to desegregate parks and theaters very seriously. They used many strategies, from claiming rights as workers needing a break, to claiming rights as responsible patriots and mothers who sought to protect children—whatever discourse was necessary to gain victory. When helpful, they also called on civil rights organizations to support their causes and filed lawsuits and opposed city councils.

Desegregating Restaurants and Buses

In both Detroit and Richmond, African American women took advantage of civil rights legislation and rulings in order to break down barriers in restaurants and public transportation. Michigan had passed a civil rights law in 1918, but Richmond established legalized segregation codes, some as recently as 1930. Still, African American women there attempted to take advantage of the 1946 Supreme Court ruling against segregation in interstate transportation by challenging segregation on intercity buses and streetcars. In both cities, women used laws in order to reinforce the power of both the state and the federal government in controlling prejudice and to secure equality. In many cases they were successful in eroding racial hierarchies.

Beginning in 1941, women in Detroit sought equality in restaurants that continued to practice segregation despite a civil rights law. Although the law specifically outlawed segregated accommodations, restaurants, and other facilities that served the public, Detroit restaurants flaunted the law by ignoring black patrons, treating them rudely enough to make them leave voluntarily, or allowing them to order take-out food but not allowing them to eat in the establishments.[24] The frenetic pace of Detroit in World War II gave women the perfect opportunity to challenge the restaurants, which remained busy serving meals to those who normally would have eaten at home but for women spending time in factories or at volunteer home-front activities. Moreover, black women found that they could easily employ positions as volunteers or war workers for the state in attempts to secure service at restaurants, which helped involve the UAW and institutions like the DCCR and

Fair Employment Practices Committee (FEPC). The women challenged restaurant proprietors by entering the businesses and demanding service and by securing the help of outside agencies when they found their rights denied.

Working-class women often turned to the UAW for help. When Cecil Whitaker, a worker at Ford's River Rouge plant, found that the Dexter Dairy Restaurant refused to serve her, she reported the incident to her Local 600. The union swore out a warrant against the restaurant on Whitaker's behalf and helped her prepare testimony for the prosecution. The owner of the restaurant received a $25 fine in court.[25] Otha Kirk, secretary to the CIO director of war relief, also used the union to help with a claim against the Old Colonial Restaurant. In 1944 she and a white friend had waited twenty minutes for service. The waitress then told the white woman, a Miss Duprey, that she could not serve Kirk. Otha Kirk received help from the National CIO Committee to Abolish Racial Discrimination, which secured a warrant against the restaurant for her.[26] At the trial, the owner of the business claimed that although he always served African Americans, his waitress had taken it upon herself to refuse service to the women. After deliberating for twenty-five minutes a jury convicted the waitress of violating the civil rights law. The owner paid the $25 fine.[27] The incident prompted the UAW-CIO to conduct an antidiscrimination drive in Detroit restaurants in order to bring organized union pressure against proprietors. Throughout the campaign, local unions boycotted restaurants outside factory gates. With union power behind such desegregation efforts, many restaurants found it expedient to serve black workers as well as white.[28]

Women also complained to the NAACP about discrimination. After documenting many complaints against Detroit restaurants, the NAACP, like the UAW, decided to launch a massive offensive against cafes, using a group of "respectable" women to try to galvanize public support against discrimination. Jessie Dillard, head of the special NAACP committee, set out with several companions to test restaurants that reportedly refused to serve African Americans. A week after the committee formed, Dillard found her test case— the Presto Restaurant, where she and five female friends went for lunch. When told that the restaurant would not serve them, they ignored the manager and settled into a booth to await service. He called officers to the scene, but the women used them to swear out a warrant against proprietor Alexander Pappis for refusing them service. Pappis, known as a virulent racist, had already been through several trials involving civil rights violations, so the NAACP scheduled a mass rally in support of the women and against continued discrimination at Presto.[29]

Evidence against the restaurant appeared to be solid, and the case seemed to be a clear-cut and undeniable example of a civil rights violation, but the prosecutor and judge conspired to defeat it, according to a subsequent UAW report. The prosecutor enabled the defense to question the accuracy of Dillard's memory by allowing him to ask about the exact placement of everything in the restaurant, from bottles to employees, without objecting to irrelevant questions or cross-examining her. Then the prosecution let the defense bring up Dillard's "criminal past." Apparently, she had been arrested while demonstrating against another incident of racial bias in a picket line. Moreover, the prosecution refused to query serious inconsistencies in defense witnesses' stories of events at the restaurant. Before the all-white jury went into deliberation, the judge reminded it that the key witness was a convicted criminal. A not-guilty verdict followed quickly.[30] Although the defeat was a crushing blow for the program to desegregate restaurants, the NAACP pledged to continue the fight and asked for community support in another mass meeting to honor Dillard and her friends.[31]

The Dillard case reveals that despite activists' best efforts, the civil rights law remained hard to enforce in the face of a hostile local white power structure. In a society where the dominant population tried to evade egalitarian laws, only the persistent efforts of African Americans gave the law any meaning. Often even activists' best efforts failed to have the desired effect. In the Dillard case, the state sided with racists when the court labeled Dillard's resistance to discrimination criminal. While she and her supporters attempted to fight for change by calling for an existing law to be enforced, the state branded such activism illegal.

Some black women went to the UAW or the NAACP, whereas others complained to the DCCR. The mayor created the commission in order to alleviate race problems and avoid another riot, but it did not have power to enforce laws. Instead, the DCCR tried to negotiated settlements between aggrieved parties and restaurants, hotels, employers, and other defendants. The group, however, was quite visible, so African American women knew their complaints would at least be docketed and addressed in some fashion. Between 1943 and 1954 at least twenty-eight women used the DCCR to support their battle against restaurant segregation.[32] In 1944, for example, six groupwork secretaries from the YWCA went directly from a Wayne University social work class to Webster Hall, a restaurant just off campus, for lunch. When the head waitress told them they could eat in the main dining room but not the luncheonette, they protested because they were between classes and only wanted sandwiches. When they asked to see the manager, the waitress ignored their request. Finally, afraid that further protest would make them late for class, they went to the main dining room and ate at an "inconspicuous" table in the corner. When the women reported the incident to the DCCR, it took the matter to Wayne University's administration because the policy had a direct effect on students, many of whom were the restaurant's clients. The school planned to challenge Webster Hall's policy and did, eventually, secure the right for students to eat there.[33] In this case, the power of the university eclipsed the power of the DCCR and backed the women's cause.

While the unions, the NAACP, and the DCCR found limited successes in their support of African American women's desegregation attempts, some black women chose to fight the restaurants themselves—and without outside help. Bessie Reynolds and Jean Roseman, a white friend, for example, went to Seward Bar, and the owner refused them service. After refusing Reynolds's request for two glasses of beer, the owner admitted, "'You can't drink beer in here because you are colored.'" Reynolds swore out a warrant for his arrest, and at the trial found support with a sympathetic judge, Paul Krause, and Assistant Prosecutor William T. Patrick, Jr. Patrick argued that "'civil rights have become a must in America'" and pointed out the irony in the fact that the owner was a veteran who fought for democracy during the war, only to deny it to a customer in Detroit. After deliberating for thirty minutes, the all-white jury fined the owner $100—the largest fine allowable for a civil rights violation. The judge commended the jury for its decision.[34] Perhaps Reynolds won because of the convincing prosecution, which took up the Double V message in its argument.

Unlike Reynolds, most women who chose to fight restaurants themselves found less success. Of three other cases in which black women brought suit against restaurants for civil rights law violations, only one other case resulted in a waitress being convicted.[35] Taken as a whole, the restaurant cases in Detroit suggest that the success or failure of black women's actions quite often rested with the sympathies of judge and jury. With a capricious judicial system that sporadically backed and often repudiated African American women's efforts to desegregate restaurants, it is unsurprising that many racist whites continued to practice discrimination and take their chances with the court.

Richmond's African American community still lived under black codes. In 1944 the NAACP unsuccessfully attempted to have segregation laws on public transportation repealed, and it continued that effort after the war. When the Supreme Court outlawed segregation on interstate transportation in 1946, however, black women in Richmond attempted to use that precedent to overturn all intracity segregation, written into law in 1930 as an exact duplicate of the 1902 interstate segregation law the court had overturned.

That law designated separate sections for black passengers on all transportation.[36]

In Richmond, African American women took the lead in trying to desegregate buses, continuing a long tradition of gendered protest against inequalities in public transportation. Historically, they had protested against the treatment they experienced at the hands of racist whites on public transportation by claiming that being segregated into dirty, dangerous railroad cars was an affront to their womanhood. Middle-class women such as Ida B. Wells asserted that their gentility allowed them access into the better white facilities, and as early as 1886 they sought the right to comfortable and safe travel environments. Clubwomen used the tenets of respectability to claim the right to equal facilities on railroads, and that contention translated into gendered protest in later eras as they demanded the right to sit unmolested on any seat on a bus.[37]

Beginning in 1947 and continuing through 1953 while educational desegregation battles gripped Richmond, African American women attempted to test the Supreme Court ruling by challenging local segregation laws on public transportation. In 1947 Lavalette Allen refused to move to the rear of a streetcar and was arrested. A twenty-year veteran of the school system, she maintained before Judge Jewett that she had been carrying groceries and the car was full, so she could not move backwards with ease. Although Jewett fined her $5 for disorderly conduct she appealed the case with the help of the NAACP, and the appellate court dismissed the matter.[38]

The next year, Willa Johnson, a nurse, refused to move from her seat when ordered by the bus driver because, as she testified, the seat he wanted her to take was just directly across the aisle, and the driver failed to explain the reasoning behind his order adequately. Apparently, a white passenger who did not want to take the empty seat next to a black person wanted Johnson to quit her seat next to a white woman who did not seem to mind sitting next to her. For some reason, Jewett decided that she had violated the segregation law, and so rather than fine her $5 for being disorderly he fined her $10 for what he considered a much more serious infraction. When Johnson and the NAACP appealed Jewett's decision, the appellate court also threw out her case, which caused controversy in Richmond. The NAACP and Johnson wanted the court to make a ruling about the segregation law, but, apparently, the court traditionally threw out cases on technicalities rather than closely examine the law itself.[39] At least Johnson did not have to pay the fine.

In both Allen's and Johnson's cases, middle-class women protested peacefully and used the judicial system and the NAACP to effect change. Their actions suggest that when they chose to defy the law, they did so in a manner consistent with the tenets of respectability. They used legal means to redress the problem, and, rather than fighting, they questioned the bus driver's orders and came up with plausible reasons for their protest. Allen's explanation was based in a gendered concept of domesticity—her arms were full of groceries.

In 1953 the arrests of seventeen-year-old Thelma Davis and eighteen-year-old Florence Robinson in a bus segregation incident galvanized Richmond's black community and became a point of serious contention between it and the local transportation commission. When Davis refused to move to the back of a bus on the way to school, the driver stopped in order to wait for an officer to come and arrest her. In a show of support, Robinson asked the driver if he could continue on or at least give her a note explaining why she was late to school. When she tried to get off the bus as the policeman attempted to board it, she was arrested for interfering with a police officer. Jewett fined her $5, and she appealed the case with the help of the NAACP.[40]

The NAACP scheduled a rally in support of the two students, and more than a thousand attended. In a continuation of the Double V theme of World War II, Robinson's mother read a letter pleading for democracy from her eldest son, who was fighting in the Korean War. Robinson and Davis also had a chance to speak out for democracy at the rally. Robinson stated:

> I was educated to believe in the "American Dream," of equal justice under the law, certain inalienable rights, life, liberty, and the pursuit of happiness. . . . I look forward to these ideals being made real in my daily life. If what I was taught is not really intended for me, then my education has been either wrong or it has been hypocritical. . . . So we youngsters are asking tonight that we have more of this kind of liberty in Richmond, Virginia. These American dreams and the Four Freedoms will be brought to Richmond, with the help of the NAACP.[41]

Although the incident occurred eight years after the conclusion of World War II, Robinson still used the discourse made available to women during the war. She claimed freedom and equality based on the country's guarantee of liberty and drew upon the Declaration of Independence to support her claim.

Although the periods during and after the war were not the first times blacks used democratic ideals to justify equality, the war did heighten contradictions in American practices and made democratic appeals more central to their discourse. Davis, for example, used the economic approach in arguing against bus segregation: "When you pay for something, you are supposed to get what you want. Everyone who rides a VTC Bus pays thirteen cents. Then, why should we sit in the back of the bus and the white people sit in the front? We are just as clean as they are. If we can cook the food they eat, surely we can sit beside them."[42]

Davis also challenged racial stereotypes of African Americans as unclean and undesirable. Although she was only seventeen, she understood the irony of the fact that African American women took care of white families but remained segregated from the same people. She also pointed out that although the black community's money seemed good enough for the transit system, African American riders failed to receive the same treatment as white ones. By questioning the logic in segregation, Davis emphasized the oppressive racial barriers that stood between the African American community and equality.

Although Robinson, Davis, and the other women who challenged the segregated buses achieved little success in the short-term, their acts of resistance placed them squarely within the modern civil rights movement. Similarly, the women who demanded service in Detroit's restaurants became part of the vanguard of activist strategists, along with CORE campaigners, in a push for civil rights movements during the 1940s. Because women appeared to be visibly affected by problems with food service and on buses, they became militant in their efforts at desegregation and often pointed out that segregated facilities violated their rights as women to be protected. Their sit-in tactics, whether spontaneous or planned, provided a model for the desegregation efforts of the following decades.

Housing Battles

At the same time that African American women in Detroit and Richmond tried to erase barriers in restaurants and public transportation, they also worked to break into all-white neighborhoods. Because both cities upheld legal or de facto segregation covenants that barred house sales to African Americans in white neighborhoods, black families found themselves in the worst areas in the cities. In Detroit in 1944, 14,795 African Americans lived in boardinghouses and residential hotels because they could not find homes. This represented a 311 percent increase over African Americans who had found no homes in 1940. Thirty percent of the 44,990 black couples in Detroit in 1944 either doubled up with families or lived in boardinghouses and hotels. By contrast, only 6 percent of Detroit's 353,155 white couples failed to locate homes.[43]

Although many African Americans could not find housing in Richmond, the city council planned massive slum clearance plans from 1940 to 1950 that threatened the existence of Jackson Ward, the main black community, at a time very few African Americans owned homes and no other neighborhoods allowed them entry. In 1940 Richmond's blacks and whites challenged each other for neighborhood space in an attempt to secure better housing.[44] In both Detroit and Richmond, both working- and middle-class black women were concerned about housing. The working-class often sought entry into new wartime housing projects, whereas middle-class women frequently contested restrictive covenants in all-white neighborhoods.

Detroit housing emerged as the "contested terrain" of a city in which discrimination determined the seriousness of the postwar urban crisis.[45] Community organizations that represented the "various constituents of the New Deal state" fought to shape neighborhoods and claim space, either by buying or stopping the sale of white-owned houses to blacks or by halting slum clearance.[46] From 1940 through the postwar period, white women were important to maintaining racial boundaries because they could use the discourse of racial purity, domestic tranquillity, and family guardianship to reinforce maintaining the status quo.[47] African American women, however, sought not only better housing in their neighborhoods but also a way to break down neighborhood race barriers.

The most significant event in Detroit's housing battles focused on the Sojourner Truth housing project. In 1942 clubwomen and working-class women joined to support black families' entry into the projects. In that same year, when the facility was ready for occupancy, the surrounding white working-class neighborhood rioted to protest the fact that the first families were attempting to move in.[48] Middle-class African Americans in the surrounding community had originally protested the projects as well because they feared the complex would hurt their property values.[49] When African American workers tried to gain occupancy, however, and faced violent protests in doing so, the middle-class finally recognized the fight as an important moment in the civil rights movement. If the state used the protests of neighboring whites to keep blacks out of a project built especially for them, then it had abandoned the black community in order to privilege the interests of its white citizens.

In a move showing the convergence between middle-class and working-class interests, black clubwomen donated money and time to aid the battle to occupy Sojourner Truth. The New Era Study Club, for example, donated to the Sojourner Truth Citizens' Committee to help fund educational programs.[50] In addition, the local chapter of Delta Sigma Theta sent a strongly worded letter to the Detroit Housing Commission to protest black tenants being barred. The sorority employed the discourse of responsible patriotism in order to point out the ironic fact that a housing project named after a famous black woman was barred to black families because of undemocratic white working-class families in surrounding neighborhoods. The Deltas demanded justice based on their participation in the war effort:

> Delta Sigma Theta Sorority, composed of thousands of Negro college women of America adds her voice to the thousands of voices already protesting the unfair, undemocratic, and prejudicial act of the housing co-ordinator in denying Negro citizens the right to occupy the government homes built for them and named for one of their prominent women. . . . The two Detroit chapters of Delta Sigma Theta comprise 140 citizens who are vitally interested in the defense of America and all it stands for. Our national organization has just purchased $5,000 worth of defense bonds, Our local chapters purchased $300 worth. We believe in America! We want America to believe in us. *Democracy, like charity, begins at home!* We urge you to bring your influence and pressure to bear in this case and see that justice is done.[51]

Working-class women were also involved in the Sojourner Truth housing fight, whether or not they tried to find spots there. Fifty YWCA industrial clubwomen went to city hall in March to join Sojourner Truth picket lines after their class in blueprint reading at the YW center. Just as the Deltas used their discourse of responsible patriotism to legitimize claims for democracy in housing, the women laid claim to the power of black workers' patriotism to support occupancy of the housing project. As one young woman explained, "'Blue Prints speed the Battle of Production, and so does our picket line against Hitler's Klan friends. When those families are in their new homes and safe from KKK terrorism they'll work better and harder in the war factories too.'"[52]

By claiming the right to housing built for them, working-class women reinforced their status as citizens as they demanded justice based on their efforts as defense workers. They joined the Sojourner Truth picket lines outside city hall in large numbers and protested for four hours every day from March 5, 1942, until African Americans finally occupied the projects several months later. The *Sojourner Truth Daily News,* a community newsletter, recognized the work that women had done: "The quiet but heroic work of the women who have given so much toward the building of the Citizen's Committee into a fighting machine in the Battle of Sojourner Truth will be spotlighted at next Sunday's mass rally." All the speakers were women who had worked for equality in the projects.[53]

Black women in Detroit were also at the forefront of neighborhood integration because they represented patriotic sacrifice and motherhood to the black and the white communities. Often mothers claimed power by calling upon the dominant white discourse of motherhood in working to legitimize themselves and the civil rights struggle. Sometimes, women gained not only legitimacy but also national publicity, as when Emmett Till's mother fought to convict her son's assailants and outlaw lynching.[54]

The women in both cities also employed their power as mothers as they tried to make a better life for their children and opposed segregated housing from 1940 to 1954. That discourse was not new to African American women because it was a major part of the definitions of domesticity during the Victorian era. Now, however, women began to claim rights based on their status as mothers and attempted to break into all-white, blue-collar neighborhoods. Maternal concerns motivated and legitimized the search for decent housing and education. The language of motherhood made the women able to claim their children's right to live in safe neighborhoods and attend schools in better districts, both during and following the war, and further gendered the language of the civil rights struggle.

As early as 1941 Mina Johnson sought to stay in her home in Ferndale, a racially mixed suburb close to Detroit where whites owned homes and some blacks rented. She called upon the government to defend her and her ten children, who had resided in the community without problems for fourteen years until she raised enough money to buy the house outright from the landlord. Apparently, white residents felt comfortable enough with African Americans as renters but considered their buying a home as too permanent a change in the neighborhood's economic hierarchy. In her interview with the *Detroit Tribune*, Johnson explained that she failed to see why the civil rights law did not protect her and mentioned that she was determined to remain on her property at all costs. In order to reinforce her "good mother" image, she emphasized that her children were law-abiding citizens who did not deserve to be run out of their own neighborhood.[55]

After the war, when African Americans had more money to buy homes and when barriers to neighborhoods were contested frequently, African American women continued to put themselves at the vanguard of the movement into all-white neighborhoods. When the NAACP took Detroit's restrictive covenant system to court in 1947, for example, the Les Verites Bridge Club led by Margurite Glenn held a cocktail party to raise money for the case. The society page reported, "Demonstrating their indignation over the injustices of racial restrictive covenants, [they] . . . pledged themselves to go about correcting this evil." The women raised $250 for the NAACP.[56] In this case, they showed support for the entire black community by earmarking the funds for the restrictive covenant litigation.

Many women who moved into all-white neighborhoods reported incidents of violence to the NAACP and the police in order to receive help when they determined to hold their ground. A Mrs. Ford, wife of an auto worker and mother of five with another on the way, returned to her new rental home in a neighborhood close to the River Rouge plant to find her telephone lines cut and her windows broken. She reported the incident to the police, who started regular patrols around the house because she and her husband refused to leave.[57] The following month, Anna Cruse reported to the DCCR incidents of violence surrounding her family's move to an all-white neighborhood. She was nervous because a fire had begun after a firecracker was thrown into her home. Someone, she feared, would succeed in burning down the house. The DCCR ensured that police patrols in the area continued.[58] The fact that the police helped in this situation confirms the capricious nature of the state. In some neighborhoods where the police sympathized with whites, they let violence go unpunished; in others, they enforced the law.

African American women sometimes called upon their respectability when justifying decisions to remain within neighborhoods. For example, a Mrs. Smith told the *Chronicle* about her attempts to desegregate her neighborhood. A typist at the Chrysler Tank plant, she found offers of buy-outs, threats of "trouble," and other terrifying messages left at her door. When white neighbors explained that they feared lower-class people moving in, she was indignant and affirmed her respectability. "'We certainly aren't low-class people,'" she commented, "'and as far as the neighborhood is concerned, all we want to do is mind our business and have other people mind theirs.'"[59] Despite the fact that Smith's pink-collar job located her within the working class, she employed a middle-class discourse of respectability to defend herself against white neighbors who constructed all blacks as poor. She also stood up for herself and others in her economic position by demanding respect and privacy from her new community.

In 1952, and as a direct result of pressure from working-class blacks, the Detroit Housing Commission repealed its race segregation policy in housing projects. In 1954, the Supreme Court outlawed restrictive covenants in a case involving Detroit litigants.[60] African Americans claimed victory in the housing battle. African American women had failed to change white prejudices, but they did help break down structural barriers to housing segregation in Detroit. Still, gains made because of desegregation were limited, and whites in every neighborhood violently opposed black incursion. Once an African American family would move onto a block, whites would move on, to neighborhoods further outside the city, and de facto segregation was retained.[61]

African American women in Richmond also opposed neighborhood racial restrictions despite the fact that the city tacitly supported residential segregation as a means of maintaining "peaceful" race relations—in other words, nonexistent ones—by virtue of no contact between the races. In 1946 Mrs. Lemuel Eggleston and her husband, a postal employee, purchased a home covered, technically, by a race-restrictive covenant and stayed there despite "neighborhood opposition." A newspaper failed to report the nature of the opposition, but because the neighborhood was a middle-class one there may have been silent hostility toward the Egglestons rather than the violent outbreaks that occurred in more working-class areas. The *Richmond Afro-American* pictured Mrs. Eggleston in her spacious garden, clipping flowers. The picture reinforced both Eggleston's femininity (in that she wore a nice dress and asserted that she spent most of her spare time among the flowers) and the middle-class stature of the family (in that the photograph included the spacious, well-kept, colonial-style home).[62] As Smith did in Detroit, Eggleston was using her status as a respectable woman to legitimize her claim to a home within a white neighborhood.

A Mrs. Crews almost started a riot on Midlothian Turnpike when she allowed her son to move into a house she had purchased in a white neighborhood. Originally, Crews had told the police about the move and asked for protection, which they refused. When she and her son were in the house, two white men fired sixteen bullets into the home. The son fired back, and a white mob surrounded the house and vandalized the property until police came. Although the police refused to arrest the two white men, Crews's son went on trial and was found guilty for unlawfully discharging a weapon.[63] Once again, Richmond police colluded with white male civilians by ignoring their illegal acts but punishing a black man trying to defend himself and his home against trespassers. Crews did, however, remain in her home despite the violent acts of her neighbors. Her determination is impressive, given the seriousness of the aggression exhibited toward her and her son.

Despite the fact that Detroit's and Richmond's African American communities faced hostility from white neighbors, the police, and the city government, some black women still attempted to purchase and remain in homes in formerly segregated neighborhoods. Despite white opposition, several, such as Cruse, Eggleston, and Smith, succeeded in staying in their homes by sheer determination. By challenging residential segregation, these women pushed against and destabilized the oppressive boundaries of each city's racial hierarchy.

Richmond Women and the Fight to Desegregate Public Facilities

Richmond's African American women fought battles in some public places in order to claim space and challenge the city's racial structure. Although segregated restrooms remained completely legal in the city, one woman challenged the system. In 1946 an unnamed "matron," after making purchases at Grant's 5 & 10, asked to use the restroom. When refused entry, she took her complaint to the board of health. Because the woman had no legal grounds to complain, she tried to have the board condemn the store for not providing sanitary facilities for all customers. The board, however, explained that facilities only needed to be provided in places where patrons stayed for more than two hours, such as theaters.[64] Although the matron was unsuccessful in her bid to equalize facilities at this store, she was creative in how she tried to challenge the racial norm.

In order to reshape race relations within local state structures, two women and their male companion spearheaded the battle to desegregate Richmond's courtrooms. In 1949 Joyce Vernon, Gladys Barrett, and Walter Smith challenged the Jim Crow seating in the notorious Carleton Jewett's police court. With the help of the NAACP and the *Afro-American,* the three staged a protest in court, seating themselves in the whites-only section of the room. The group filed suit against the judge when the bailiff forcibly removed them and held them in a room for questioning without notifying them of their rights.[65] Jewett answered the lawsuit by arguing that he provided completely equal facilities, the only stipulation the U.S. and the Virginia Constitutions required. The plaintiffs replied that the judge had the right to control his own courtroom, but he could not restrict their freedom of movement, which his Jim Crow courtroom clearly did.[66] After the defendants' lawyers delayed the case several times, a judge finally considered it. Although the Fourth District Court failed to publish the final verdict and has no record of trying the case, the *Afro-American* determined that the issue did not seem promising. The presiding judge had rightly decided that a favorable ruling would open the door to ending all Jim Crow practices in public areas.[67] The group fought to change the state's power structure and thus faced a losing battle because the state overtly supported segregation in Virginia.

Because agents of the state, including the courts and the police, enforced the Jim Crow laws in Richmond, it is significant that any black women attempted to desegregate public facilities. In each case the activists believed they could employ a valid reason and sway the white community, whether because they patronized a certain store or believed in a system of blind justice. Despite the fact that targeted public spaces remained segregated, African American women in Richmond provided a blueprint of activist strategies that a new generation would take up during the late 1950s and early 1960s.

Street Fights

With so many African American women in Detroit and Richmond seeking space, dignity, and equality during and after World War II, it is unsurprising that tensions emerged and violence often broke out over racial slights. Both working-class and middle-class women were involved in pitched battles, whether as aggressors or by defending themselves against white civilians and policemen in hostile situations. In these situations, public transportation and city streets were transformed into literal battlegrounds on which many African American women fought for respect and their rights.

In both Detroit and Richmond, many fights began on and around the public transportation system. In his study of the Birmingham bus system, Robin Kelley terms the transportation system of World War II a "theater of violence" in which African Americans' informal but important acts of resistance played out in front of a captive audience, often with "military" involvement as police entered into the situations. He asserts that public transportation proved symbolic of the dangerous and undemocratic public space of the wartime city, which was fraught with problems for African Americans trying to survive in overcrowded war conditions and trying to negotiate racially oppressive boundaries. Moreover, because buses failed to maintain fixed dividing lines, Kelley notes that African Americans easily contested space within them as they challenged what were already fluid boundaries.[68]

The "bus battles" that took place in Birmingham during the war also occurred in Detroit and Richmond, and, as in Birmingham, participants tried to change racial boundaries and restrictions in a very real way. In both cities, African American women instigated many skirmishes, often making riding on public transportation a dangerous proposition.

Although Kelley explains the shifting boundaries on buses during the war, he fails to see the gendered aspects of bus fights. Public transportation has always been a gendered domain, as Ida B. Wells revealed at the turn of the twentieth century when she literally fought for the right to sit with white women in the first-class car of a train in Tennessee rather than in a dirty and disreputable smoking car. During World War II, women were the primary participants in bus fights because buses were also gendered space. Women negotiated bizarre and often unpredictable routes in order to shop, take children to day care, and get to work. Often they spent hours on buses daily to accomplish personal business and get to paid work. The buses remained perpetually overcrowded, which led to men and women being in close proximity and created a situation where women's space was often violated. This violation could be especially dangerous to black women, because the white community, by definition, excluded them from constructions of virtue and saw them as available to white men. Moreover, buses became theaters where African American women claimed the same privileges as respectable white women while navigating wartime transit systems. In this way, the protests were as much about claiming autonomy and the right as women to be protected as they were about claiming equality.

In Detroit, buses appeared to be war zones wherein black female passengers fought white conductors, black female conductors fought white passengers, and black and white passengers fought each other. In the first month of 1944, thirty-seven African American women involved themselves in violent incidents and were considered the aggressors in twelve of those cases. In the first six months of 1945, sixty-six women fought pitched battles on public transportation, and twenty-one instigated the violence.[69]

Often, women contested conductors' interpretations of procedural issues, such as how to use transfers and where stops were located. In 1945 Mary Doctor reported to the police commissioner that the conductor of a bus on which she rode had screamed at a group of very young schoolgirls who, apparently, had accidentally ripped their transfers. When Doctor came to their aid, the conductor threatened to throw her off and told a white passenger, "That's the trouble with them, we try to be nice to them and they knife us in the back; the flock of monkeys ought to be back in Africa where they belong." The indignant schoolteacher filed complaints with Detroit Street and Railways (DSR) system, the police commissioner, and the DCCR.[70] When another black woman tried to have a driver stop to let her on at a place that was not, according to the driver, on the schedule, he refused. She went to the next scheduled stop, entered the bus, and began arguing with him. She then hit him and threatened to crack him over the head with the bottle of wine she carried. The police removed her from the bus, and she later received a $15 fine.[71] Mabel Bruns also argued over a procedural snafu with a transfer, but instead of receiving a fine herself she sued the driver and DSR. Bruns maintained that the driver harassed her for not paying a fare although she told him she had a transfer. Moreover, she had shown the transfer to him but then lost it in the crowded bus. She said that his accusation wounded her reputation because she was an upstanding and respectable woman who participated actively in civic, church, and community affairs. Although police charged her with disturbing the peace in the fight, Bruns tried to sue the driver and DSR for $20,000 for defamation of character.[72] In these situations, African American women attempted to receive redress from the company that allowed its drivers to abuse them. None of the women achieved success, but their actions were important. In filing against the company, they defined themselves not just as slighted women but as dissatisfied consumers who had a right to decent treatment.

African American women on Detroit's public transportation contested their treatment on buses as well as in society by opposing bus drivers, symbols of white male authority. By publicly displaying displeasure over problems with fares and procedures, the women ensured an audience for their grievances. Moreover, by standing up for what they perceived to be their rights, the women claimed power for themselves in a society that often provided little chance of speaking against oppression. Although most faced the consequences of arrest and subsequent fines, the women enjoyed moments of inverted traditional power relations.

Several African American working-class women in Detroit experienced day-to-day power reversals when the city employed black women as streetcar and bus conductors. The women often engaged in pitched battles with passengers, but they had the power and called upon their official "conductor" status to justify their actions. In 1943 one black female conductor antagonized white passengers by refusing them entry to the bus until all African Americans had boarded, gave rude answers to the white passengers, and missed stops that they needed. Many witnesses attested to her behavior, and the police questioned her, yet the conductor faced no punishment.[73] That same year, another black female conductor reported, "Woman asked me why I didn't call Newport. I told her I had called it. She got very insulting and started calling me names. I asked her not to do it any more. She did, so I hit her."[74] In such incidents African American women used their status to claim power over white passengers. They had experienced the racism of bus drivers so often in Detroit that being able to act out against hostile whites in similar situations must have seemed divine justice.

Other African American women who worked on buses became the targets of racial antagonism because they signified a changing racial climate in Detroit. A black female conductor, for example, involved herself in a dispute with a white man over a transfer that she refused to give him. In her police report, she stated, "Passenger called me a b—— and said that I couldn't treat white people that way."[75] Apparently, the white man was enraged by the fact a black woman had refused to let him have his way and not pay for a transfer. The refusal was a blow to his privileged existence in Detroit's race and gender hierarchy.

In one week in October 1944, two African American women conductors disputed with unruly white passengers. One reported that when a white woman dropped transfer money into the fare box instead of giving it to the conductor, the black conductor refused to give her a regular transfer. Instead, she gave her one marked "emergency," which apparently infuriated the white woman, who jerked the conductor's cap down over her face. When the conductor pushed the white woman's hand away from the cap, the woman's mother apologized and said her daughter was sick and did not know what she was doing. Several hours later, another black female conductor refused to give a man a transfer for another bus because he had already used one transfer to get on her bus and needed to purchase a new one. After arguing for some time, the man cursed and hit the woman in the eye. Although she did not return the blow she secured witnesses to aid in his prosecution.[76] These physical disputes signified not just an assertion of authority on the part of conductors but an attempt by whites to reorder their world in order to reassert their authority. Black women conductors symbolized many whites' belief that a world of privilege was slipping quickly away.

Passengers in Detroit also fought among themselves, which added to an already tense situation on public transportation. It is very likely that many disputes resulted from earlier factory fights that escalated outside factory walls; contested space in factories could easily turn into contested space in buses and streetcars. In 1943 a white man began an argument with a black female conductor. Violence escalated, and a black woman came to her aid, purportedly to help the conductor collect the man's fare. When the man swung at the black passenger, she stabbed him in the stomach and was later charged with aggravated assault.[77] In the summer of that year and just after the Detroit riot, two factory workers returning home on the bus engaged in a battle when the women, one white and one black, fought over a stolen watch. Both had to be removed from the bus when they started pulling each other's hair.[78] In 1944, Mary Blair, who was white, made a derogatory comment about the color of Laura Crawford's hair. Crawford, an African American returning home from work, beat up Blair on the Woodward Avenue bus and was charged with assault and battery. Apparently, the buses proved so dangerous that at least one African American took to carrying weapons to protect herself. The police found them after she picked a fight by swearing at white women and pushing against them. When the police searched the unnamed woman they found a set of knives with five- and six-inch steel blades.[79] On Detroit's crowded, dirty, and unpleasant buses, passengers and conductors contested for space with words, hands, and even weapons.

Richmond buses and streetcars also saw their fair share of violence as African American women fought both drivers and passengers in racially charged incidents concerning seating, fares, and everyday insults. Richmond buses differed from Detroit's, however, in that Jim Crow statutes created racialized space, and the contested space seemed much less fluid. In several cases, African American women sued Richmond's transit company for indignities they had faced during physical altercations. In 1943 a bus driver told Marjorie Forbes, a student at Armstrong High School, to move to the back of his vehicle. When Forbes claimed that the bus was too crowded for her to move to do so, the driver grabbed her and attempted to throw her off. Forbes refused to budge and pushed him away, and black and white passengers supported her. The driver then refused to drive. Although Forbes had created a scene, the police refused to arrest her, and she claimed a small victory for her community.[80] Forbes won her battle with the driver on the same day Aretha Glass found herself facing a $10 fine and thirty-day suspended sentence for a small act of defiance on a bus. When the driver blamed her for incorrectly signaling for a stop, although it was a white woman who had done so, Glass went to the front of the bus and cursed at the driver until police arrived to arrest her.[81] The differing experiences of Forbes and Glass suggest that the success of an African American woman's actions often depended upon whether she could secure white passengers' support.

Other Richmond women were also fined for being physically or verbally abusive to bus drivers, although most claimed they had only retaliated in self-defense. A Mrs. Parrish received a fine for disorderly conduct when she protested against an abusive streetcar driver. When she did not move through the turnstile fast enough for him, he slapped her, called her a "n——r," and accused her and other African Americans of "trying to run the streetcars."[82] According to Parrish, she had merely protested verbally to the driver; other passengers, however, admitted that she hit him in self-defense. Parrish received a $5 fine for disorderly conduct, but the judge dismissed the charges against the bus driver.[83] Sadie Boling received a more severe sentence after fighting with a bus driver over the change due from her child's fare. After he refused her change, she accused him of abusing her and struck him. Boling received a $25 fine and a three-month suspended sentence.[84] She experienced the same injustice that Jessie Dillard had when she tried to desegregate Detroit restaurants. Instead of filing charges against white instigators, police focused on black criminality in situations where African Americans tried to challenge the racial hierarchy.

As in Detroit, African American women in Richmond opposed white passengers in attempting to renegotiate racially defined space on segregated city buses and streetcars. In 1941 Helen Johnson became an object of pity in the *Afro-American* when she displayed her torn coat and a cut on her head she had received from a white man on a bus. Although the newspaper called her a "matron," a term denoting respectability, she had engaged in physical violence. Apparently, the man kicked her, and she then slapped him. After that, he followed her off the bus and hit her with a brick. She obtained a warrant for his arrest. Because the Richmond city court purged its records from the

1940s and 1950s, it is impossible to know whether the charges were dismissed. It is likely, however, given the justice in Carleton Jewett's courtroom, that the man failed to receive punishment for his actions.[85]

In 1943 Addie Walker not only fought with white women on the bus but also resisted arresting officers and in the end became a victim of police brutality. One morning, on the way to the factory where she worked, she spotted several white women with babies, in line for the bus. She told them that it was improper to have babies out in the hot, humid weather, and one woman slapped her. When Walker threatened retaliation, the women called Richmond police, who fought with her when she resisted arrest and then beat her on the way to the station. Although the NAACP took on Walker's case, she received a $20 fine and lost her appeal.[86]

Johnson and Walker both claimed authority based on their motherhood and in each case did not receive justice. The fact that they asserted their autonomy based on claims to motherhood, however, suggests that mothering and social justice continued to be intertwined, whether in battles over welfare entitlements or bus space. It also reinforces the fact that protests over public space became gendered as the women fought for equal treatment from white society.

Other African American women in Richmond sued passengers and the bus company over injuries they received in public transportation battles. In one case, termed "The Battle of the Bus" by the local press, Virginia Rose Sadler won $300 from an abusive passenger in a lawsuit against him. When Sadler boarded a bus on which the only vacant back seat was next to a white man, L. B. Rigsby, she asked him to move to the front of the bus, where there were several vacant seats. The insurance agent ignored her request, so she sat down. Rigsby then pushed her onto the floor, and she pushed him back. He grabbed her dress and hit her in the face, and she punched him in the eye. When the police arrested both of them for being disorderly, Rigsby allegedly told the officer, "'Give me your gun and I'll finish her.'" Although the officer affirmed that Rigsby had indeed made that comment, he denied doing so in court. In characteristic fashion, Judge Carleton Jewett threw out Rigsby's case and fined Sadler $5. She received justice, however, when an all-white jury awarded her $300 in a civil court claim against Rigsby and an appellate court judge overturned the fine, stating that no black person needed to give up a seat to anyone if she sat in the back of a Richmond bus.[87] The case suggests that the right judge and jury could, in some cases, help black women challenge whites, revealing the permeable and changeable nature of the state on the issue of racial justice. Still, in this case Sadler failed to truly challenge the racial hierarchy; the battle occurred at the back of the bus.

Sadler was not the only woman to win money in a civil court case concerning bus violence in Richmond. Phila White brought suit against a Virginia Electric and Power streetcar company for the abuse she endured at the hands of a driver. When she boarded his full car, he grew angry because he had told her to wait for the next car to arrive. He pushed her against the wall, verbally abused her and her two companions, and then refused to let her off the car until he called the police. When she explained the situation to the arriving officers, they decided not to arrest her. White settled her lawsuit against the company out of court for an undisclosed amount of money.[88] Clara Roane received not only money from the Virginia Transit Company but also a public apology over her treatment by a bus driver in 1953. An assistant pastor of St. James Baptist Church, Roane fell asleep on a bus after a revival meeting. The driver roughly awakened her, pushed her, and called her a "N———r." Roane claimed that the incident caused her to become hysterical and suffer a nervous breakdown, which necessitated being hospitalized. The company agreed to pay her medical bills and made a public apology in an out-of-court settlement.[89] Although African Americans found their freedoms severely restricted by Jim Crow segregation and popular prejudice in Richmond, black women still had the right to sue, and they used it to reaffirm their right to be treated with dignity and respect. In these situations, they claimed their womanhood and respectability, continuing a long tradition of gendered bus protest that climaxed with the actions of Rosa Parks in 1955.

Occasionally, in both Detroit and Richmond violence failed to remain contained in public transportation and became brawls, melees, and even riots. African American women often fought with whites in the streets in very visible bids to claim space in hostile city environments. The most violent event that occurred in Detroit stopped production there for three days and ended only after federalized Michigan guard troops shut down the city. On June 20, 1943, a riot broke out at Belle Isle, a popular recreational spot, after African Americans heard rumors that a black woman and her child had been thrown from a bridge. Gladys House, who may have been the first to pinpoint the real start of the riot, explained that late in the day she saw a black boy being chased by a group of white men. When she attempted to rescue him, whites threw her down and rioting broke out around her. After the rioting was over, the police counted thirty-one dead, seven hundred wounded, and 1,400 who had been arrested (1,200 of whom were black).[90] The riots shook the country as businesses counted thousands of production hours lost in the three-day melee.

African American women instigated few of the fights during the riots but often found themselves targets of aggression and willingly informed on white perpetrators in the three days of chaos. A worker at the Roxy Theater, Ann Easley, watched in horror as a group of white women beat an old black woman on the street, and she then hid from a mob that entered the theater looking for blacks to beat up. She received the help of the manager, who turned the crowd away and drove her home when the people left the area. Middle-class women also found themselves in the middle of pitched battles as they conducted business on Detroit's main street. Director of Emergency Welfare Beulah Whitby, for example, opened centers for food and information during the riot but needed aid as she waited out the mobs that roamed Woodward and targeted African Americans. She relied on white friends to bring her food until the rioting was over.[91] Easley and Whitby came from different socioeconomic backgrounds, but their common experiences during the riots indicate that the events affected all Detroiters, not just those who were poor.

Whether they witnessed violence or were victims of violence, women reported the acts to the NAACP and the DCCR in order to claim justice against the perpetrators. Lillian Thomas, who lived across from the state armory, reported to the NAACP that on the first night of the riot she had witnessed snipers shooting at a black man on the street. The next evening, when she went out to attempt to help a black man running from debris thrown from the armory, she found herself the target of the rifle fire. Thomas displayed her understanding of the newly devised discourse of responsible patriotism when she told the DCCR that she believed that troops in the armory had impeded her in doing her duty as a citizen and volunteer. She was, after all, a member of the Office of Civilian Defense block squad trying to investigate a problem. When the NAACP reported the incident to the brigadier-general in charge of the armory, he claimed that debris thrown from the windows came from inmates housed there and denied that rifle fire had come from the windows, despite the fact that Detroit police called to the scene had found bullets.[92] Thomas stood up as a witness to state-perpetrated violence, but the lax law enforcement of the case suggests that the state was unwilling to blame the agents, although they had exhibited clear signs of aggression toward innocent African Americans.

Other women complained to the groups that brutal policemen denied them their basic rights when trying to quell riots. Parrish reported to the DCCR that she and six companions were stopped as they drove down Holbrook Street. Although the seven had done nothing wrong, the police searched their car, took them to the station, and locked them away without reading them their rights. Parrish had taken a pocketknife from her brother when she saw that the police planned to stop the car, thus keeping him from receiving too harsh a sentence, but all seven went to court. Apparently, a piece of concrete, which the driver used as a carjack, was found in the trunk along with a beer bottle. The group was tried in less than five minutes and found guilty, but, according to Parrish, they never knew the charges against them. She and her female companion received two years' probation, but the men received sentences of ninety days each in the city prison. She protested the fact that they never understood the charges and had received no contact with outside help, including lawyers.[93]

All in all, at least seventeen women reported violence against themselves or other African Americans or unfair treatment by police in an attempt to bring some of the whites involved in the riot to justice.[94] The reports did not alter what happened to the women, but they did return some power to individuals who tried to oppose the whites who had taken away their civil rights and personal pride.

The Detroit riots struck fear into the hearts of city mayors across the country as rumors of planned race riots circulated throughout the nation. In Richmond, white fears exaggerated black power in the city after the Detroit riots. Gov. Colgate W. Darden of Virginia, who had heard rumors about African Americans in Richmond planning a race riot for July 4, called in the FBI to investigate the matter. Apparently, the director of public safety had heard that maids were coordinating a strike intended to begin a civil disobedience campaign on that day. Riots were to spread from the black neighborhoods outward to coincide with this strike. Although the FBI agent interviewed many African Americans and found the rumors to be unfounded, it is significant that middle-class whites feared the power of their maids in 1943. Dora Parker, an African American who owned a boardinghouse, told the agent that recent reports in white newspapers of riots seemed to be the work of Axis agents trying to stir up trouble, a position reiterated by many other interviewees. Still, the fact that FBI agents traveled to Richmond to investigate rumors of domestics striking and the populace rioting indicates the tensions among the black and white populations of Richmond and the fear of the chaos that would ensue if black women claimed power.[95]

Although Detroit and Richmond women were not usually aggressors in riot situations, they did participate in many street brawls, especially after tensions were heightened in the wake of the Detroit riot and the rumors of riot in Richmond. In Detroit almost a year after the riots occurred, an African American woman became so enraged at the comments of a white man that she could not remain silent and complacent. She hit him with bottles, cut his face, and continued to beat him until the police arrived. A sympathetic observer suggested that a rude comment from the man had likely triggered the burst of violent energy, but it also seemed to be the result of the woman having had to endure many similar comments throughout her life. After taking as much as she could from whites, she finally snapped. She took control of her life from white male aggressors by attacking a man who had targeted her for verbal abuse.[96] Although many street fights may have gone unreported, the DCCR and the NAACP recorded at least four other incidents between 1944 and 1952 that involved women who refused to back down when aggravated by hostile whites.[97]

Although women in Richmond did not appear to be the aggressors in street fights, they did oppose their assailants in court in order to try to have them convicted of assault. Local court cases from 1948 to 1953 suggest that African American women faced physical danger, in each situation resulting from their attackers' belief that white men should have complete sexual access to black women. When Helen Morton, who worked at the Western Union telegraph center, exited her building after work, a white man grabbed her and asked if she wanted to make a dollar. She slapped him, and he and several friends dragged her into the alley, purportedly to sexually assault her. A black man who happened by helped Morton to safety, and she pressed charges against the group. When she refused to drop the charges at the judge's request, he dismissed the case on the grounds that the men were drunk and therefore could not know what they were doing.[98] He thus defined the woman as being available because he ascribed the men's violation to "drunkenness."

One African American woman secured a court victory against a man who exhibited signs of road rage in 1951. In doing so she claimed her right to drive in the city without being molested by a white male, despite his position as a city worker or his state of mind. One night as Theola Hall, a McGuire Hospital night shift nurse, drove to work she noticed that a car was following her. She sped up and went to her in-laws' home in order to escape the man in the car, but he followed. Gordon Jarding, an off-duty firefighter, grabbed her as she rang the doorbell and said, "'I want to talk to you and you want to talk to me.'" The terrified woman ran inside when her father-in-law came to the door, and Jarding fled the scene. When the police caught up with him, he claimed that Hall had cut him off. He was charged with and convicted of interfering with the nurse when the police explained to the judge that he was a "show-off" and had confused the duties of firefighter and policeman.[99] Despite that fact that many whites in Richmond did not believe African American women had rights, in this case a black woman won a victory in court. She was not the only woman to win a victory in Richmond's court system.

The fact that several women in Detroit and Richmond were successful in bringing cases against white men suggests that each city's oppressive racial climate had shifted slightly in order to accommodate black women as citizens who had some rights. The importance of single judges and juries in such cases cannot be underestimated. It was their acceptance of black women's lawsuits against white aggressors that enabled the women to enter into successful negotiations with the state over what sort of protection they could expect under the law. In every case of street violence, the women struggled to assert authority in a hostile world that failed to see African Americans as citizens and equals.

Protesting Police Brutality

African American women negotiated segregated public facilities, neighborhoods, and courtrooms both during and after World War II. They also traveled via the dangerous terrain of public transportation and on the streets, where tensions often led to physical violence. Yet they had one more battle to face in Detroit and Richmond: police brutality. In both cities, women accused of minor charges or those who were falsely arrested faced assault by racist white officers. In many cases, however, they refused to accept such violence as a fact of life and usually brought suit against individual officers and the police force. In one Richmond case, a woman did succeed in securing a criminal conviction against the offending officers.

In Detroit, African American women contested unfair and often brutal treatment by police officers. Often they used their status as mothers and respectable citizens and war workers in order to highlight the cruelty they faced when dealing with the police. As when they sought housing, they portrayed themselves as upstanding individuals who received unfair treatment at the hands of prejudiced government personnel. Moreover, they focused on their status as citizens to point out how police trampled the rights of law-abiding Americans. For example, Pearlie Battle, who defined herself to the press as a mother of four and a war worker, went Christmas shopping in a downtown store, and a white woman tried to steal her purchases. When Battle slapped her, the security guard and a clerk held Battle, allowing the thief to escape. "'I don't care what she's done,'" they said. "'You had no business slapping a white woman. You niggers shouldn't talk back to a white woman let alone slap one.'" The *Detroit Tribune* supported Battle and depicted her as a citizen caught in an unjust state system of racism. She was described as a "woman citizen . . . mother . . . and war worker," and the newspaper demanded help on her behalf from the mayor's office in order to apprehend the thief. When Battle asked an officer for help and he refused, she "pushed the issue" and he kicked her and dragged her to the curb before stealing her money. Not only did Battle lose her purchases and money, but she was also punished for disturbing the peace.[100] She apparently believed that she had little recourse in the court system, because she failed to file charges against anyone. She did, however, take the story to black newspapers in order to highlight how the police had treated such a patriotic citizen and good mother.

From 1943 to 1952 at least nine women in Detroit either filed lawsuits or complaints against the brutal treatment they had received at the hands of officers. In many of these cases they were falsely accused of stealing or disturbing the peace, and the arresting officers arrived and humiliated them with strip searches or beatings.[101] Although most of the cases appear to have been unresolved or thrown out of court, the women used the systems available to them in the form of either civil court or investigative committees to try to effect positive outcomes in their dealings with the police.

Richmond's African American women also experienced police brutality, and in almost every case they gained the support of their communities and sued the police for unfair treatment. Sometimes they found efforts to file civil or criminal charges against the police thwarted by the department itself. For example, 1946 seemed to be a particularly brutal year in Richmond, and the women involved in police disputes filed criminal and civil lawsuits against the arresting officers. Geraldine Polite, an innocent bystander and witness to police brutality, tried to step in and stop officers from beating a black woman accused of shoplifting. When Polite intervened, however, she, the mother of a ten-month-old child, found herself at the center of the controversy. When she resisted arrest the officers beat her in the head with nightsticks and, according to one witness, kicked her while she was on the ground before taking her to the station. Although Polite attempted to file criminal charges against the police, the department refused to provide the names of the officers involved, so she could not sue them.[102]

While Polite proved a sympathetic character because of her middle-class matron status, Louella Tazewell failed to receive quite the positive press response from her encounter with police. Several months after the Polite incident, an officer at the Greyhound station attempted to arrest Tazewell for using vulgar language. When she resisted, she asserted, an officer carried her to a small room, knocked her down, sat on her chest, and hit her in the mouth several times. He did not deny the charges, but a witness did tell the press that Tazewell was "'cursing a blue streak, some of the most vile language I have ever heard,'" so the court deemed the arrest justified. Tazewell received a $5 fine, and the NAACP helped her file a complaint against the officer with the director of public safety and the chief of police.[103]

One other woman tried to sue the police for brutality during arrests in

1946, and she was unsuccessful as well.[104] The lawsuits did, however, highlight the fact that Richmond had problems with police brutality, and when a severe case occurred at the end of 1946 even white citizens stood up for the civil rights of the woman involved.

In December 1946, Nannie Strayhorne, a wife and mother, involved herself in a fight with a man who had offered to drive her home from a party at a minister's house. She soon found herself the victim of sexual assault by two police officers. Although many southern whites considered sexual assault by white men against black women rather commonplace and completely acceptable, Strayhorne fought for her rights and her dignity during an explosive trial. Apparently, the two officers involved in the incident saw Strayhorne exiting her escort's car and ordered her to get into their patrol car. Carl Burleson and Leon Davis then drove Strayhorne to a remote area in a Richmond neighborhood and raped her. She reported the incident. During the ensuing trial, the racism that African American women had tried to fight for centuries became the defense's leading argument. Burleson's and Davis's attorney argued that she was obviously "easy" because she had been in the car with another man, returning from a party. The incident was not rape, because Strayhorne had not fought back (as evidenced from the lack of bruises on her body). Furthermore, he said, she had to be a prostitute, because "'no respectable woman would be leaving a drinking party at two o'clock in the morning.'"[105] Despite the facts that the officers were white and the defense attorney had attacked Strayhorne's character, the all-white jury returned a guilty verdict and sentenced each man to seven years in prison. Perhaps the jury did so because the case brought dishonor to the city in a way that belied the rhetoric of "cordial race relations" that many white Richmonders embraced.

The verdict proved a shock to the city and a huge victory for African American women. It shook the very basis of race and gender power relations that had functioned in the South for years. Many white Richmonders protested the verdict, and the prosecutor, Lynwood Smith, received death threats for even taking on the case.[106] The defense continued by arguing that Strayhorne willingly submitted to the police officers. In the appeal, the attorney stressed, "It was preposterous to think that a white man would be guilty of criminally attacking a woman who is not white."[107]

When the appellate court rejected the defense's argument, a fundamental shift occurred in the way Richmond's white community constructed African American women as being sexually available to men. The court was forced to acknowledge that white men could rape black women—and in the city of Richmond. Although Burleson escaped and remained an at-large fugitive with the help of racist friends, Davis served his term. The case also opened the way for other black women to contest the treatment they received from police and judges. From 1947 to 1954, two successfully prosecuted civil and criminal cases against arresting officers.[108] Their success is further proof that African American women were making headway in Richmond in the struggle for civil rights by using the justice system to effect change.

In Detroit and Richmond, African American women opposed police brutality by calling upon their rights—as mothers, citizens, and workers—to fair treatment. The fact that a Richmond court found police officers guilty of violations is significant in that the state reprimanded its own agents of power. In many cases, sympathetic judges and juries determined the suits' outcomes, reinforcing the facts that the state is not a monolith and that persistent agitation against a dominant order sometimes dislodges aspects of state power.

* * *

In working to claim space between 1940 and 1954, African American women from all socioeconomic stratas called upon new definitions of themselves as citizens, workers, and mothers to lend legitimacy to their battles, launching their claims to space into the national black consciousness by gaining publicity in major black newspapers. Not only did they contribute greatly to the ability of African Americans to vote in local and national elections, but they also "engendered" their protests over desegregation. As women, they asserted, they had the right to protection and the right to be safe in public. Although African American women had used the discourse of motherhood and respectability in order to claim rights before 1940, the fact that they merged citizenship, motherhood, and patriotic work gave their struggles a new tone as they struggled for rights that were, they maintained, inherent and owned by all. If the modern civil rights movement can be defined as a time when large numbers of people directly confronted symbols of oppression by staging sit-ins and filing suit in order to claim equality in public space despite white institutional opposition, the women who participated in activities to desegregate Richmond and Detroit from 1940 to 1954 played an important role in that movement.[109]

Conclusion

By 1954 the racial structures of Richmond and Detroit were still oppressive but had shifted slightly. African American women's discourse of responsible patriotism and self-identification as potential war workers enabled them to engage with the state to negotiate new freedoms. These freedoms included entry into neighborhoods, industries, and establishments previously closed to them, as well as such state and private entitlements as child care, monetary benefits, and housing. They required constant reinforcement through formal politics, such as electoral participation and filing lawsuits, and informal protests, including sit-ins. Although the activities claimed the attention of the nation from 1954 through the 1960s, it is clear that the African American women who sought equality from 1945 to 1954 sparked a new level of protest activity and helped found the modern civil rights movement.

The women in Richmond and Detroit remained largely responsible for many changes made in each city. Women's voter registration efforts almost quadrupled the number of black voters in Richmond. That city's African American canvassers managed to get eight thousand blacks to vote by 1946, up from 1,527 in 1936. The fact that noted civil rights leader Oliver Hill won a seat on Richmond's city council in 1948 is a testament to women's political organizing efforts.[1] Voting in Detroit's predominantly black areas decreased from 40.1 percent of the total eligible voting population in 1948 to 33.7 percent in 1950. In contrast, the white community registered only a 37.5 percent vote in 1948—31.7 percent in 1950.[2] Moreover, the money female canvassers raised for the NAACP throughout the entire period no doubt played a significant role in funding the NAACP's school desegregation lawsuits throughout the 1950s.

Middle-class women redefined themselves as responsible patriots and enacted programs that pressed hard for civil rights. In some cases, as with various public restaurants and parks and the USO in Detroit, women succeeded in claiming greater access to public facilities for the African American community. Women's groups formed interracial coalitions in each city. The YWCA in Richmond led efforts to desegregate its community by holding many interracial functions after 1945. Its interracial board, desegregated since the 1930s, promoted many more activities between the black and the white branches in order to bring women of both races together. Urged on by African American board members, the YWCA promoted civil rights legislation and interracial understanding. As leaders noted, "Realizing that human hearts cannot be legislated [we must] find more ways of translating the common needs of all into practices and habits of living and understanding."[3] In Detroit, clubwomen were again at the vanguard of civil rights progress when, in 1950, they negotiated with white women and desegregated both the YWCA and the Girl Scouts. By contrast, the YMCA and the Boy Scouts remained segregated as late as 1954.[4]

Working-class women also secured their rights by using government and industrial institutions to bolster their claims to equal employment opportunity and equal access to social welfare benefits. In Detroit before 1942, fewer than a hundred women worked in manufacturing. By 1950, however, 6,751 did so, one-fifth of all working women in the city. In addition, 8,643 women worked in service industries outside domestic work by 1950. The number in manufacturing and service work topped the total number of women in domestic work by 3,090.[5] In Richmond, the number of black women working as operatives in factories actually declined from 2,998 in 1940 to 2,217 in 1950. Their number increased, however, in positions other than domestic work. Although the number of black women in the workforce remained relatively stable throughout the decade, from 16,342 in 1940 to 14,268 in 1950, the number of women employed as domestics dropped dramatically, from 7,759 in 1940 to 4,906 in 1950. In nondomestic work, women in Richmond made significant gains, from 1,976 to 3,610, from 1940 to 1950.[6]

While working-class African American women found themselves largely abandoned by the unions by the 1950s and lost the Fair Employment Practices Committee after the war, they still managed to make gains in nondomestic work by continuing to press for the right to equal work and equal treatment within industries. In addition, they constructed themselves as citizens within the state, claiming welfare rights and negotiating slum clearance issues. In some cases, women bargained with the government and with private institutions for better housing and welfare benefits. Like middle-class women, working-class women also sought the right to equal public facilities; their actions helped destabilize racial structures in Detroit and Richmond.

African American women's protests failed to alter fundamentally the racial structures of either city. Legal segregation remained in place in Richmond before the Civil Rights Act of 1964, and the city opposed integration after 1954 with rezoning laws and simple intimidation. Even now, Richmond retains some of the most segregated school systems in the country as a result of white flight to suburbs that surround the city.[7] In Detroit, de facto segregation remained a problem in public institutions and neighborhoods. Most restaurants remained closed to blacks in 1954, and protective leagues, claiming rights of citizenship through freedom of association and property rights, sprang up to defend white neighborhoods from black encroachment.[8]

In both cities, slum clearance decimated historical black neighborhoods, usually by way of expressways designed to cut wide swaths through black-dominated areas. In Richmond between 1955 and 1957, more than seven thousand African Americans—10 percent of the population—moved to make way for expressways built through the heart of Jackson Ward. Richmond city development still threatens the historic district to such an extent that the National Historic Trust named the area one of the country's eleven most endangered historic sites.[9] It would take the mass mobilization of the African American community, along with media focus on the civil rights struggle, to effect changes for which African American women had fought throughout the twentieth century.

The women did not create vast changes in either Richmond or Detroit. They did, however, create the discourse upon which the modern civil rights movement grounded itself. Moreover, they backed the discourse with activities that promoted equality, including canvassing for voter registration, participating in sit-ins to protest equality, and using state structures to gain equal employment opportunities. Their language of dissent and protest, based on immediate demands for citizenship fostered by participation within the state and backed with activism in promoting equality, was a turning point in the civil rights movement. No longer were African Americans supplicants to the state; they were a vital part of the wartime and cold war state by nature of contributions to both home fronts.

By constructing a new concept of citizenship, African American women of all socioeconomic levels gave the movement a language of protest and a template for public activism. As they protested against inequalities by staging formal and informal demonstrations against various forms of inequality in public facilities, public transportation, government institutions, and industrial workplaces from 1940 to 1954, the women began a program of nonviolent activism used by later civil rights leaders in the 1950s and 1960s.

The new discourse and programs of middle-class women, linked with the attempts of working-class women to gain and retain jobs and better living conditions, contributed to a new sense of militancy and urgency within the civil rights movement of the 1940s and early 1950s. By attempting to claim their rights based solely on their status as citizens within the state, African American women greatly contributed to creating the groundwork and the ideology of the modern civil rights movement, which would continue with more civil rights campaigns in the 1950s and 1960s. Their initial forays into desegregating restaurants, jobs, transportation, and housing created momentum for the entire African American community's postwar struggles. The women's activist strategies and methods met with more success as thousands of African Americans continued to promote civil rights throughout the next two decades.

Notes

Abbreviations

ACWP   Records of the Automotive Council for War Production, National Automotive History Collection, Detroit Public Library

AKA   Alpha Kappa Alpha Sorority, Inc. Archives, Moorland Spingarn Research Center, Howard University, Washington, D.C.

CASW   Records of the Civilian Aide to the Secretary of War, RG 107, National Archives and Records Administration, College Park, Md.

CFM   Children's Fund of Michigan Collection, Bentley Historical Library, University of Michigan, Ann Arbor

CHP   Citizens' Housing and Planning Council Records, Burton Historical Collection, Detroit Public Library

CRCM   Civil Rights Congress of Michigan Collection, Wayne State University, Detroit

CWD   Office of the Governor, RG 3, Colgate W. Darden (1942–1946) Collection, box 75, Race Problems, folder 1: Memorandum for the Officer in Charge, Racial Situation in the City of Richmond, VA, file 17074, RI State Records Collection, Archives Research Services, The Library of Virginia, Richmond

DCCR   Detroit Commission on Community Relations Collection, Wayne State University

DNAACP Detroit Chapter of the National Association for the Advancement of Colored People, Wayne State University

DUL   Detroit Urban League Papers, Bentley Historical Library, University of Michigan, Ann Arbor

FAK   Francis Albert Kornegay Papers, University of Michigan, Ann Arbor

FEPC   Records of the President's Committee on Fair Employment Practices, RG 228 National Archives and Records Administration, College Park, Md.

GCP	Gloster Current Papers, Wayne State University
HWL	Records of the Housewives League of Detroit, Burton Historical Collection, Detroit Public Library
JANB	Records of the Joint Army and Navy Boards and Committees, RG 225, National Archives and Records Administration, College Park, Md.
JWB	Jeanetta Welch Brown Papers, Mary McLeod Bethune Council House, Washington, D.C.
LBT	Larus and Brother Tobacco Collection, Virginia Historical Society, Richmond
NA	National Archives and Records Administration, College Park, Md.
NAACP	National Association for the Advancement of Colored People Papers
NACW	Records of the National Association of Colored Women, Bethesda, Md., University Publications International
NCNW	National Council of Negro Women Papers, Mary McLeon Bethune Council House, Washington, D.C.
NLRB	Records of the National Labor Relations Board, RG 25, National Archives and Records Administration, College Park, Md.
OCWS	Records of the Office of Community War Services, RG 215, National Archives and Records Administration, College Park, Md.
RGP	Rosa Gragg Papers, Burton Historical Collection, Detroit Public Library
SBC	Second Baptist Church Collection, Bentley Historical Library, University of Michigan, Ann Arbor
TC	Thalhimer Collection, Virginia Historical Society, Richmond
TWIU	Archives of the Tobacco Workers' International Union, Special Collections, University of Maryland Libraries, College Park
UAW7	UAW Local 7 Collection, Wayne State University
UAW80	UAW Local 80 Collection, Wayne State University
UAWCD	UAW Chrysler Department Collection, Wayne State University
UAWFD	UAW Ford Department Collection, Wayne State University
UAWFP&AD	UAW Fair Practices and Anti-Discrimination Department Collection, Wayne State University
UAWFP&ADWB	UAW Fair Practices and Anti-Discrimination Department—Women's Bureau Collection, Wayne State University
UAWRC	UAW Research Department Collection, Wayne State University
UAWWD	UAW War Department Bureau Collection, Wayne State University
UAWWP	UAW War Policy Division Collection, Wayne State University
UCS	United Community Services Central File Collection, Wayne State University
VUUSC	Virginia University Special Collections, Virginia Commonwealth University, Richmond
WB	Records of the Women's Bureau, RG 86, National Archives and Records Administration, College Park, Md.
WMC	Records of the War Manpower Commission, RG 211, National Archives and Records Administration, College Park, Md.

WWII   World War II History Commission, RG 68 box 7, Labor File, "Domes-
                        tic Help Runs Short as Women Take Men's Jobs," *Richmond News-
                        Leader,* 25 Sept. 1942, State Records Collection, Archives Research
                        Services, The Library of Virginia, Richmond
YWCA   YWCA Collection, Virginia Commonwealth University, Richmond

Introduction

1. Capeci and Wilkerson, *Layered Violence,* 69, 169. The authors derived their numbers
from arrest records and eyewitness accounts.

2. Giddings, *In Search of Sisterhood,* 209–10.

3. "The Scene of the Crime," *Richmond Afro-American,* 1 Mar. 1941, 24.

4. Corrigan and Sayer, in *The Great Arch,* discuss the state as a fluid entity that orders
social relations in order to maintain its polity. Works that consider citizenship as it is traditionally gendered male include Mouffe, "Feminism, Citizenship, and Radical Democratic Politics"; Smith-Rosenberg, "Dis-Covering the 'Great Constitutional Discussion'";
Kerber, *No Constitutional Right to Be Ladies;* Mettler, *Dividing Citizens;* Randall, *Women
and Politics,* 129; Sassoon, "Women's New Social Role"; Balbo, "Crazy Quilts"; and Bredbenner, *A Nationality of Her Own.*

Although Smith-Rosenberg (369–84) argues that the American Constitution granted
white male citizens the benefits of state services, including the protection of speech and
property and the right to a fair trial, it marginalized women and people of color in order
to frame the white male as the primary citizen. Kerber (11) explains that the state defined
women as subordinate citizens and reproductive laborers and subsumed women's obligations to the state under their obligations to husband and family, enabling men to maintain the state by perpetuating family stability. Bredbenner (43) discusses the fact that although foreign-born wives of American citizens were naturalized not to give them
citizenship but to enable the state to support the husband's control over the family, it took
away the rights of American women who married foreigners. Moreover, after women won
the vote in 1920 it revoked automatic citizenship for foreign-born wives because citizenship now meant more than being an agent of a patriarchal family. Sassoon (171) maintains that the success of the capitalist state depends on women's unpaid labor providing
services the state will not.

5. Higginbotham, "African-American History and the Metalanguage of Race"; Mink,
The Wages of Motherhood; Baker, "The Domestication of Politics."

6. These issues are discussed in Mink, *The Wages of Motherhood;* Hunter, *To 'Joy My
Freedom;* Wolcott, *Remaking Respectability;* and Hicks, "Northern Crime/Southern Parole."

7. Zinn and Dill, "Theorizing Racial Differences from Multiracial Feminism," 326–27;
Anderson, *Changing Woman,* 9. Zinn and Dill argue that women of color are situated in
socially constructed gendered categories of overlapping and connecting inequalities based
on economic location, regional identity, and sexual orientation. Anderson contends that
women of color cannot split identities into mutually exclusive categories because of the
multitude of oppressions they face at any given time based on different economic, social,
and ideological frameworks.

8. These issues are addressed in Hine, "An Angle of Vision," 194–201, 203; Salem, *To Better Our World*, 104–13, 125; and Higginbotham, "Club Women and Electoral Politics in the 1920s," 134–55.

9. Higginbotham, *Righteous Discontent*, 14.

10. White, *Too Heavy a Load*; Gilmore, *Gender and Jim Crow*.

11. Kevin Gaines discusses the struggles black women endured over trying to balance public activities with self-constructed normative roles (*Uplifting the Race*, 231–32).

12. Wolcott, *Remaking Respectability*, 8–9. Chateauvert maintains that the wives of sleeping car porters often called upon the discourse of respectability to claim rights for themselves and their families (*Marching Together*, xiii, 84–85, 178).

13. Gaines, *Uplifting the Race*; Ladd-Taylor, "My Work Came out of Agony and Grief"; Boris, "The Power of Motherhood."

14. Gaines, *Uplifting the Race*, 107, 114–17, 250–53; White, *Too Heavy a Load*, 118–37, 148–51.

15. Wolcott, *Remaking Respectability*, 165–77; Shaw, *What a Woman Ought to Be and Do*, 209–10.

16. Hunter, *To 'Joy My Freedom*. These issues are discussed fully in Wilentz, *Chants Democratic*; Roediger, *The Wages of Whiteness*; and Baron, "An 'Other' Side of Gender Antagonism at Work." White male laborers had historically connected their control over the labor process with their citizenship. During the late 1700s men lost control over the crafts trades as skilled journeymen positions transformed into unskilled piecework positions. White men called upon the state to defend them against losing control over their work product. They cited their ability to control their own labor as a characteristic of white male freedom in a democratic society. That definition continued through the nineteenth century as working men juxtaposed their position against slaves when protesting factory conditions. During the late nineteenth century unions also connected white men's abilities to control their own labor with citizenship as the unions strove to connect the right to bargain and democratic ideals.

17. Tera Hunter discusses this issue at great length in *To 'Joy My Freedom*.

18. Wolcott, *Remaking Respectability*, 3–4, 179–80, 209–10, 227–29; Fehn, "African American Women and the Struggle for Equality in the Meatpacking Industry," 46–49, 60; Clark-Lewis, *Living In, Living Out*, 166–77.

19. Kelley, *Race Rebels*, 4–7.

20. Brown and Kimball, "Mapping the Terrain of Black Richmond," 97–102; Hunter, *To 'Joy My Freedom*, 60–67, 132–33, 225–27.

21. White, *Too Heavy a Load*; Dalfiume, *Desegregation of the U.S. Armed Forces*; Wynn, *The Afro-American and the Second World War*; Reed, *Seedtime for the Modern Civil Rights Movement*; Payne, *I've Got the Light of Freedom*; Lawson, *Running for Freedom*; Blum, *V Was for Victory*.

22. Lichtenstein, *Walter Reuther*, 211–19. Lichtenstein also discusses the problems with the no-strike pledge in *Labor's War at Home*.

23. Honey, ed., *Bitter Fruit*, 16–17.

24. Wynn, *The Afro-American and the Second World War*, 101.

25. Ibid.; Dalfiume, *Desegregation of the U.S. Armed Forces*; Scott and Womack, *Double V.*

26. Wynn, *The Afro-American and the Second World War;* Payne, *I've Got the Light of Freedom;* Scott and Womack, *Double V;* Dalfiume, *Desgregation of the U.S. Armed Forces;* Harvard Sitkoff, "African American Militancy in the World War II South," 70–92; Fairclough, *Race and Democracy,* 105; Dittmer, *Local People,* 105.

27. Kerber, *No Constitutional Right to Be Ladies,* 248–60.

28. Lawson, *Running for Freedom,* 29; Morris, *The Origins of the Civil Rights Movement,* x–xi. Other authors who focus on the modern civil rights movement in the post-1954 era include Sitkoff, *The Struggle for Black Equality;* and Payne, *I've Got the Light of Freedom.* In *Local People,* Dittmer sees *Brown v. Board of Education* (1954) as the galvanizing point for the Mississippi civil rights movement (41). John Higham observes that although no one can pinpoint the exact start of the civil rights movement, many have focused on a single event, often *Brown v. Board of Education,* as the catalyst for the modern movement ("Introduction," 3).

29. Gaines discusses the ambivalence of blacks during World War I, when Du Bois called upon all African Americans to stand behind an administration that segregated government workplaces and support the war. This caused debate about what was appropriate support for the state (*Uplifting the Race,* 154–56).

30. Anderson, "Last Hired, First Fired," 82–83.

31. Wynn, *The Afro-American and the Second World War;* Anderson, *Wartime Women;* Campbell, *Women at War with America;* Hartmann, *The Homefront and Beyond;* Milkman, *Gender at Work;* Anderson, "Last Hired First Fired," 83–95. These authors discuss the problems that women faced during the war. Although white women had to contend with industries that constructed their work as specifically gendered female and ephemeral in order to maintain constructions of women predominantly as caretakers (and to pave their way back into the home after the war was over), African American women had a hard time getting any jobs.

32. Gabin, *Feminism in the Labor Movement,* 88–89; Lemke-Santangelo, *Abiding Courage,* 4–5.

33. Sitkoff, *The Struggle for Black Equality,* 12–13.

34. "FEPC Probe Given Funds to Probe Job Discrimination in Five Cities," *Richmond Afro-American,* 5 Dec. 1942, 12. Daniel Kryder discusses the positive and negative aspects of the FEPC in *Divided Arsenal,* 96–98.

35. White, *Too Heavy a Load;* Giddings, *In Search of Sisterhood;* Thomas, *Riveting and Rationing in Dixie.*

36. "During the Last Six Months 5,782 Workers Put in 145,552 Hours of Knitting," *Richmond Times-Dispatch,* 15 Mar. 1942, 9.

37. "President's Message," *Ivy Leaf* 18 (Aug. 1940): 3.

38. White, *Too Heavy a Load,* 148–52.

39. Ibid., 155–57.

40. Giddings, *In Search of Sisterhood,* 199.

41. Silver, *Twentieth-Century Richmond,* 121–22; "Tension Files, Detroit," OCWS, Master Locator Record (hereafter MLR), entry 37, box 448, Labor file, NA; Sugrue, *The Origins of the Urban Crisis,* 23.

42. Hill, *The Big Bang,* 91–135, 146; National Association for the Advancement of Colored People, *NAACP Annual Report,* 1951, 15; Murray, ed., *Negro Handbook, 1946–47,* 43;

Wolcott, *Remaking Respectability,* 49–50, 132; Finch, *The NAACP,* 69–70, 111; National Urban League, *Fortieth Anniversary Yearbook,* 63, 115; Weiss, *The National Urban League, 1910–1940,* 114–26, 169.

43. Ovington, *The Walls Came Tumbling Down;* Branch and Rice, *Pennies to Dollars,* 67–9, 87; Wolcott, *Remaking Respectability,* 151, 210; Hine, *Hine Sight,* 73, 78–79, 81.

44. Background information on Richmond can be found in Lutz, *Richmond in World War II;* Gavins, *The Perils and Prospects of Southern Black Leadership;* and Davis, *The World of Patience Gromes.* Gavins and Davis offer two different looks at the black community. While Gavins finds that the fortunes of black leaders rose with the increased political power of blacks during the 1970s, Davis concludes that the politics of the 1960s and 1970s destroyed communities of poor black homeowners through slum clearance policies and lackluster police enforcement of drug-related neighborhood crime problems. The most complete history of Richmond and its racial tensions can be found in Tyler-McGraw, *At the Falls.*

45. Silver, *Twentieth-Century Richmond,* 11.

46. Silver and Moeser, *The Separate City.*

47. Silver, *Twentieth-Century Richmond,* 144–54.

48. Gaines, *Uplifting the Race,* 42.

49. Brown and Kimball, "Mapping the Terrain of Black Richmond," 94.

50. Wynn, *The Afro-American and the Second World War,* 51–52.

51. Silver and Moeser, *The Separate City,* 58.

52. Brown and Kimball, "Mapping the Terrain of Black Richmond," 85–90.

53. Gaines, *Uplifting the Race;* Brown and Kimball, "Mapping the Terrain of Black Richmond," 86–88; Janiewski, "Seeking a 'New Day and a New Way,'" 161–78.

54. Sugrue, *The Origins of the Urban Crisis,* 33–55, 57–89.

55. Meier and Rudwick, *Black Detroit and the Rise of the UAW,* 16, 18, 21, 34–61; Lichtenstein, *Labor's War at Home,* 124–25; Zieger, *The CIO, 1935–1955,* 123.

56. Gabin, *Feminism in the Labor Movement,* 1–11, 64–78.

57. Anderson, "Last Hired, First Fired."

58. Gabin, *Feminism in the Labor Movement,* 88.

59. Gaines (*Uplifting the Race*) and Gilmore (*Gender and Jim Crow*) discuss both the problems and the benefits of black elites allying with white sympathizers in order to gain more political and social power.

60. Meier and Rudwick, *Black Detroit and the Rise of the UAW,* 43–86.

61. Sugrue, *The Origins of the Urban Crisis,* 73.

62. Johnson, "Gender, Race, and Rumours," 263–64; Capeci and Wilkerson, *Layered Violence,* 16–18, 26–27, 73, 94, 104–5, 146, 156, 181, 184.

63. Capeci and Wilkerson, *Layered Violence,* 54–55, 71–72.

64. Payne, "Men Led, but Women Organized," 1–12; Robnett, *How Long? How Long?* 20–21.

65. These authors historicize women's networks of activism, placing them at the centers of struggles for equality. Gilmore, *Gender and Jim Crow;* Robnett, *How Long? How Long?* Giddings, *When and Where I Enter;* and Brodkin, *Caring by the Hour.* Sitkoff details the impact of a woman on the march on Washington movement in *A New Deal for Blacks,* 314.

66. For more information about the activities of women during the war, see Hartmann, *The Homefront and Beyond;* Campbell, *Women at War with America;* Anderson, *Wartime Women;* Honey, ed., *Bitter Fruit;* Honey, *Creating Rosie the Riveter;* Anderson, "Last Hired, First Fired"; Thomas, *Riveting and Rationing in Dixie;* Lemke-Santangelo, *Abiding Courage;* and Milkman, *Gender at Work.*

Chapter 1: Engaging with the State

1. Dorothy Boulding Ferebee, "Negro Women in the National Crisis," *Ivy Leaf* 19 (Sept. 1941): 3.

2. Ferebee, "Negro Women in the National Crisis."

3. Higginbotham, *Righteous Discontent,* 14.

4. Carby, *Reconstructing Womanhood,* 104–5, 164–67.

5. "Message from Dorothy Boulding Ferebee," *Ivy Leaf* 18 (Sept. 1940): 3–4.

6. "The President's Message," *Aframerican Women's Journal* (Winter 1941): 1, ser. 13, box 1, folder 9, NCNW.

7. "President's Message," *The Aurora* 7 (Spring 1942): 10.

8. "NCNW Speaker Would Seek Standard Democracy," *Richmond Afro-American,* 24 Oct. 1942, 16.

9. "YWCA Unit Will Meet at Forum," *Richmond Afro-American,* 3 Oct. 1940, 4.

10. "Message from the Editor," *National Notes* 1 (Oct. 1941): 1, 4.

11. "Delta Sorors Hear Women's Challenge," *Detroit Tribune,* 3 Jan. 1942, 1.

12. "Delta Sorors Hear Women's Challenge," 4.

13. Beulah Whitby, "The Increasing Awareness of Our Social Responsibility," minutes of the twenth-third annual Boule, 36, box 1, AKA.

14. Information about Whitby can be found on the African American Biology Database <http://abd.chadwyck.com.>, accessed on 10 Feb. 2003.

15. Interview with Beulah Whitby, 36.

16. "Delta Sorors Hear Women's Challenge," 4.

17. Antoinette Bowler to Mrs. Norman, 19 Mar. 1941, ser. 4, box 1, folder 18, NCNW.

18. "Message from Beulah Whitby," *Ivy Leaf* 20 (Dec. 1942): 4.

19. Rhea Talley, "Tues. and Wed. Set for Women's Defense," *Richmond Times-Dispatch,* 23 Mar. 1941, 9.

20. Women's Army for National Defense Summary, ser. 18, box 8, folder 9, NCNW.

21. Ibid.

22. "128 Delegates Attend Zeta Regional Session," *Richmond Afro-American,* 16 May 1942, 16; "Eastern Stars to Buy $10,000 U.S. Bonds," *Richmond Afro-American,* 8 Aug. 1942, 19; "Delta Bond Investment Now $25,000," *Richmond Afro-American,* 8 Mar. 1943, 16; "AKA's Purchase $25,000 in Bonds," *Richmond Afro-American,* 15 May 1943, 16; "Detroit Deltas Win Northwest Trophy," *Detroit Tribune,* 2 May 1942, 4; "Club Invests in War Bond," *Richmond Afro-American,* 31 Oct. 1942, 9.

23. "Walker Will House Red Cross Workers," *Richmond Afro-American,* 5 Oct. 1940, 24; "Red Cross Seeking War Relief Funds," *Richmond Afro-American,* 18 May 1940, 3; *Ivy Leaf* 21 (Dec. 1943): 10; "War Bond Rally to Open AKA Sorority Activity," *Richmond Afro-American,* 2 Oct. 1943, 16; "AKA Unit Sells $10,000 in Bond and Stamp Drive," *Richmond*

Afro-American, 16 Oct. 1943, 7; "Bond Rally for South Richmonders," *Richmond Afro-American*, 16 Sept. 1944, 7; "War Bond Rally Yields $2150," *Richmond Afro-American*, 9 Sept. 1944, 6.

24. "War Widows' Whist Party a Success," *Michigan Chronicle*, 3 Apr. 1943, 16; "War Widows Closed Drive with Party," *Michigan Chronicle*, 1 May 1943, 15; "Raise over Twenty Thousand in Bond Sale," *Michigan Chronicle*, 14 Aug. 1943, 9; "Gallant Awarded Certificate for Selling War Bonds," *Michigan Chronicle*, 11 Mar. 1944, 8.

25. Frances Leonard, "Women's Doings," *Michigan Chronicle*, 18 Sept. 1943, 16.

26. "Red Cross Workers Keep Busy at Work," *Richmond Afro-American*, 12 Sept. 1942, 24; "AKA Unit Will Roll Bandages at St. Philip," *Richmond Afro-American*, 20 Feb. 1943, 6; "Beauties Stitch," *Detroit Tribune*, 24 Jan. 1942, 5; "Mrs. Stephens Instructor," *Michigan Chronicle*, 6 Feb. 1943, 16.

27. "Va. Hospital Plans Nurse Aide Class," *Richmond Afro-American*, 18 Sept. 1943, 6.

28. "Win Home Hygiene Certificates," *Richmond Afro-American*, 10 May 1941, 4; "They Believe in Preparedness," *Richmond Afro-American*, 7 Feb. 1942, 3; "Thirty-nine Graduated from Nursing Class," *Richmond Afro-American*, 28 Mar. 1942, 24.

29. "Finish Red Cross Nursing Course," *Richmond Afro-American*, 3 Mar. 1945, 6.

30. "Ready for Defense Emergency," *Detroit Tribune*, 14 Aug. 1941, 2; "Advanced First Aid Grads Are Given Certificates," *Detroit Tribune*, 13 June 1942, 2.

31. "Home Nursing Courses Open at Two Centers," *Michigan Chronicle*, 18 Sept. 1943, 9.

32. "Home Nursing Class Organized Last Week," *Michigan Chronicle*, 4 Mar. 1944, 11.

33. "AKA Group to Help Nutrition Program," *Richmond Afro-American*, 14 Mar. 1942, 3; "Meat Specialist Planning Nutrition Demo," *Richmond Afro-American*, 25 Apr. 1942, 24; "Nutrition Group Will Have Meeting at Bethlehem," *Richmond Afro-American*, 9 May 1942, 24; "Canning Instruction Slated at Bethlehem," *Richmond Afro-American*, 24 Apr. 1943, 6.

34. "YW News," *Michigan Chronicle*, 3 Apr. 1943, 17; "Classes in Nutrition Given at Club House," *Detroit Tribune*, 15 Jan. 1944, 5; "Five Canning Centers Open for Six Weeks," *Michigan Chronicle*, 7 Aug. 1943, 15.

35. "Women Given Rationing Aid by Specialist," *Richmond Afro-American*, 17 Apr. 1943, 16; "History of Detroit Housewives League," 3, box 1, History file, HWL.

36. Jeanetta Welch to Mark McCloskey, 13 Nov. 1941, MLR 18, box 1, Negro Problems file, JANB.

37. "History of the Leigh Street USO," 1947, box 4B, folder 66, WWII.

38. "Old Monroe School Serving as Negro Activities Center," *Richmond Times-Dispatch*, 16 Aug. 1942, box 15, USO file, WWII; "'Our War' Is Attitude of State Negroes," *Commonwealth of Virginia Civilian Defense News* 1 (Oct. 1942): 3, box 1A, folder 1, WWII; "Deltas Give $100 to USO," *Detroit Tribune*, 4 July 1942, 4; "Miss Helen Watson Gave $250 to USO Club Room," *Michigan Chronicle*, 3 Apr. 1943, 10; "Three Honor Students Get World Fellowships," *Detroit Tribune*, 20 June 1942, 2; "Women Raise $1200 for Club Rooms," *Detroit Tribune*, 1 Aug. 1942, 6; "USO Recognition Service at YWCA," *Michigan Chronicle*, 31 July 1945, 5.

39. "USO Group Hears National Official," *Richmond Afro-American*, 29 Apr. 1944, 5.

40. "Leigh St. USO Notes," *Richmond Afro-American*, 14 Oct. 1944, 10.

41. "USO Hostess Club Will Crown Queen," *Richmond Afro-American*, 29 Apr. 1944, 12.

42. "Young Ladies Anxious to Win Pin-Up Crown," *Michigan Chronicle*, 25 Dec. 1944, 15.

43. Anderson, *Wartime Women*, 96–106.

44. "Leigh Street USO Activities," *Richmond Afro-American*, 29 July 1944, 6; "Notes on USO Activities," *Richmond Afro-American*, 28 Oct. 1944, 5.

45. "Girls Hand-Picked for Service Work," *Detroit Tribune*, 5 Sept. 1942, 9.

46. R. L. Bradby to Mrs. Ardenah Stephens, 8 Dec. 1943, reel 3, SBC.

47. Smith, ed., *Notable Black American Women: Book 2*, 253–55.

48. Frances Leonard, "About Women," *Michigan Chronicle*, 1 May 1943, 17.

49. "Defense Service Unit to Be Host," *Richmond Afro-American*, 9 May 1942, 12.

50. USO Roll of Service in Leigh Street YMCA 1943–1947, box 4B, folder 43, WWII; "USO Forms Servicemens' Wives' Club," *Richmond Afro-American*, 25 Mar. 1944, 4.

51. "Party Line," *Michigan Chronicle*, 12 June 1943, 15; "War Widows Plan for Summer Affair Soon," *Michigan Chronicle*, 23 July 1943, 21; "Sapphire Club to Celebrate Twentieth Year," *Detroit Tribune*, 19 Feb. 1944, 5; "Entre Nous Celebrate Twenty-one Years Growth," *Michigan Chronicle*, 15 Apr. 1944, 10.

52. "USO Plays Host to Hill Troops," *Richmond Afro-American*, 30 May 1942, 5.

53. "Leigh Street USO Club Has Dance," *Richmond Afro-American*, 6 Feb. 1944, 3; "USO Celebrates St. Patrick's Day," *Richmond Afro-American*, 25 Mar. 1944, 6; "They Relax at USO Barnyard Frolic," *Richmond Afro-American*, 1 Apr. 1944, 2; "USO Club Sponsors Pre-Easter Dance," *Richmond Afro-American*, 15 Apr. 1944, 2; Leigh Street USO Club Activities," *Richmond Afro-American*, 10 June 1944, 11 (see also same article, same publication, 15 July 1944, 11, 2 Sept. 1944, 6, and 4 Nov. 1944, 5); "Hundreds Visited USO Center Saturday," *Michigan Chronicle*, 6 Mar. 1943, 9; "USO Club to Have Party on March 20," *Michigan Chronicle*, 20 Mar. 1943, 18; "Movies Shown on Nutrition and the War," *Michigan Chronicle*, 3 Apr. 1943, 17; "National Negro Health Week," *Michigan Chronicle*, 1 Apr. 1944, 9; "USO Group to Hold Sweetheart Ball," *Detroit Tribune*, 2 Mar. 1944, 5; "Voguettes Do Honor to Men of Services," *Michigan Chronicle*, 21 July 1945, 10; "USO Hostesses Hold Tea," *Detroit Tribune*, 15 Dec. 1945, 5.

54. "Leigh Street USO Revamps Program," *Richmond Afro-American*, 18 Mar. 1944, 3; "Hostesses Bring Smokes for Servicemen," *Richmond Afro-American*, 29 Apr. 1944, 5; "Co-Ettes Play Santa to Soldiers, Needy," *Detroit Tribune*, 2 Jan. 1943, 6.

55. "Seven Dances in Two Weeks at Camp Lee," *Richmond Afro-American*, 8 Nov. 1944, 5; "USO Girls Guests at Camp Lee," *Richmond Afro-American*, 27 June 1942, 7; "USO Girls Attend Camp Lee Dance," *Richmond Afro-American*, 13 May 1944, 11; "Girls Attend Camp Lee Picnic," *Richmond Afro-American*, 1 July 1944, 8; "YWCA-USO Gives Party at Oscada," *Michigan Chronicle*, 22 May 1943, 14; "The Day of Military Tea Draws Near for YWCA," *Detroit Tribune*, 25 July 1943, 6; "Girls Go to Fort Brady," *Detroit Tribune*, 22 Aug. 1942, 6; "Social USO," *Detroit Tribune*, 24 Oct. 1942, 6.

56. "Monroe Center Makes Soldiers Feel at Home in Richmond," *Richmond Afro-American*, 10 Oct. 1942, 5.

57. "Boys in Khaki, Girls in Lace Strictly Chaperoned by USO," *Richmond Afro-American*, 23 Jan. 1943, 12.

58. All of the previously listed articles from various newspapers detail events and participants in a manner that indicates the respectability of the efforts.

59. "Monroe Center Makes Soldiers Feel at Home."

60. Ibid.; "Volunteers for Soldiers' Lounge Sought," *Richmond Afro-American*, 12 Dec. 1942, 9; "Fifth Street Unit Serves Breakfast to Servicemen," *Richmond Afro-American*, 13 June 1942, 7; "Service Men Hear Musical Group," *Richmond Afro-American*, 31 Mar. 1945, 6; "Christmas Treat Given Men at OCD Center," *Richmond Afro-American*, 2 Jan. 1943, 24.

61. "Deltas Stuff Boxes," *Detroit Tribune*, 27 Dec. 1943, 1; "War Widows Progress in Their Plans," *Detroit Tribune*, 10 Apr. 1943, 18; "Contributions Must Be Made by Dec 10," *Michigan Chronicle*, 4 Dec. 1943, 2; "Choicettes Pack Overseas Boxes," *Michigan Chronicle*, 21 Oct. 1944, 11; "Local Deltas Exceed Book Drive Goal," *Michigan Chronicle*, 12 June 1943, 17; "Girl Reserves in Fashion Show at Y," *Michigan Chronicle*, 18 May 1943, 3; "Cookies to USO," *Michigan Chronicle*, 6 Mar. 1943, 13; "Sorors Plan to Feature Stamp Rally," *Detroit Tribune*, 20 Dec. 1941, 1–2; "Red Cross Canteen Serves Two Thousand Soldiers," *Detroit Tribune*, 25 Sept. 1943, 4; souvenir program from Fourth Anniversary of the Clubhouse of the Detroit Association of Women's Clubs, 2–8 Apr. 1946, box 33, NACW Detroit and Michigan Literature folder, RGP; "Ladies' Society Served Dinner to Servicemen," *Michigan Chronicle*, 12 June 1943, 16.

62. Leigh Street USO Honor Roll, box 4B, folder 43, WWII; "John R. Hostesses Give to Wounded," *Michigan Chronicle*, 9 June 1945, 17.

63. Telegrams and letters from AKA chapters, 1941, MLR 17, box 1, AKA file, WB; form letter from Women's Bureau, MLR 36, box 22, Negro Organizations file, WB; "Charge Secretary Perkins Snubbed AKA Job Request," *Richmond Afro-American*, 1 Nov. 1941, 17.

64. Norma Boyd and Jeanetta Welch to FDR, 1 Apr. 1942, MLR 25, box 210, AKA file, FEPC.

65. "Women's Council Rebukes War Department for Snub," *Richmond Afro-American*, 25 Oct. 1941, 14.

66. NCNW News Release, 30 June 1943, ser. 5, box 30, folder 10, NCNW.

67. Mary McLeod Bethune to Antoinette Bowler, 11 June 1943, ser. 17, box 28, folder 3, NCNW.

68. "Listen America Week Planned to Show Other Side of Picture," *Richmond Afro-American*, 21 Nov. 1942, 16.

69. "Mrs. Downs Heads Deltas," *Richmond Afro-American*, 2 Sept. 1944, 16; "Sigma Sorors Will Hold 1945 Meeting in Balto.," *Richmond Afro-American*, 2 Sept. 1944, 12; "Mrs. B. T. Whitby Speaks before House for FEPC," *Michigan Chronicle*, 17 June 1944, 8.

70. In *Too Heavy a Load,* Deborah Gray White discusses the growing power of black women within the state during the 1930s and attributes it to Bethune's networking abilities.

71. "Civil Liberties Program Held by Local Elks," *Richmond Afro-American*, 13 Jan. 1940, 24; "Schools Take Lead in History Events," *Richmond Afro-American*, 17 Dec. 1940, 4; "Citizenship Rally Scheduled at YW," *Richmond Afro-American*, 17 Dec. 1940, 6.

72. "First Line of Defense on Feminine Shoulders," *Richmond Afro-American*, 31 May 1941, 17; annual chapter meeting program, 28 Apr. 1941, box 1, AKA Non-Partisan League folder, JWB; "Struggle for Integration, Lobbyist Pleads," *Richmond Afro-American*, 6 Nov. 1943, 10.

73. The riot lasted three days, wasted hundreds of hours in war labor, and caused hundreds of thousands of dollars in damage in the black community as well as the lives of

dozens of men. The event heightened Detroiters' awareness of the pervasive race problems in the community. Capeci and Wilkerson, *Layered Violence,* give the most detailed account of the riot.

74. "Mrs. G. Bledsoe Main Speaker," *Michigan Chronicle,* 27 Jan. 1943, 9; "B & P Girls in Panel Discussion," *Michigan Chronicle,* 4 Dec. 1943, 2; "Dedicate Plans to Greater Aid in War Effort," *Michigan Chronicle,* 17 June 1944, 10; "Keeping Up with Members, Detroit Metropolitan Council," *Aframerican Women's Journal,* Mar. 1945, 9, ser. 13, box 1, folder 16, NCNW; "Intercultural Observance at YW Draws Crowd," *Michigan Chronicle,* 24 Mar. 1945, 15.

75. "1300 Added in NAACP Drive," *Richmond Afro-American,* 25 May 1940, 1–2; "Goal Topped by NAACP in Campaign," *Richmond Afro-American,* 26 Apr. 1941, 1–2; "1,790 Enrolled in NAACP Drive," *Richmond Afro-American,* 23 May 1942, 12; "NAACP Closes Drive with 3,350 Members," *Richmond Afro-American,* 31 July 1943, 10; "Richmond NAACP Enrolls 3,452 in Annual Campaign," *Richmond Afro-American,* 28 Oct. 1944, 10; "Pioneers Christian, Lawson Celebrated," *Richmond Afro-American,* 8 Jan. 1983, 1; Senora Lawson obituary, *Richmond News-Leader,* 2 Jan. 1983, 4.

76. "NAACP Ball Here on Friday, Feb. 11," *Michigan Chronicle,* 29 Jan. 1944, 3; "Mrs. Lampkin Stresses Need for Support," *Michigan Chronicle,* 2 June 1945, 2.

77. "School Board Salaries Rise, but Retain Race Inequalities," *Richmond Afro-American,* 14 Feb. 1942, 24.

78. "All Teachers Back Petition on Equality," *Richmond Afro-American,* 7 Dec. 1940, 2.

79. "Teachers Offer Five-Year Plan on Equal Salary," *Richmond Afro-American,* 26 July 1941, 7.

80. "Teachers Given Their Contracts," *Richmond Afro-American,* 4 Oct. 1941, 1–2; "Virginia Teachers Plan Pay Suit," *Richmond Afro-American,* 8 Nov. 1941, 1.

81. "Teachers' Pay Decree Signed," *Richmond Afro-American,* 24 Jan. 1942, 1–2.

82. "The Negro Teachers' Suit," *Richmond Times-Dispatch,* 31 Dec. 1941, 10.

83. "Five-Year Plan Accepted by Teachers," *Richmond Afro-American,* 21 Feb. 1942, 1–2.

84. "Only Legal Kinks Delay Action," *Richmond Afro-American,* 2 May 1942, 24.

85. "$13,846 in Bond and Stamp Sales," *Richmond Afro-American,* 15 May 1943, 12; "YCWA Clubs Engage in War Stamp Drive," *Richmond Afro-American,* 5 May 1945, 3; "All Were in Good Health," *Richmond Afro-American,* 20 May 1943, 3; "Victory Corps Class Collects 7,317 Cans," *Richmond Afro-American,* 24 Mar. 1945, 10; "Children Salvage Materials to Assist in the War Effort," *Richmond Afro-American,* 20 June 1942, 12.

86. "Children Contribute," *Michigan Chronicle,* 30 Dec. 1944, 5; "Dealers in High Finance," *Michigan Chronicle,* 6 May 1945, 3; "Girls to Aid in Civilian Defense Work," *Michigan Chronicle,* 6 Feb. 1943, 15.

87. "AKA Fights for Child Care Bill," *Michigan Chronicle,* 31 July 1943, 16. Elizabeth Rose argues that state recognition for child day care reached a turning point during the war, when women's war work had to be legitimated (*A Mother's Job,* 153–81). State recognition of day care enabled black women to enter into negotiations with the state over funding issues.

88. "Nursery Sponsored by College Women," *Richmond Afro-American,* 27 Dec. 1940, 9; "They're Doing Good Deed," *Richmond Afro-American,* 9 Oct. 1943, 7; "Phi Delta Kappas Open Rec Center Room," *Richmond Afro-American,* 28 Apr. 1945, 21.

89. "Annual Report of Peter Pan Nursery of Detroit, Inc., June 1943–Dec. 1950," printed in 1951, 1, box 12, Peter Pan Nursery School file, CFM.

90. "Sorority Plans Youth Center," *Detroit Tribune,* 25 Mar. 1944, 4.

91. "Mothers Warned of Delinquency Problem," *Michigan Chronicle,* 19 Oct. 1943, 5.

92. "Y to Hold Ninth Youth Canteen," *Richmond Afro-American,* 9 Dec. 1944, 9; "To Open New Canteen at Garfield High," *Michigan Chronicle,* 3 July 1943, 17; "Girl Reserves Entertain Boys," *Michigan Chronicle,* 2 Dec. 1944, 16; Sept. 1944 Chestnut Center Memo to Mrs. Weldon from Sutler, box 5, July–Sept. 1944 general file, DUL; Anderson, *Wartime Women,* 96–106.

93. "Association's Services Given 138 Youngsters," *Richmond Afro-American,* 15 Feb. 1941, 24.

94. In reality, only 4 percent of the rioters arrested were women, and they were usually charged with looting after the initial vandalism to stores, according to Capeci and Wilkerson (*Layered Violence,* 65, 71–73, 169). Still, evidence shows that the Deltas believed that many young women were involved, hence the need for a home for delinquents.

95. Delta Sigma Theta Home for Girls Prospectus, 1–2, box 15, Slade–Gragg Academy Correspondence (1) folder, RGP.

96. Delta Sigma Theta Home for Girls Prospectus.

97. Ibid.

98. Jessica Kimball, "Delta Sigma Theta Home for Girls," box 23, file 5, UCS.

99. Speech to AKAs, Apr. 1944, ser. 18, box 1, folder 1, NCNW.

100. "Ninth Workshop of NCNW in Washington," *Michigan Chronicle,* 11 Jan. 1944, 12.

101. Middle-class activists had always believed in providing industrial training for working-class African Americans. Some programs' sole focus on industrial training over liberal arts training suggests a class bias in jobs the middle-class thought appropriate for those lower on the economic ladder (Gaines, *Uplifting the Race,* 19–67).

102. Zatella Turner, "AKA's Wartime Program," *Aframerican Women's Journal* (Summer 1943): 22–23, ser. 13, box 1, folder 11, NCNW; "Wartime Delta Conference Places Emphasis on Needs during Crisis," *Michigan Chronicle,* 8 May 1943, 17.

103. Statement from Jeanetta Welch Brown, 9 Feb. 1942, MLR 22, box 36, Negro Organizations file, WB.

104. "Mrs. Gragg Offers Victory Plan on Employment to FDR," *Detroit Tribune,* 5 Oct. 1942, 5; memo of Women in Industry, Employment in Detroit Subsection, box 32, Women's Auxiliaries 1943–1945 folder, UAWRC.

105. "Four Groups Co-operate on Vocational Drive," *Richmond Afro-American,* 6 Apr. 1940, 4; Richmond Urban League *Messenger* 9 (Jan. 1942), box 1B, folder 92, WWII.

106. "Message from Lillian Payne," *St. Luke Fraternal Bulletin* 13 (Aug. 1944): 4.

107. Executive Board Minutes, 9 Nov. 1942, box 1, Executive Board Minutes 1942 file, GCP.

108. YWCA Interracial Practices Questionnaire, 1943 work copy, box 28, Interracial Committee Information 1936–1944 folder, YWCA; "Week of Charm Scheduled at Y," *Richmond Afro-American,* 25 May 1940, 5.

109. *Ivy Leaf* 20 (June 1942): 12; "Adult Activities at Y Offer Personality Help," *Michigan Chronicle,* 25 Mar. 1944, 19.

110. *Double V Begins with Me* (flyer), box 1, Executive Board Minutes 1942–1944 file, HWL.

111. Meier and Rudwick, *Black Detroit and the Rise of the UAW,* 86–93.

112. Jeanetta Welch Brown to Rosa Gragg, 23 July 1943, ser. 5, box 13, folder 12, NCNW.

113. President's Address, 1943 meeting, 3–4, ser. 2, box 1, folder 19, NCNW.

114. Wartime Employment Clinics Memo, 1943, 3–4, ser. 5, box 11, folder 11, NCNW.

115. *Wake Up! Your Job Is in Danger* (pamphlet), Message to Negro Workers, 1943, ser. 5, box 11, folder 11, NCNW.

116. Lawson, *Running for Freedom,* 9.

Chapter 2: Working for Democracy

1. "Workers—Shortage Cry Is Farce to Trained Jobless Women," *Detroit Tribune,* 24 Oct. 1942, 1.

2. "Workers—Shortage Cry Is Farce."

3. Anderson, *Changing Woman,* 14–15; Janiewski, "Seeking 'a New Day and a New Way,'" 772–74; Fehn, "African American Women and the Struggle for Equality in the Meatpacking Industry," 46–47, 48–49, 60.

4. Milkman, *Gender at Work,* 9.

5. Transcript of Women's Conference, 7 Feb. 1942, 40, box 2, UAWWP.

6. Eileen Boris discusses the problems between white women and black women regarding factory employment in "'You Wouldn't Want One of 'Em Dancing with Your Wife,'" 86–87, 94, 96. George Lipsitz also addresses this issue when he contends that white women especially resisted black women's entry into the workforce as a "means of maintaining distance, even when it gave them no economic advantage" (*Rainbow at Midnight,* 50). In addition, he discusses the reactive hate strikes launched against African Americans entering the workforce (69–95).

7. Memo to files from Father Roche, 28 June 1944, re: Field Visit to Wortendyke Manufacturing Co., MLR 25, box 10, Richard Roche file, FEPC.

8. Milkman, *Gender at Work,* 55.

9. *National WTUL Life and Labor Bulletin,* Dec 1942, MLR 22, box 185, Human Interest Stories file, WB.

10. Will Maslow, Weekly Report, 13 Jan. 1944, MLR 25, box 258, file 4, 1943–1944, FEPC.

11. Federal Security Agency Richmond Locality Report, Myrtle Cohen to Irving Posner, 18 Nov. 1944, 2, MLR 51, box 11, War Area Reports and Correspondence, Richmond file, OCWS.

12. Cohen, *Making a New Deal,* 256–61.

13. NAACP Press Release, 12 Sept. 1941, based on letter from Lela Leverette to FEPC, 4 Sept. 1941, box A333, Detroit Discrimination file, NAACP.

14. Final Disposition Report, 15 May 1944, case 5GR1210, MLR 25, box 240, case 5GR1210 file, FEPC.

15. "A Challenge from Bellwood," *Richmond Afro-American,* 17 Oct. 1942, 9.

16. Elizabeth Smith to *Afro-American Weekly,* 24 Sept. 1942, MLR 25, box 109, Richmond Quartermaster Depot file, FEPC.

17. Ora Branch to FDR, 10 Sept. 1942, MLR 25, box 109, Richmond Quartermaster Depot file, FEPC.

18. Memo from George Johnson, 6 Apr. 1943, MLR 25, box 109, Richmond Quartermaster Depot file, FEPC.

19. George Johnson to Murray Body, 24 Nov. 1942, MLR 5, box 6, FEPC; George Johnson to Dorothy Simmons, 10 Nov. 1942, MLR 5, box 6, FEPC; George Johnson to Murray Body, 19 Oct. 1942, MLR 5, box 5, FEPC; Final Disposition Report, 1 June 1945, case 5BR1356, MLR 25, box 239, case 5BR1356 file, FEPC.

20. Final Disposition Report, 28 Nov. 1944, case 5BR1052 and case 5BR1292, MLR 25, box 240, cases 5BR1052 and 5BR1292 files, FEPC.

21. "Manufacturer Defies FDR's Orders Won't Hire Colored," *Richmond Afro-American,* 16 May 1942, 8.

22. Gaines (*Uplifting the Race*) provides the most complete account of how black institutions reflected the concerns of their middle-class leaders in the first half of the twentieth century.

23. Roundtable Meeting, 7 Apr. 1943, 10–11, MLR 25, box 168, Detroit file, FEPC.

24. George Johnson to Gloster Current, 4 Dec. 1942, MLR 5, box 7, FEPC; George Johnson to Jack Burke, 26 Dec. 1942, MLR 5, box 7, FEPC; NAACP Press Release, "Telephone Company Admits Discrimination Cite More Cases," Detroit, 30 Nov. 1942, box 87, 1942 (2) file, NAACP; "Protest Phone Firm Urge Jobs for Negroes," *Detroit Tribune,* 21 Nov. 1942, 1.

25. Detroit Discrimination Record, 1942, 5, group 2, box C86, Detroit 1942 (2) file, NAACP.

26. "Workers Join in Fight on Racial Bias," *Michigan Chronicle,* 3 Apr. 1943, 3.

27. "Workers Join in Fight."

28. "Thousands Demand Equal Rights for Negro Workers," *Detroit Tribune,* 17 Apr. 1943, 1; "Four Women Turned Down by Eight Plants," *Michigan Chronicle,* 15 May 1943, 4.

29. "Labor Source Not Utilized by Plants," *Michigan Chronicle,* 25 Sept. 1943, 3.

30. George Johnson to J. M. Tinsley, 24 Oct. 1942, MLR 5, box 7, FEPC; Memo to Joseph Evans, 15 Oct. 1943, MLR 5, box 16, FEPC; George Johnson to J. M. Tinsley, 29 July 1942, MLR 5, box 3, FEPC.

31. Richmond Urban League *Messenger* 2 (Jan. 1944): 6–7, ser. 13, box 26, Richmond file, NUL.

32. August Meier and Elliot Rudwick give the most complete account of race relations and the UAW from its inception in the 1930s through the war years in *Black Detroit and the Rise of the UAW.*

33. "Applicants for Defense Accuse Ford of Bias," *Detroit Tribune,* 21 Feb. 1942, 1.

34. Special Meeting of the UAW Interracial Committee with the Ford Motor Company, 1 June 1942, box 14, folder 11, UAWFP&AD.

35. Final Disposition Report, 24 Aug. 1945, case 5BR1440, MLR 25, box 239, case 5BR1440 file, FEPC.

36. Demonstration Flyer, 20 Aug. 1942, box 4, July–Dec. 1942 general file, DUL.

37. "Work in a Defense Plant: Chases Wolf from Her Door," *Detroit Tribune,* 28 Nov. 1942, 1–2.

38. Harry Koger to Lawrence Cramer, 3 Oct. 1942, MLR 25, box 104, file L, FEPC.

39. For a more detailed description of the race categories assigned in the tobacco industry, see Janiewski, *Sisterhood Denied.*

40. George Johnson to Harry Koger, 30 Oct. 1942, and Harry Koger to George Johnson, 5 Nov. 1942, both in MLR 25, box 104, file L, FEPC.

41. George Johnson to Harry Koger, 13 Nov. 1942, MLR 25, box 104, file L, FEPC.

42. George Johnson to Charles Reed, 5 Nov. 1942, MLR 25, box 104, file L, FEPC.

43. Answer of Larus Tobacco to TWIU Case 4–8007, Local 219, 6 July 1944, ser. 3, box 32, Local 219 Agreements file, TWIU.

44. Clipping from *Richmond News-Leader,* 18 Oct. 1941, box 7, Tobacco Workers' Strike, Clippings and Affidavits, 1941, LBT.

45. Brief of the ACLU, cases 5R1413 and 5R1437, 2 Nov. 1944, ser. 3, box 32, Local 219 1944–1945 Reports file, TWIU.

46. Ibid.; Answer, from Larus and Brothers Company and Local 219, by John Jacobs, 13 Feb. 1945, 19, ser. 3, box 32, Local 219 1944–1945 Reports file, TWIU.

47. Testimony, 31 July 1945, in the Matter of Larus and Brothers, Co. and TWIU Locals 219 and 219B, case 5R1413, RE: Case R1413 *CIO vs. AFL in the Matter of 219 and 577,* RG 25, MLR 156, box 4004, NLRB.

48. Ibid., 277–78, 307.

49. Ibid., 544, 546.

50. Ibid., 306–8, 557–59.

51. Boris, "'You Wouldn't Want One of 'Em Dancing with Your Wife,'" 94; Anderson, "Last Hired, First Fired," 86–89.

52. G. James Fleming to George Johnson, and G. James Fleming to Montague Clark, both 4 Mar. 1943, MLR 25, box 228, Fleming file, FEPC.

53. Report on Packard Work Stoppage, 3 Mar. 1943, MLR 25, box 228, Fleming file, FEPC.

54. G. James Fleming to Earl B. Dickerson, 15 May 1943, MLR 25, box 228, Fleming file, FEPC.

55. "Protested Four Colored Girls in Department," *Michigan Chronicle,* 20 Feb. 1943, 1–2; Report on Packard Work Stoppage.

56. Will Maslow to Consolidated Brass, 18 Aug. 1943, MLR 5, box 15, FEPC; Minutes of Local 80 Meetings with Company, 16 Sept. 1942–7 Nov. 1945, Meeting on 19 Jan. 1944, 19–20, UAW80; Detroit Progress Report, 5 Mar. 1943, MLR 25, box 228, Fleming file, FEPC.

57. Detroit Progress Report, 5 Mar. 1943.

58. Interview with Jess Ferrazza, 19–20.

59. "Murray Body Employee's Lunch Stolen, Face Slapped, Is Fired," *Detroit Tribune,* 16 Mar. 1943, 1.

60. Oscar Noble, Discharge at Murray Body Report, box 29, Local 2 file, UAWWD; Final Disposition Report, 24 Nov. 1943, case 5BR1043, 23 Nov. 1943, case 5BR1056, both in MLR 25, box 251, Region 5 1005–199 file, FEPC.

61. "Defense Worker Says Guard Tore Her Coat Sleeve," *Michigan Chronicle,* 18 Mar. 1944, 18.

62. Final Disposition Report, 31 Oct. 1944, case 5BR1367, MLR 25, box 239, case 5BR1367 file, FEPC.

63. G. James Fleming to Lawrence Cramer, 13 Mar. 1943, MLR 25, box 228, Fleming file, FEPC.

64. Ibid.

65. Incident Report and Follow Up, 25 Mar. 1945 to 25 June 1945, part 1, ser. 2, box 3, Incident Reports 1944–1945 folder, DCCR.

66. Memo to G. James Fleming and Jack Burke, 12 Feb. 1943, re: Vickers, MLR 25, box 228, Fleming file, FEPC; Detroit Progress Report and G. James Fleming to George Johnson, both 5 Mar. 1943, MLR 25, box 228, Fleming file, FEPC.

67. Final Disposition Reports 5BR1233, 29 June 1945, 5GR1317, 1 June 1945, 5BR1241, 28 Nov. 1944, and 5BR1497, 20 June 1945, all in MLR 25, box 239, files for cases 5BR1233, 5BR1317, 5BR1241, and 5BR1497, FEPC; Final Disposition Report 5GR1392, 20 Dec. 1944, MLR 25, box 240, 5GR1392 file, FEPC.

68. Velum Smith to FDR, 8 Nov. 1944, MLR 22, box 179, Defense 1944 file, WB.

69. Mary Anderson to Velum Smith, 21 Nov. 1944, MLR 22, box 179, Defense 1944 file, WB.

70. Sworn Statements of Dorothy Smith, Sue Ellen Oglesby, and Nellie Wimberly and Memo to Director of Civilian Personnel and Training from Truman K. Gibson, 1 May 1943, MLR 188, box 233, CASW; Filed Reports Complaint file; First Quarter of the Fair Practices Committee, box 1, folder 24, UAWFP&AD; Final Disposition Report, case 5BR1301, 30 June 1944, MLR 25, box 240, case 5BR1301 file, FEPC.

71. Clarence Mitchell to Joseph Evans, MLR 5, box 23, FEPC; Memo to Will Maslow and Joseph Evans, 3 July 1944, MLR 25, box 10, Richard Roche file, FEPC; Truman Gibson to Clarence Mitchell, 14 Feb. 1945, MLR 25, box 167, Region 4 file, FEPC.

72. "545 Promoted at Richmond Army Service Forces Depot," *Richmond Afro-American,* 18 Apr. 1944, 3.

73. Final Disposition Report, case 5BR1439, 22 Dec. 1944, MLR 25, box 240, case 5BR1439 file, FEPC.

74. Grievance 338, Oct. 1944, box 101, folder 7, UAWCD.

75. "Males Protest Firing of Two Colored Girls," *Detroit Tribune,* 30 Jan. 1943, 1.

76. Book 3, 13 Mar. 1942–12 Aug. 1943, 1427, box 1, UAW7; Answer to Grievance 1427, 6 Apr. 1943, box 3, folder 7, UAW7.

77. "Race Workers Strike over 'Woman Issue,'" *Michigan Chronicle,* 3 Apr. 1943, 9.

78. John Wood, "Inside Story of Chrysler Plant Strike," *Michigan Chronicle,* 27 Mar. 1943, 2.

79. Wood, "Inside Story."

80. "Packard Strikers Return to Jobs," *Detroit Tribune,* 27 Mar. 1943, 1; NAACP Annual Report, 1943, box 8, Mayor's Interracial Committee 1944 (1) folder, CFM; Edward Swan, Weekly Report for Week Ending 6 May 1944, MLR 25, box 259, Detroit file, FEPC; Strike Memo, Apr. 1944, MLR 25, box 110, Richard Roche file, FEPC.

81. "Threatened Strike at Hudson's Called Off," *Michigan Chronicle,* 20 Mar. 1943, 1.

82. Women's Bureau, *Negro Women War Workers,* 3.

83. *Current Observations of Detroit,* 7 Dec. 1943, box 5, Aug.–Dec. 1943 general file, DUL.

84. Manpower Supply Committee, War Production Board Field Information Circular 46, 14 Feb. 1944, 11, ACWP.

85. "Four Thousand Jobs Go A-Begging," *Richmond Afro-American,* 23 Oct. 1943, 1–2.

86. *TBI Fights* 5 (July 1945): 6, and *TBI Fights* 5 (Nov. 1944): 5, both in section 6, Personnel box 2, folder 44, TC.

87. "Domestic Help Runs Short as Women Take Men's Jobs," *Richmond News-Leader,* 25 Sept. 1942, box 7, Labor file, WWII.

88. Richmond Urban League *Messenger* 12 (Jan 1945), box 1B, folder 92, WWII.

89. Ann Folkes, "The Future of Domestic Help," *Richmond News-Leader,* 23 May 1944, 18.

90. Folkes, "The Future of Domestic Help."

91. Annual Descriptive Report for the Year 1945, 27, Industrial Department 1941–1945 folder, YWCA.

92. Annual Descriptive Report for the Year 1945, 31.

93. "Provisions Made to Care for Children of Mothers Who Work," *Michigan Chronicle,* 22 May 1943, 10; "New Day Nursery to Open for War Workers," *Michigan Chronicle,* 9 Oct. 1943, 16.

94. John Dancy to Mrs. Fred Johnson Charitable Fund, 31 Jan. 1944, box 5, Jan.–June 1944 general file, DUL.

95. Ann Chapman to John Dancy, 23 Nov. 1943, box 5, Aug.–Dec. 1943 general file, DUL.

96. Minutes from Board of Directors Meeting, 3 Dec. 1943, box 61, Board of Directors Minutes 1943 folder, DUL.

97. "Nursery School Fees Lowered," *Michigan Chronicle,* 12 Dec. 1944, 2.

98. "Nursery Schools and Day Care Centers Aid Working Mothers," *Richmond Afro-American,* 14 Aug. 1943, 14.

99. "City to Expand Nursery, Child Care Centers," *Richmond News-Leader,* 14 Mar. 1945, box 29, Nursery file, WWII.

100. "Women Workers in World War II: How to Counsel Them Series," 25, 8, MLR 22, box 205, Plant and Community Facilities file, WB.

101. McClusky and Smith, eds., *Mary McLeod Bethune,* 282.

Chapter 3: Looking Ahead

1. *Trade Week Guide,* 20–27 Nov. 1946, 1, box 5, Trade Week Guide file, HWL.

2. Address of Beulah Whitby, Proceedings, twenty-eighth annual Boule, 27–31 Dec. 1948, Morning Session, 24–25, box 1, AKA.

3. NCNW *Telefact* 7 (Dec. 1949): 1, ser. 13, box 2, folder 6, NCNW.

4. "Women Must Achieve Ideals of Democracy, Says NCNW Head," *Richmond Afro-American,* 13 June 1950, 10.

5. "Women Must Achieve Ideals of Democracy"; Fairclough, *Race and Democracy,* 112–13, 123–26, 153; Fairclough, *Better Day Coming,* 213.

6. "AKA Lobbyist Warns America on Home Front," *Michigan Chronicle,* 24 Nov. 1945, 5.

7. Thirteenth Annual Conference Minutes, 1948, 1–2, ser. 2, box 3, folder 40, NCNW.

8. Rogin, *Ronald Reagan,* 66–71.

9. Schrecker, *Many Are the Crimes,* 375, 389–93.

10. "Robeson Does Not Speak for Negro Women—Bethune," *Michigan Chronicle,* 30 Mar. 1949, 5.

11. Schrecker, *Many Are the Crimes,* 389–93; Report of the National President, Proceedings, twenty-eighth biennial session of the NACW, 1952, 18–19, reel 2, NACW.

12. Mink, *The Wages of Motherhood;* Sklar, "Historical Foundations," 43–94; Baker, "The Domestication of Politics," 55–91.

13. Gordon, "Black and White Visions of Welfare," 157–85; Boris, "The Power of Motherhood," 213–45.

14. May, *Homeward Bound,* 10–11, 91.

15. "Zetas View an Ideal Woman in Commemoration of Finer Womanhood Week," *The Panther,* 18 Apr. 1950, 3, VUUSC.

16. Mary Belle Rhodes, "Women Must Set Example for Children," *Michigan Chronicle,* 12 July 1947, 2.

17. Kevin Gaines addresses the problem of such earlier reformers as Alice Dunbar Nelson, who wrestled with trying to promote a domestic ideal without necessarily applying that ideal to themselves, which they understood as problematic for themselves (*Uplifting the Race,* 209–21).

18. "AKA Delegates Discuss Methods for Friendship," *Richmond Afro-American,* 26 Apr. 1947, 9.

19. Bonnie Parker, "Hampton Professor Tells Women of Future Role," *Richmond Afro-American,* 17 May 1947, 20.

20. The importance of maternalism to peace movements is discussed in Alonso, *The Women's Peace Union and the Outlawry of War;* Jensen, "All Pink Sisters," 199–219; Evans, *Born for Liberty;* and Ruddick, *Maternal Thinking.*

21. "Mrs. Bethune to Give Up Gavel during Women's Council Session," *Richmond Afro-American,* 24 Sept. 1949, 11.

22. "Peaceful World to Start at Home, She Tells Women," *Michigan Chronicle,* 21 July 1949, 22.

23. "Peaceful World to Start at Home."

24. Elaine Tyler May discusses these issues at great length in *Homeward Bound* (16, 30, 96–101, 109).

25. Boris, "The Power of Motherhood," 222–28.

26. Gaines asserts that there were significant problems with the middle-class using science to categorize and deem pathological working-class behavior because middle-class elites failed to see that the problems the working-class faced stemmed from structural economic issues rather than behavioral ones (*Uplifting the Race,* 152–79).

27. Bonnie Parker, "School Needs Public Funds to Remain Open," *Richmond Afro-American,* 8 Feb. 1947, 10.

28. "Local AKA Chapter Gives $600 Donation to Nursery," *Richmond Afro-American,* 15 Mar. 1947, 7; "Zetas Celebrate Womanhood Week," *Richmond Afro-American,* 6 Mar. 1948, 7; "Church in Community Day Nursery Celebrate at Halloween Fete," *Richmond Afro-American,* 12 Nov. 1949.

29. "Annual Report of Peter Pan Nursery of Detroit, Inc., June 1943–Dec. 1950," printed in 1951, 10, box 12, Peter Pan School file, CFM.

30. "March 30 Tea Will Launch New Campaign," *Michigan Chronicle,* 29 Mar. 1947, 3.

31. "Children's Play to Benefit Nursery," *Michigan Chronicle,* 17 Nov. 1951, 16; "Caption of Peter Pan Pictures," *Michigan Chronicle,* 20 Mar. 1954, 13; "Peter Pan Auxiliary in Initial Bridge," *Michigan Chronicle,* 26 June 1954, 15; "Izetta Ray Captures the 'Miss Peter Pan' Crown," *Michigan Chronicle,* 28 Aug. 1954, 16.

32. "AKA's Donate $1,500 to Equip Playgrounds," *Michigan Chronicle*, 4 June 1949, 6; "Camperships to Go to Selected Girls in Project," *Michigan Chronicle*, 22 June 1946, 5; "150 Tots Feted at YWCA Party," *Michigan Chronicle*, 26 Dec. 1953, 9.

33. "Girls Observe Y-Teen Roll Call with Varied Activities," *Richmond Afro-American*, 16 Oct. 1948, 13; "Youth Canteen Organized for Boys and Girls," *Michigan Chronicle*, 11 Oct. 1947, 2.

34. "Girls Observe Y-Teen Roll Call with Varied Activities"; Answers to Questionnaires for Teen Age Department, 1953, box 2, Executive Director Phillis Wheatley Branch Communications 1950–1953 folder, YWCA.

35. "Midwinter Conference for Girl Reserves," *Michigan Chronicle*, 6 May 1946, 11.

36. "Y Group Fights Delinquency," *Michigan Chronicle*, 14 Aug. 1954, 5.

37. Delta Home for Girls, Summary of Study Covering Years 1947–1954, 2, box 23, file 7, UCS.

38. Delta Home for Girls, Summary, 3.

39. Ibid., 5, 7.

40. "Report of Chairman, Delta Home For Girls," May 1952–53, box 41, Delta Home for Girls folder, DUL.

41. "Annual Report, 11 May 1955," box 41, Delta Home for Girls folder, DUL.

42. "Report of Chairman, Delta Home for Girls," May 1952–53.

43. Solinger, *Wake Up Little Susie*, discusses the fact that white women could be "rehabilitated" if they went to maternity homes and gave up their children for adoption. The women learned the skills that social workers thought would make them good mothers and wives during their stays in the homes.

44. "Delta Dinner," *Michigan Chronicle*, 8 May 1954, 19.

45. May, *Homeward Bound*, 103–7.

46. "Red Cross Plans Nursing Classes," *Richmond Afro-American*, 29 Nov. 1947, 9.

47. "Ten Home Nurses Get Certificates," *Richmond Afro-American*, 14 Feb. 1948, 3.

48. "Red Cross Class Has 100 Percent Record," *Richmond Afro-American*, 29 Oct. 1949, 3.

49. "First Nurses' Aides Are Graduated: Red Cross Trainees Eight Women for CD," *Richmond Afro-American*, 28 Aug. 1951, 20; "Nurses' Aides at St. Phillip," *Richmond Afro-American*, 9 Aug. 1951, 18.

50. "Red Cross Aide Trainees," *Michigan Chronicle*, 3 Nov. 1951, 6; "Receive Nursing Certificates," *Michigan Chronicle*, 14 Feb. 1953, 7.

51. "Praises Job Done by Red Cross," *Michigan Chronicle*, 25 Sept. 1954, 23.

52. "Leigh St. USO to Close Sept. 30," *Richmond Afro-American*, 6 Sept. 1947, 7; "USO Transit Lounge Closed," *Richmond Afro-American*, 19 Apr. 1947, 9.

53. "USO Dead, Women Volunteers Carry on Work in Richmond," *Richmond Afro-American*, 14 Feb. 1948, 11.

54. "Holiday Cheer for Hospitalized Veterans," *Richmond Afro-American* 23 Apr. 1949, 10; "Members of GSO Display Yule Stockings," *Richmond Afro-American*, 7 Jan. 1950, 1; Olivia Daniels to Miss Ella Turner, 27 Dec. 1954, box 2, Executive Director Associated Agencies Richmond USO 1954 folder, YWCA.

55. "Organization First Formed as YWCA-GSO," *Michigan Chronicle*, 28 Dec. 1946, 3; "John R. USO Hostesses Give Formal Party," *Michigan Chronicle*, 26 Mar. 1946, 10; "USO Host to Navy at Park," *Michigan Chronicle*, 23 Aug. 1952, 26; "New Year's Dinner Success,"

Michigan Chronicle, 10 Jan. 1953, 15; Jeannie Kemp, "Just Visit the USO," *Michigan Chronicle,* 2 May 1953, 15.

56. "Charity Club to Aid Armed Forces Members," *Michigan Chronicle,* 26 July 1952, 26.

57. "Young Women, the USO Needs You!" *Michigan Chronicle,* 27 Mar. 1954, 21.

58. "USO Junior Hostesses Tread Glory Road," *Michigan Chronicle,* 10 Apr. 1954, 15.

59. "Just Visit the USO."

60. Minutes and Records of the twenty-fifth National Convention, 27 July–2 Aug. 1946, 68, reel 2, NACW.

61. Emma Bradslaw, "Mrs. Lawson Civic Leader for Ten Years," *Richmond Afro-American,* 5 Nov. 1949, 9; "AKA Lobbyist to Speak at FEPC Meeting Sunday," *Richmond Afro-American,* 26 May 1945, 6; "Drive for $2,750 FEPC Fund Set to Open Friday," *Richmond Afro-American,* 6 Oct. 1945, 8; "Local FEPC Council Will Present Singer at Rally," *Richmond Afro-American,* 11 May 1946, 7.

62. "Gloster Current at Panhellenic Council Meet," *Michigan Chronicle,* 25 May 1946, 19.

63. "Co-Ette's Mother and Daughter Tea," *Michigan Chronicle,* 18 May 1948, 13.

64. "Raises $100 for the NAACP," *Richmond Afro-American,* 26 Feb. 1949, 3; "NAACP Membership Campaign Launched in Meeting at Local Church," *Richmond Afro-American,* 14 May 1949, 18.

65. "Navy Hill Teachers 100 Percent behind NAACP," *Richmond Afro-American,* 14 Apr. 1951, 8; "Moore School Faculty Gets behind NAACP," *Richmond Afro-American.* 5 May 1951, 13.

66. "NAACP Membership Drive Gets Going," *Michigan Chronicle,* 11 May 1946, 2; "Local Branch Hopes to Make 25,000 Quota," *Michigan Chronicle,* 28 June 1947, 2.

67. "Beauties Boost NAACP Cause," *Michigan Chronicle,* 6 May 1950, 1.

68. "Fight for Freedom," *Michigan Chronicle,* 10 Apr. 1954, 3.

69. Hill, *The Big Bang,* 91–135.

70. "Women Gather to Aid Fund Drive," *Richmond Afro-American,* 24 Sept. 1949, 10.

71. "Women March on Capitol, Urge Anti-Poll Tax Bill," *Richmond Afro-American,* 3 Aug. 1946, 19.

72. Non-Partisan Political Forum, Reports of the 1948 NACW Convention, reel 11, NACW.

73. NCNW *Telefact* 7 (July 1948): 2, ser. 13, box 2, folder 9, NCNW.

74. NCNW *Telefact* (Sept.–Oct. 1952): 5, ser. 13, box 2, folder 9, NCNW.

75. Lula Patterson, "Towards the Distaff," *Richmond Afro-American,* 2 Mar. 1946, 2.

76. "Deltas Aid in Hill Campaign," *Richmond Afro-American,* 24 Apr. 1948, 11; "Deltas Observe May Week," *Richmond Afro-American,* 5 June 1948, 10.

77. Tyler-McGraw, *At the Falls,* 282–84.

78. "Radio, Block, and Finance Committees of the Women for Ransome Group," *Richmond Afro-American,* 30 July 1949, 1; "Richmond Women Plan Permanent Civic Group," *Richmond Afro-American,* 3 Sept. 1949, 13.

79. "Women Workers Aid Diggs Campaign," *Michigan Chronicle,* 30 Oct. 1954, 10; "Congressman Diggs," *Michigan Chronicle,* 13 Nov. 1954, 23.

80. Bradslaw, "Mrs. Lawson Civic Leader for Ten Years."

81. "Organizing Women," *Michigan Chronicle*, 1 June 1946, 16; "Benefit Tea at Boston Home Draws Women," *Michigan Chronicle*, 8 June 1946, 10.

82. "Elk Temple to Sponsor Civil Liberties Parley," *Richmond Afro-American*, 25 Jan. 1947, 20; "Beta Upsilon," *Delta Journal* 18 (1948): 91; NCNW *Telefact*, Apr. 1950, 4, ser. 13, box 2, folder 7, NCNW.

83. "Miss Burroughs to Speak at Interracial Meeting," *Richmond Afro-American*, 27 Sept. 1947, 3; "YWCA Business, Professional Girls Hold Interracial Fete," *Richmond Afro-American*, 6 Apr. 1946, 12; Minutes of Board of Directors, 15 Dec. 1948, 2, box 8, Minutes of Board of Directors 1948 folder, YWCA.

84. Summary of Meeting of the Chairman, Discussion Leaders, Recorders, 13 Nov. 1946, ser. 2, box 2, folder 28, NCNW; Beulah Whitby to Rev. A. A. Banks, 19 Apr. 1949, reel 3, SBC.

85. Statement of Bethune before Ways and Means Committee, 13 Mar. 1946, ser. 5, box 11, folder 8, NCNW.

86. Ida Coker Clark, "Security for the Negro Woman Worker," *Aframerican Women's Journal*, Sept. 1945, 12, ser. 13, box 1, folder 18, NCNW.

87. Clark, "Security for the Negro Woman Worker," 30.

88. Statement of Bethune before House Education Committee, 20 May 1949, ser. 5, box 11, folder 9, NCNW.

89. Gaines studies the class bias inherent in elites' focus on industrial training, as they believed that only a small group of talented leaders should receive a classical education and then go on to represent the multitudes. These leaders believed that all other African Americans would do well to have a skill that they could perform well in order to maintain a certain degree of economic autonomy (*Uplifting the Race*, 19–67).

90. J. E. Bradston, "Pupils Learn to Sell in Class and on Job," *Richmond Afro-American*, 8 Oct. 1952, 3.

91. "Job Opportunity Campaign Organized," *Richmond Afro-American*, 20 Feb. 1954, 18.

92. "NAACP Executive to Address Delta Sorors," *Michigan Chronicle*, 20 Feb. 1947, 2; Thelma Radden to Alpha Pi Sigma and Tau Chapters of Delta Sigma Theta, 7 Apr. 1949, box 1, general file Mar.–Apr. 1949, FAK; "Job Clinics Feature of Meet," *Michigan Chronicle*, 13 Mar. 1948, 4; "Seventeenth Anniversary Program Planned for Detroit Urban League Campaign," *Michigan Chronicle*, 12 Mar. 1949, 3; "Experts Help Youths Plan for Careers," *Michigan Chronicle*, 18 Mar. 1950, 18.

93. "Career Clinic Holds Interest of Sherrard Student Group," *Michigan Chronicle*, 26 May 1951, 15; "Students Tour A. W. Curtis Plant," *Michigan Chronicle*, 7 Mar. 1951, 4.

94. "Recommended Standards for Household Employment," *Richmond Afro-American*, 2 Oct. 1948, 12; "Housewives Level Criticism at Employment Survey Report," *Richmond Afro-American*, 9 Oct. 1948, 4.

95. "League Sponsors Household Course," *Richmond Afro-American*, 25 Sept. 1948, 1.

96. Minutes of Board of Directors, 27 Oct. 1948, 2–3, box 8, Board of Directors Minutes folder, YWCA.

97. "YWCA to Offer Varied Program for Domestics," *Michigan Chronicle*, 20 Sept. 1947, 3.

98. "Mrs. Rosa Gragg Is Bethel AME Speaker," undated, box 17, Bethel AME Church 1947–1957 folder, RGP.

99. Slade–Gragg Academy of Practical Arts Bulletin, 1950–1951, 8, box 2, Correspondence 1950s (2) folder, RGP.

100. Ibid.

101. "Gragg Institute and Dorm for Students and Working Girls," box 15, Correspondence folder, RGP.

102. "New Project Opened for Public Survey," undated clipping, box 15, Slade–Gragg Academy (2) folder, RGP. Rosa Gragg followed Washington's example by arguing that vocational education would best help the African American community thrive.

103. "Zeta Presents Charm School," *Michigan Chronicle*, 18 Mar. 1950, 13; "Mrs. Lillian Hatcher Named Woman of the Year by Zeta Sorority," *Michigan Chronicle*, 8 Mar. 1952, 6.

104. "Deltas Order Tobacco Ban," *Richmond Afro-American*, 19 Jan. 1946, 13.

105. Vivienne, "Hear City Commissioners at Delta Brunch," *Michigan Chronicle*, 24 Nov. 1945, 9.

Chapter 4: Trying to Hold On

1. "Women War Workers Find New Interests," *Michigan Chronicle*, 8 Sept. 1945, 2.

2. Minnie Wilson Complaint Case file, box 14, folder 8, UAWFP&AD.

3. Anderson, "Last Hired, First Fired," 95–97.

4. Fried, *Nightmare in Red*, 164.

5. Many works discuss America's move to the right and the effects that had on personal freedoms. They include Fried, *Nightmare in Red*; Rogin, *Ronald Reagan*; and May, *Homeward Bound*.

6. Fried, *Nightmare in Red*; Sugrue, *The Origins of the Urban Crisis*, 153–79.

7. Lichtenstein, *Walter Reuther*, 252.

8. Ibid., 282–87; Brown, *Race, Money, and the American Welfare State*, 164. Lipsitz maintains that the CIO pulled back from organizing efforts in the South because of a fear of communism and that union, government, and business actively worked to remove women from lucrative jobs as well as suppress democracy in factories (*Rainbow at Midnight*, 193, 336).

9. Sugrue, *The Origins of the Urban Crisis*, 47–55; Silver, *Twentieth-Century Richmond*, 184–85.

10. Excerpts from Minutes of the Detroit Urban League Industrial Associates, 12 Dec. 1944, 5, box 5, Industrial Associates folder, DUL; Richard Dier, "Twenty Million Women Workers Vanish," *Richmond Afro-American*, 20 July 1946, 8; Minutes, War Manpower Priorities Committee, Richmond-Petersburg Area, MLR 59, box 15, Richmond file, WMC, NA; "60,000 Workers Idle as Unemployment Rises," *Michigan Chronicle*, 12 Feb. 1949, 8; "Chronicle Continues Probe into Plant Hiring Practices," *Michigan Chronicle*, 17 July 1953, 5.

11. Sweetie Hall to Albert Cobo, 12 Oct. 1950, pt. 1, ser. 1, box 7, folder 50–48E, DCCR.

12. For Hall's case, see pt. 1, ser. 1, box 7, folder 50–48E, DCCR.

13. Report of Meeting re: Discrimination in Retail Trades, 5 Dec. 1945, pt. 3, ser. 7, box 74, folder 75–11, DCCR.

14. "Sam's Cut Rate Hires First Negro Saleswoman," *Michigan Chronicle*, 10 May 1952, 1.

15. Kaye Alford to Earnest Brown, 12 Jan. 1951, box 4, Discrimination file, FAK; Industrial Relations Committee Minutes, 27 Mar. 1951, 3, box 5, Industrial Relations of Urban League 1951 file, FAK; Departmental Reports 1946, box 61, Departmental Reports 1946 file, DUL.

16. Testimonial of Johnnie Kendrick, 1948, Testimony of Pauline Adkins, 19 Feb. 1948, Testimony of Ruth Price, 28 Apr. 1948, Testimony of Annie Mae Little, 26 July 1948, and Letter from Miss A. J. Moore to James Webber, 29 Nov. 1948, all in box 5, J. L. Hudson Company file, FAK.

17. Miss A. J. Moore to Mrs. Louis Frank, box 5, J. L. Hudson Company file, FAK.

18. "Department Store Employees," *Michigan Chronicle,* 9 May 1953, 18; Vocational Services Department Report Digest, box 1, Jan.–Apr. 1953 file, FAK.

19. "Brotherhood in Action," *Michigan Chronicle,* 21 Feb. 1953, 5.

20. Anderson, "Last Hired, First Fired," 95.

21. "Announce Plan to Hire Help without Bias," *Michigan Chronicle,* 12 Oct. 1946, 1, 19; "Detroit Girls Get Hundreds of Calls a Day," *Michigan Chronicle,* 21 Jan. 1950, 9; Doris Burney to Francis Albert Kornegay, 2 Mar. 1953, box 1, Jan.–Apr. 1953 file, FAK; Irma Robinson to Francis Kornegay, box 2, May–Dec. 1953 file, FAK.

22. Minutes, Manpower Priorities Committee, 26 May 1944, 1–2, MLR 59, box 15, Richmond file, WMC, NA.

23. Quality Services Flyer, box 1, Executive Director Associated Agencies Richmond Race Relations folder, YWCA.

24. "Blazing Trail for Others," *Richmond Afro-American,* 12 June 1948, 3.

25. Wilentz, *Chants Democratic;* Montgomery, *The Fall of the House of Labor;* and Roediger, *The Wages of Whiteness* all discuss the ways in which white working-class men defined citizenship by their relative control over their own labor.

26. Beatrice Woodruff to Guy Nunn, 22 Nov. 1952, box 14, folder 11, UAWFP&AD.

27. William Oliver to Al Musilli, 10 Dec. 1952, box 14, folder 11, UAWFP&AD.

28. Open Letter, *Dodge Main News,* 7 Aug. 1948, 1; William Oliver to Michael Lacy, 1950, box 15, folder 35, UAWFP&AD; William Oliver to Francis Albert Kornegay, 20 Mar. 1951, box 4, Discrimination Cases file, FAK; William Oliver to Caroline Davis, 20 Mar. 1951, box 15, folder 25, UAWFP&AD; Minutes of National Advisory Council of Fair Practices and Anti-Discrimination Department, 14–15 Apr. 1953, 3, box 26, folder 9, UAWFP&AD.

29. "Auto Plant Bias under Attack by UAW-CIO," *Michigan Chronicle,* 22 Nov. 1952, 1, 4.

30. William Oliver to Richard Leonard, 30 July 1946, and Richard Leonard to William Oliver, 19 Aug. 1946, both in box 16, folder 33, UAWFP&AD.

31. "Two Women Re-Instated, Get $2000.00 Back Pay," *Michigan Chronicle,* 27 Oct. 1945, 1.

32. Louise Hamilton to William Oliver, 5 Nov. 1946, box 8, Local 600–Aircraft folder, UAWFD.

33. Richard Leonard to Peter Casper, 21 Nov. 1946, box 8, Local 600–Aircraft folder, UAWFD; Louise Hamilton to William Oliver, 23 Dec. 1946, box 7, folder 26, UAWFP&AD.

34. Report of John Clark, Local 961, Case of Thelma Hubert, box 16, folder 19, UAWFP&AD; Memo from Lillian Hatcher to William Oliver, 22 Feb. 1950, box 15, folder 39, UAWFP&AD; William Oliver to Arthur Johnson, 1 Sept. 1953, box 14, folder 11, UAWFP&AD.

35. Meeting of Case and Clearance Committee, 21 Nov. 1945, pt. 3, ser. 7, box 75, folder 75–11, DCCR; Case 52–20Ec, 11 July 1952, pt. 1, ser. 1, box 9, folder 52–20Ec, DCCR.

36. Richard Leonard to Joseph Ritivoy, 7 Mar. 1945, box 3, folder 17, UAWFP&AD.

37. Interview with Fannie Brown, 10 Apr. 1947, and letter from Lillian Hatcher to Peter Kasper, 22 May 1947, box 14, folder 24, UAWFP&AD; Fair Practices Committee Report, Case of Fannie Brown, 13 July 1947, box 14, folder 24, UAWFP&AD.

38. "Thirty-one Women vs. the Giant Chrysler Corp.," *Dodge Main News,* 12 June 1948, 3–4.

39. Memo Regarding Employment Practices at Murray Corp., box 15, folder 25, UAWFP&AD; Hubert MacEwen to William Oliver, 9 Dec. 1946, box 15, folder 30, UAWFP&AD; E. M. Carey to Lillian Hatcher, 6 Jan. 1947, box 16, folder 8, UAWFP&AD; GM Fleetwood Plant Johnnie Wash and Emma Glover Case, 17 May 1948, box 16, folder 20, UAWFP&AD; "Union Sues Briggs for Wage Claim," *Michigan Chronicle,* 13 Nov. 1948, 3; Charles Wartman, "On the Labor Line," *Michigan Chronicle,* 5 Feb. 1949, 9; Report of Fair Practices Sub-Committee, 21 Nov. 1952, box 16, folder 31, UAWFP&AD; "Women Laid-Off Sue for $500,000," *Michigan Chronicle,* 31 July 1954, 6.

40. Gabin, *Feminism in the Labor Movement,* 136.

41. Lichtenstein, *Walter Reuther,* 287.

42. "Va. Workers Get $25,000 Pay Hike," *Richmond Afro-American,* 22 Sept. 1945, 1, 19.

43. "Five Organizers Appointed by CIO," *Richmond Afro-American,* 21 Sept. 1946, 24.

44. "Officers of Local 216 A.F. of L.," *Richmond Afro-American,* 16 Mar. 1946, 3; Pauline Christianson to John O'Hare, 21 Apr. 1949, Settlement in Matter between Local 216 and Christianson, and Synopsis of Case with Reference to the Recall of Mrs. Hattie Hubbard, ser. 3, box 31, Local 216 1949–1961 file, TWIU.

45. George Crockett to Bruce Dodge, 22 Apr. 1946, box 14, folder 18, UAWFP&AD; transcript of Sammons Case against Local 36, 14, 15, 21–22, 29, 122, box 6, folder 3, UAWFP&AD; Case 7, Fair Practices Committee Decisions, box 2, folder 10, UAWFP&ADWB.

46. "Va. Tobacco Firm Sued by Worker for $10,000," *Richmond Afro-American,* 23 Oct. 1949, 1–2.

47. Josephine McCloudy to William Oliver, 31 Jan. 1947, box 15, folder 36, UAWFP&AD; "Employees Segregated in Richmond P.O. Cafeteria," *Richmond Afro-American,* 4 Sept. 1945, 1–2.

48. "Negro Beauty Is Voted Local 600 Contest Winner," *Michigan Chronicle,* 23 Aug. 1947, 1; Charles Wartman, "On the Labor Line," *Michigan Chronicle,* 17 Jan. 1948, 13.

49. "Girls Strike to Get Raise at Viviano's," *Michigan Chronicle,* 27 July 1946, 2; "Accuse Pair of Striking Woman with Picket Sign," *Michigan Chronicle,* 27 Nov. 1948, 3; "Policy Holders Plan Action in Insurance Fight," *Michigan Chronicle,* 18 Dec. 1948, 3; "Great Lakes Strike Fizzles, UOPWA Deserts Girls," *Michigan Chronicle,* 2 Apr. 1949, 1, 4; Charles Wartman, "On the Labor Line," *Michigan Chronicle,* 30 Apr. 1949, 9; *Ford Facts 600,* 20 Nov. 1948, 1.

50. "Harper Patients Snack, AFL Strike Cuts Diets," *Michigan Chronicle,* 13 Nov. 1948, 1, 4; "Still Walking after Two Weeks," *Michigan Chronicle,* 20 Nov. 1948, 1; "Harper Hospital Superintendent Says Union Threatened Workers," *Michigan Chronicle,* 8 Jan. 1949, 2; Case 48–137, 15 Nov. 1948, pt. 1, ser. 1, box 4, folder 48–137, DCCR.

51. "Patrons Urged to Avoid Three Plants," *Richmond Afro-American,* 16 Nov. 1946, 3;

"115 Workers Cheat Death in Laundry Wall Cave-In," *Richmond Afro-American,* 15 Mar. 1947, 16; "Workers Say Laundries Employ Ruthless Tactics," *Richmond Afro-American,* 11 Nov. 1947, 5.

52. "Women Picket Pie Shop," *Richmond Afro-American,* 5 Sept. 1951, 14.

53. Anderson, "Last Hired, First Fired," 97.

54. Report of Urban League Vocational Services Department, 1948, box 68, Departmental Reports 1948 file, DUL.

55. Detroit 1950s Monthly Reports, ser. 7, box 55, Detroit 1950s Monthly Reports file, NUL.

56. Annual Report, Richmond Urban League *Messenger,* ser. 1, box 26, Richmond file, NUL.

57. Annual Report, Richmond Urban League *Messenger,* ser. 1, box 123, Richmond file, NUL.

58. Mildred Williams, "Local Domestic Help Supply Found Better," *Richmond News-Leader,* 29 Aug. 1946, 21.

59. Reports of Vocational Service Department, Vocational Service Department files 1947, 1948, 1949, 1950, 1951, 1952, box 6, FAK.

60. Vocational Services Department Employment of Negroes with the Following Bakeries in Detroit, 20 June 1950, box 1, Apr.–Dec. 1950 file, FAK; "Key Placements," 21 Sept. 1951, box 1, Apr.–Dec. 1951 folder, FAK; Francis Albert Kornegay to Morlean Helen Austin, 3 Oct. 1945, box 1, general file Sept.–Oct. 1945, FAK; Vocational Services Department Program Report, 13 May 1954, box 2, Jan.–June 1954 file, FAK.

61. Hale, *Making Whiteness,* 125.

62. *TBI Talks* 7 (Apr. 1947): 7–8, *TBI Talks* 8 (July 1948): 8, *TBI Talks* 9 (Dec. 1949): 7, *TBI Talks* 10 (Apr. 1950): 11, and *TBI Talks* 10 (Nov. 1950): 3, 11, all in section 6, box 2, folder 45, TC.

63. Richmond Urban League *Messenger,* Annual Report 1946, 9.

64. Many historians and sociologists have addressed the issue of African American working poor women as activists as they negotiate state welfare systems in order to get benefits for themselves and their families, including Stack, *All Our Kin;* Gordon, *Pitied but Not Entitled;* Polatnick, "Diversity in Women's Liberation Ideology," 679–706; Amott, "Black Women and AFDC," 281–98.

65. Goodwin, *Gender and the Politics of Welfare Reform,* 23, 57.

66. Ibid., 185; Gordon, *Pitied but Not Entitled,* 5–11.

67. Gordon, *Pitied but Not Entitled,* 5; Brown, *Race, Money, and the American Welfare State,* 70, 82, 85; Goodwin, *Gender and the Politics of Welfare Reform,* 188; Mettler, *Dividing Citizens,* 20–25, 45, 143–76.

68. Brown, *Race, Money, and the American Welfare State,* 106–9, 127. It is impossible to know how many African American women were on welfare in Detroit from 1940 to 1954 because the Department of Public Welfare, now the Family Independence Agency, did not classify cases by race or gender during that period.

69. Abbie Veal to Appeals Board, 12 Oct. 1949, Interoffice Communication, 8 Nov. 1949, box 20, DPW folder, RGP.

70. "East Side Groups Hit Welfare Department Rules," *Michigan Chronicle,* 4 Mar. 1950, 2.

71. "Widow Comforts Self and Destitute Family of Eight with Trust in God for Providing Money for Food and Clothing," *Michigan Chronicle,* 11 Nov. 1950, 9.

72. "Nursery School Fight Takes Form of Picket Line," *Michigan Chronicle,* 13 Oct. 1945, 5; "Nursery School for Mothers Is Expanded," *Michigan Chronicle,* 10 Oct. 1953, 3.

73. "Families Facing Tragedy Because of Living Costs," *Richmond Afro-American,* 18 Oct. 1947, 3.

74. Richmond's Welfare Department kept cost disbursements in its annual reports but failed to note who received those disbursements. The Department of Health kept records on how many women attended clinics. Many more African American women than white women demanded vaccinations for their children, as well as the services of visiting nurses and prenatal care, between 1940 and 1950, which suggests they were conscious of their rights to benefits and more than willing to work to get those benefits. Information can be found in Richmond Department of Public Health Reports, Annual City Reports, and Richmond Department of Welfare Reports, Virginia State Library and Archives, Richmond.

75. Caseworker note by Louise Blaine, box 20, E.H. folder, YWCA.

76. M.L.P. Caseworker file, 27 Nov. 1951, box 21, M.P. folder, YWCA.

77. A.H. to Rebekah Lee, 21 July 1948, 1949, and 1951, Caseworker Report, box 20, A.H. folder, YWCA.

78. Jean Collmus to Rebekah Lee, 14 Feb. 1947, box 21, I.S. folder, YWCA.

79. Case files, boxes 19–21, quotations come from B.B. file and J.C. folder, YWCA.

80. I.J. to Community Chest, 19 May 1952, box 20, M.F. folder, YWCA.

81. Report to Lumsden Committee from Family Services Committee, 6 June 1949, box 20, P.B.L. folder, YWCA.

82. Ethel Chambers, Caseworker, to Hazel Ormsbee, 23 June 1950, box 19, A.A. folder, YWCA.

83. Mayor's Interracial Committee, *Analysis and Recommendations Regarding the Racial Occupancy Policy and Practice of the Detroit Housing Commission,* 24 May 1952, 5, box 38, Community Services Mar.–June 1952 file, DUL. Sugrue discusses the origins of the Detroit housing crisis in *The Origins of the Urban Crisis,* 41–55.

84. "'We Want a Home!'" *Michigan Chronicle,* 7 Oct. 1950, 3.

85. Willie Johnson to Urban League, 31 Oct. 1951, box 38, Community Services June–Dec. 1951 file, DUL.

86. Silver and Moeser discuss the housing policies of Richmond, Memphis, and Atlanta in *The Separate City.*

87. "Creighton Court Apartments Open," *Richmond Afro-American,* 29 Nov. 1952, 14.

88. Complaints file from Visiting Nurses Association, box 58, Complaints file, CHP.

89. Block Unit Reports, 1945, and "Forms First Block Clubs," clipping, 18 Aug. 1945, both in box 62, Departmental Reports 1945 file, DUL; Dec. 1948 Block Unit Bulletin, box 37, Community Service Department July–Dec. 1948 general file, DUL; "Winning Supervisors in Clean Block Contest," *Michigan Chronicle,* 15 Sept. 1945, 13; "Clean Block Campaign Nears Close," *Michigan Chronicle,* 31 Aug. 1946, 20; "Detroit to Select Clean-Up Queen," *Michigan Chronicle,* 7 May 1951, 7.

90. "Report of Housing Situation as It Affects the Community in the Gratoit Redevel-

opment Area," ser. 3, box 54, Detroit Housing file, NUL; Naomi Witherspoon, "See Proposal as Start of New Problems," *Michigan Chronicle,* 31 Aug. 1946, 27.

91. *Analysis and Recommendations Regarding the Racial Occupancy Policy.*

92. Memo about the Douglass–Jeffries Move, Feb. 1950, box 37, Community Service Department, Jan.–Mar. 1950 file, DUL; City of Detroit Housing Commission to Circuit Court Commissioner, box 37, Community Service Department, July–Dec. 1950 file, DUL; "250 Tenants Win Eviction Delay," *Michigan Chronicle,* 27 May 1950, 6.

93. "Complete Facts Not Known by Residents," *Richmond Afro-American,* 21 June 1951, 13; *Analysis and Recommendations Regarding the Racial Occupancy Policy;* Memo about the Douglass–Jeffries Move; City of Detroit Housing Commission to Circuit Court Commissioner, box 37, Community Service Department, July-Dec. 1950 file, DUL; "250 Tenants Win Eviction Delay," *Michigan Chronicle,* 27 May 1950, 6.

94. Sugrue discusses the importance of neighborhood activism in the face of expressway construction and slum clearance in *The Origins of the Urban Crisis* (47–51).

Chapter 5: Claiming Space

1. "Appeal Planned for Two Fined for Sitting in Front of Whites," *Richmond Afro-American,* 6 Mar. 1943, 20.

2. "Refuse Teacher Café Service, She May Get Warrant," *Michigan Chronicle,* 15 July 1944, 1–2.

3. "Democrat Women Ask Registration of Voters," *Michigan Chronicle,* 30 Sept. 1944, 16.

4. NCNW *Telefact* 1 (Sept. 1943), ser. 13, box 2, folder 1, NCNW.

5. "Deadline Is Set on Vote by League," *Richmond Afro-American,* 11 May 1940, 4; "NAACP to Hold Poll Tax Drive," *Richmond Afro-American,* 21 Sept. 1940, 3; "Mrs. Bethune Calls Vote Chief Weapon," *Richmond Afro-American,* 18 Oct. 1941, 13.

6. "League Told Vote Will Net Progress," *Richmond Afro-American,* 26 Apr. 1941, 13.

7. Jeanetta Welch, "About Women," *Michigan Chronicle,* 20 Feb. 1943, 7.

8. "NAACP Volunteers Registered Voters," *Michigan Chronicle,* 23 Oct. 1943, 5.

9. "Salvation via Votes," *Richmond Afro-American,* 15 Feb. 1947, 9.

10. "Council Peps Up Suffrage Drive," *Richmond Afro-American,* 26 Apr. 1947, 7; "Council Speeds Up Registration," *Richmond Afro-American,* 7 June 1947, 3.

11. "Civic League Launches Drive to Get Out the Vote," *Richmond Afro-American,* 19 May 1949, 3; "Registering Voters," *Richmond Afro-American,* 6 Aug. 1949, 8; "Delver Women's Club, Only Four Years Old, Has Grown Up," *Richmond Afro-American,* 6 May 1950, 10.

12. Thompson, *Whose Detroit?* 14–15.

13. "Women's Club to Hold Vote Institute," *Michigan Chronicle,* 22 Oct. 1949, 14.

14. "National Officer Addresses CIO Women's Group," *Michigan Chronicle,* 22 June 1946, 2.

15. "Local 216, A.F. of L., Elects Vote Committee," *Richmond Afro-American,* 20 Apr. 1946, 7.

16. "Boat Co. Refuses to Take Negro Reserves," *Michigan Chronicle,* 12 Aug. 1944, 1.

17. "Files Complaint with Prosecutor's Office," *Michigan Chronicle,* 30 June 1945, 1–2.

18. "Judge Maher Denies New Trial to Bob-Lo Boat Company," *Michigan Chronicle*, 8 Dec. 1945, 1.

19. Case 47–51CR file, pt. 1, ser. 1, box 4, folder 47–51CR, DCCR.

20. "Two Families Lose Cases against Restrictions," *Michigan Chronicle*, 26 Apr. 1947, 1–2.

21. "'White,' 'Colored' Bond Tickets to Sinatra Show," *Richmond Afro-American*, 29 Dec. 1945, 1–2.

22. "'White,' 'Colored' Bond Tickets."

23. "Jim Crow Mars Recital by Camilla Williams at Mosque," *Richmond Afro-American*, 15 Feb. 1947, 8.

24. Charles Wartman, "Restaurant Policy Takes Three Forms," *Michigan Chronicle*, 6 Aug. 1949, 1, 4.

25. "White Restaurant Owner Fined for Refusing to Serve Colored Girl," *Detroit Tribune*, 16 Sept. 1941, 1.

26. "Refused Service, CIO Secretary Enters Complaint," *Michigan Chronicle*, 8 July 1944, 1, 5.

27. "Second Guilty Verdict Given in Five Years," *Michigan Chronicle*, 5 Aug. 1944, 1, 4.

28. "CIO Group to Conduct Drive in Restaurants," *Michigan Chronicle*, 18 Aug. 1944, 1, 4.

29. "Mrs. Jessie Dillard Gives Report on Branch Project," *Michigan Chronicle*, 15 Oct. 1949, 9; "NAACP Opens Drive to Wipe Out Café Bias," *Michigan Chronicle*, 22 Oct. 1949, 1, 4.

30. Case 1, NAACP Committee to Fight Restaurant Discrimination, *Dillard v. Presto*, box 6, folder 7, UAWFP&AD.

31. "NAACP Schedules Mass Meeting to Fight Bias," *Michigan Chronicle*, 29 Oct. 1949, 6.

32. The following are all in pt. 1, ser. 1, DCCR: Incident Report, 3 Apr. 1945, box 3, Incident Reports 1944–1945 folder; case 131, 13 Oct. 1948, box 4, folder 48–131; Civil Rights Report 118, 9 Sept. 1948, box 5, folder 48–118; Civil Rights Report 111, 16 Aug. 1948, box 5, folder 48–118; Report on 4 May 1949, box 6, folder 49–20CR; Albert Lehman to George Sherman, 23 June 1948, box 5, folder 48–108; Case Report no. 49, 6 May 1947, box 4, folder 47–49CR; Case Report no. 47, 28 Apr. 1947, box 4, folder 47–47CR; Incident Report, 3 Apr. 1945, box 3, Incident Reports 1944–1945 folder; and Report on 4 May 1949, box 6, folder 49–20CR; see also "NAACP Schedules Mass Meeting to Fight Bias," 6.

33. Incident Reports, *Community Barometer*, 26 Oct. 1944, 1–2, pt. 1, ser. 1, box 1, Reports 1944 folder, DCCR.

34. "Bar Owner Refuses to Serve Woman," *Michigan Chronicle*, 23 Aug. 1952, 6; "Bar Owner Fined $100 Race Bias," *Michigan Chronicle*, 4 Oct. 1952, 1.

35. "Waitress Given Probation after Refuses Service," *Michigan Chronicle*, 7 July 1945, 7; "Jury Acquits Two of Civil Rights Snub in Tavern," *Michigan Chronicle*, 27 Mar. 1954, 1–2; Clippings from *Michigan Chronicle*, 14 Apr. 1951, pt. 1, ser. 1, box 8, folder 51–27CR, DCCR.

36. "Leaders Will Not Postpone Efforts till 1946," *Richmond Afro-American*, 29 Jan. 1944, 1–2; "Va.'s Jim Crow Bus Law Enacted in 1930," *Richmond Afro-American*, 8 June 1946, 1–2.

37. White, *Too Heavy a Load*, 92–93. This issue is also discussed by Welke ("When All Women Were White," 261–316).

38. "Ingram to Study Segregation Case," *Richmond Afro-American,* 27 Sept. 1947, 13; Annual Report, Richmond NAACP Activities, 1948, box C278, Richmond file, NAACP.

39. "Nurse Appeals $10 Fine for Violating Segregation Law," *Richmond Afro-American,* 10 Jan. 1948, 9.

40. "Attorneys Appeal Girl's Conviction," *Richmond Afro-American,* 30 May 1953, 1.

41. "The Pupils Speak of How They Feel," *Richmond Afro-American,* 23 May 1953, 1.

42. "The Pupils Speak."

43. "Doubled Up Families" memo, box 15, Detroit Housing folder, UAWRC. Sugrue also discusses the problems urban blacks faced in Detroit in *The Origins of the Urban Crisis.*

44. Silver and Moeser, *The Separate City,* 136, 135, 148–49.

45. Sugrue, *The Origins of the Urban Crisis,* 5.

46. Ibid., 59, 62–66.

47. Ibid., 250–53. Wolcott suggests (*Remaking Respectability,* 141) that white women were intrinsic to maintaining racial boundaries as early as the interwar period because they fought black incursions into their neighborhoods.

48. Sugrue, *The Origins of the Urban Crisis,* 73–76.

49. Ibid., 73.

50. "Victory Program Launched," *Detroit Tribune,* 28 Mar. 1942, 5.

51. President and Corresponding Secretary of Alpha Pi Chapter of Delta to Detroit Housing Commission, 22 Jan. 1942, ser. 7, box 67, Sojourner Truth 1942 no. 2 folder, CRCM.

52. *Sojourner Truth Daily News,* 6 Mar. 1942, ser. 7, box 67, Sojourner Truth News file 1942 folder, CRCM.

53. *Sojourner Truth Daily News,* 1 Apr. 1942, ser. 7, box 67, Sojourner Truth News file 1942 folder, CRCM.

54. Feldstein, "'I Wanted the World to See,'" 148–56.

55. "Threat Made to Burn Home of Colored Woman," *Detroit Tribune,* 2 Aug. 1941, 1.

56. "Emergency Declared for Restrictive Battle," *Michigan Chronicle,* 3 May 1947, 19.

57. "Police Alerted as Negro Family Occupy House," *Michigan Chronicle,* 27 July 1947, 1.

58. File 47–60, pt. 1, ser. 1, box 4, folder 47–60, DCCR.

59. "Resentment against Negro Families Flares in Two Previously White Neighborhoods," *Michigan Chronicle,* 11 Sept. 1954, 5.

60. "Housing Commission Bans Race Segregation Policy," *Michigan Chronicle,* 19 Apr. 1952, 1, 4; Charles Wartman, "Housing, Hospital, School Patterns Face Scrutiny Here," *Michigan Chronicle,* 19 May 1954, 1, 16.

61. Sugrue, *The Origins of the Urban Crisis,* 181–258.

62. "Defied Hate Covenant and Won," *Richmond Afro-American,* 21 Sept. 1946, 11.

63. "Midlothian Pike Disorder Scene," *Richmond Afro-American,* 13 Aug. 1949, 2; "Two White Men Freed in Housing Flareup," *Richmond Afro-American,* 27 Aug. 1949, 3.

64. "Restrooms for 'White Only' at Grant's 5–10 Cent Store," *Richmond Afro-American,* 4 May 1946, 19.

65. "Segregation in Courtroom Hit," *Richmond Afro-American,* 24 Sept. 1949, 7.

66. "Jewett Files Answer to Court Segregation Suit," *Richmond Afro-American,* 15 Oct. 1949, 23; "Court Studies AFRO's Suit against Segregation Practice in Va. Justice," *Richmond Afro-American,* 15 July 1950, 7.

67. "Court Studies AFRO's Suit."

68. Kelley, *Race Rebels*, 55–61.

69. Data Sheet, First Six Months of 1944–1945, 20 July 1945, pt. 1, ser. 1, box 1, Reports 1945 folder, DCCR.

70. Letter to Mayor's Interracial Commission and police commissioner, 9 Feb. 1945, pt. 1, ser. 1, box 3, Special Reports 1945 folder, DCCR.

71. DSR Police Report, 2 Feb. 1945, pt. 1, ser. 1, box 2, Police Reports Jan.–June 1945 folder, DCCR.

72. "Sues DSR City and Bus Driver for $20,000," *Detroit Tribune*, 3 Apr. 1943, 1.

73. Summary of Incidents 11 Aug. 1943, pt. 1, ser. 1, box 2, DSR Police Reports 1943 folder, DCCR.

74. Summary of 15–21 Nov. 1943, pt. 1, ser. 1, box 2, DSR Police Reports 1943 folder, DCCR.

75. Summary of Racial Disturbances for Week Ending 26 Aug. 1944, pt. 1, ser. 1, box 2, DSR Police Reports 7/44–12/44 folder, DCCR.

76. Summary of Racial Disturbances Received Week Ending 14 Oct. 1944, pt. 1, ser. 1, box 2, DSR Police Reports 7/44–12/44 folder, DCCR.

77. 2 Feb. 1943 Roundup Report, pt. 1, ser. 1, box 2, DSR Police Reports 1943 folder, DCCR.

78. Summary of Incidents 11 Aug. 1943, pt. 1, ser. 1, box 2, DSR Police Reports 1943 folder, DCCR.

79. DSR Police Department Special Investigation Squad Report, 17 Oct. 1944, and DSR Summary of Racial Disturbances, 1 Nov. 1944, both in pt. 1, ser. 1, box 2, DSR Police Reports 7/44–12/44 folder, DCCR.

80. "Student Balks Bus Driver in Attempt to Oust Her," *Richmond Afro-American*, 30 Jan. 1943, 10.

81. "Student Balks Bus Driver."

82. "Woman Abused on Trolley, Arrested," *Richmond Afro-American*, 3 Mar. 1945, 1.

83. "Woman Fined $5 in Bus Case," *Richmond Afro-American*, 24 Mar. 1945, 3; "Woman Fined in Street Car Case," *Richmond Afro-American*, 5 May 1945, 7.

84. "Mrs. Boling Fined $25 in Bus Case," *Richmond Afro-American*, 14 Apr. 1945, 3.

85. "Matron and Scene of Brick Attack," *Richmond Afro-American*, 1 Mar. 1941, 24.

86. "NAACP Will Appeal Bus Case Fine," *Richmond Afro-American*, 26 June 1943, 9; "State Appeal in Bus Case Given Study," *Richmond Afro-American*, 31 July 1943, 10.

87. "Ingram Frees Pair in 'Battle of the Bus,'" *Richmond Afro-American*, 15 Jan. 1949, 1, 3; "Woman Wins $300 in Bus Case," *Richmond Afro-American*, 1 Oct. 1949.

88. "Richmond Matron Wins Case against Virginia Bus Co.," *Richmond Afro-American*, 29 Dec. 1945, 19.

89. "Bus Co. Apologizes, Pays Bills," *Richmond Afro-American*, 19 Sept. 1953, 20.

90. "Riot Started from Fight over Child," *Michigan Chronicle*, 26 June 1943, 2; National Urban League Report of Detroit Race Riots, box 5, June–July 1943 general file, DUL.

91. "Hid in Attic, Girl, Eighteen, Eludes Mob," *Michigan Chronicle*, 26 June 1943, 9; interview with Beulah Whitby, 25, 28.

92. Lillian Thomas Report, pt. 1, box 1, Lillian Thomas file, Archives of Labor and Urban Affairs, Wayne State University, DNAACP.

93. Riot Report by Herdacine Parrish, 27 June 1943, pt. 1, ser. 7, box 70, Affidavits–Detroit Riots 1943 folder, DCCR.

94. Riot reports by Mildred Raskin, Pearl Doch, Miriam Wellington, Theresa Ann Thomas, and Mrs. Stalworth, pt. 1, ser. 7, box 70, Affidavits–Detroit Riots 1943 folder, DCCR; Cora Lee Affidavit, Mrs. Eva Gordon deposition, Maude Johnson deposition, Mrs. Ruby Thomas Deposition, pt. 1, box 1, Civil Rights Complaints (2) folder, DNAACP; Opal McAdoo Affidavit, incident reports by two anonymous housewives, pt. 1, box 1, Civil Rights Complaints (3) folder, DNAACP; Hallie Young Deposition, pt. 1, box 1, Civil Rights Complaints (4) folder, DNAACP.

95. Memorandum for the Officer in Charge, Racial Situation in the City of Richmond, Va. file 17074–RI, Race Problems folder 1, CWD.

96. 12 May 1944 Report, pt. 1, ser. 1, box 3, Incident Reports 1944–1945 folder, DCCR.

97. Summary of incidents for 3/6–3/13 1944, pt. 1, ser. 1, box 2, DSR Police Reports 1/ 44–6/44 folder, DCCR; NAACP Report of Executive Secretary Detroit Chapter, Oct. 9– Nov. 13, 1944, box 87, 1944 (3) folder, NAACP; "Slapped Man Who Pinched Her Arm," *Michigan Chronicle,* 3 Feb. 1945, 17; Interracial Committee Work Sheet case 52–28, 17 Sept. 1952, pt. 1, ser. 1, box 9, folder 52–28CP, DCCR.

98. "Va. Court Frees White Man Called Matron's Attacker," *Richmond Afro-American,* 28 Aug. 1948, 4.

99. "Story of the Week," *Richmond Afro-American,* 2 June 1951, 1.

100. Harriet Robinson, "Woman Relates a Bitter Encounter with Brutal Cops," *Detroit Tribune,* 15 Jan. 1944, 3.

101. Interracial Committee Worksheet, case 53–32, 9/2/53, pt. 1, ser. 1, box 9, folder 53– 32CR, DCCR; "Loses Child, Ill for Months after Beating," *Michigan Chronicle,* 14 June 1947, 1, 23; "In the Crimelight," *Michigan Chronicle,* 6 Sept. 1947, 4; "Seeking Aid, Woman Gets Police Slaps," *Michigan Chronicle,* 8 Mar. 1949, 2; Interracial Committee Worksheet, case 50–30ACB, 8/17–8/22/50, pt. 1, ser. 1, box 7, folder 50–30ACB, DCCR; "Accuse Cop of Disrobing Her in Big Store," *Michigan Chronicle,* 27 Mar. 1943, 1, 5; "Acquitted, She Files Suit to Ask $100,000," *Michigan Chronicle,* 10 Apr. 1943, 23; Interracial Committee Worksheet, case 52–1, 1/11/52–2/29/52, pt. 1, ser. 1, box 9, folder 52–1, DCCR; Interracial Committee Worksheet, case 53–32, 9/2/53, pt. 1, ser. 1, box 9, folder 53–32CR, DCCR; "Loses Child, Ill for Months after Beating"; "In the Crimelight," *Michigan Chronicle,* 6 Sept. 1947, 4; "Seeking Aid, Woman Gets Police Slap," Interracial Committee Report, pt. 1, ser. 1, box 7, folder 50–30ACD, DCCR.

102. "Woman Remains in Bed as Result of Police Beating," *Richmond Afro-American,* 6 July 1946, 19; "Woman Beaten, Lodged in Jail," *Richmond Afro-American,* 29 June 1946, 2.

103. "Woman Beaten; Cop Draws Fine," *Richmond Afro-American,* 14 Sept. 1946, 6.

104. "Newsie, Brother Given Grilling," *Richmond Afro-American,* 23 Mar. 1946, 3.

105. "Richmond Pair Given Seven Years," *Richmond Afro-American,* 25 Jan. 1947, 2.

106. "American Nazis in Richmond?" *Richmond Afro-American,* 1 Feb. 1947, 1.

107. "Court Upholds Conviction of Cops on Attack Charge," *Richmond Afro-American,* 29 Mar. 1947, 20.

108. "Girl Wins $275 Settlement from Store in False Arrest," *Richmond Afro-American,* 8 Jan. 1949, 3; "Warrants Issued for Two Officers," *Richmond Afro-American,* 1 Aug. 1953, 1.

109. My definition of the modern civil rights movement is derived in part from Morris, *The Origins of the Civil Rights Movement,* x–xi.

Conclusion

1. Tyler-McGraw, *At the Falls,* 283–84.

2. Project 802, 24 June 1953, box 2, May–Dec. 1953 file, FAK.

3. Report of the Executive Director, Phillis Wheatley, 1954, box 4, Executive Director Phillis Wheatley Community Administration 1954 folder, YWCA.

4. Charles Wartman, "Second Class Citizenship Plagued Negroes in the Forties," *Michigan Chronicle,* 14 May 1953, 3.

5. U.S. Department of Commerce, *Seventeenth Census of the United States,* vol. 2, pt. 22.

6. U.S. Department of Commerce, *Sixteenth Census of the United States,* vol. 2, pt. 7; U.S. Department of Commerce, *Seventeenth Census of the United States,* vol. 2, pt. 46.

7. Pratt, *The Color of Their Skin.*

8. Wartman, "Second Class Citizenship Plagued Negroes in the Forties"; Sugrue, *The Origins of the Urban Crisis.*

9. Sugrue, *The Origins of the Urban Crisis;* Silver, *Twentieth-Century Richmond,* 185; "Alarm Bell," *Richmond Times-Dispatch,* 26 June 2001, 12.

Bibliography

Manuscript Collections

Alpha Kappa Alpha Sorority, Inc. Archives, Moorland-Spingarn Research Center, Howard University, Washington, D.C.

Archives of the Tobacco Workers' International Union, Special Collections, University of Maryland.

Children's Fund of Michigan Collection, Bentley Historical Library, University of Michigan.

Citizens' Housing and Planning Council, Burton Historical Collection, Detroit Public Library.

Civil Rights Congress of Michigan Collection, Archives of Labor and Urban Affairs, Wayne State University.

Detroit Chapter of the National Association for the Advancement of Colored People, Archives of Labor and Urban Affairs, Wayne State University.

Detroit Commission on Community Relations Collection, Archives of Labor and Urban Affairs, Wayne State University.

Detroit Urban League Papers, Bentley Historical Library, University of Michigan.

Francis Albert Kornegay Papers, Bentley Historical Library, University of Michigan.

Gloster Current Papers, Archives of Labor and Urban Affairs, Wayne State University.

Jeanetta Welch Brown Papers, Mary McLeod Bethune Council House, National Historic Site, Washington, D.C.

Larus and Brother Tobacco Collection, Virginia Historical Society.

National Association for the Advancement of Colored People Papers, Manuscript Division, Library of Congress, Washington, D.C.

National Council of Negro Women Papers, Mary McLeod Bethune Council House, National Historic Site, Washington, D.C.

Office of the Governor, RG 3, Colgate W. Darden (1942–1946), State Records Collection, Archives Research Services, The Library of Virginia, Richmond, Virginia.

Records of the Automotive Council for War Production, National Automotive History Collection, Detroit Public Library.

Records of the Civilian Aide to the Secretary of War, RG 107, National Archives, Washington, D.C.

Records of the Housewives League of Detroit, Burton Historical Collection, Detroit Public Library.

Records of the Joint Army and Navy Boards and Committees, RG 225, National Archives, Washington, D.C.

Records of the National Association of Colored Women, Bethesda, Md., University Publications International, 1992.

Records of the National Labor Relations Board, RG 25, National Archives, Washington, D.C.

Records of the National Urban League, Manuscript Collection, Library of Congress, Washington, D.C.

Records of the Office of Community War Services, RG 215, National Archives, Washington, D.C.

Records of the President's Committee on Fair Employment Practices, RG 228, National Archives, Washington, D.C.

Records of the War Manpower Commission, RG 211, National Archives, Washington, D.C.

Records of the Women's Bureau, RG 86, National Archives, Washington, D.C.

Rosa Gragg Papers, Burton Historical Collection, Detroit Public Library.

Second Baptist Church Collection, Bentley Historical Library, University of Michigan.

Thalhimer Collection, Virginia Historical Society.

UAW Chrysler Department Collection, Archives of Labor and Urban Affairs, Wayne State University.

UAW Fair Practices and Anti-Discrimination Department Collection, Archives of Labor and Urban Affairs, Wayne State University.

UAW Fair Practices and Anti-Discrimination Department—Women's Bureau Collection Archives of Labor and Urban Affairs, Wayne State University.

UAW Ford Department Collection, Archives of Labor and Urban Affairs, Wayne State University.

UAW Local 7 Collection, Archives of Labor and Urban Affairs, Wayne State University.

UAW Local 80 Collection, Archives of Labor and Urban Affairs, Wayne State University.

UAW Research Department Collection, Archives of Labor and Urban Affairs, Wayne State University.

UAW War Department Bureau Collection, Archives of Labor and Urban Affairs, Wayne State University.

UAW War Policy Division Collection, Archives of Labor and Urban Affairs, Wayne State University.

United Community Services Central File Collection, Archives of Labor and Urban Affairs, Wayne State University.

World War II History Commission, RG 68, State Records Collection, Archives Research Services, The Library of Virginia, Richmond, Virginia.

YWCA Collection, Special Collections and Archives, James Branch Cabell Library, Virginia Commonwealth University.

Oral Histories

Beulah Whitby interview by Jim Keeney and Roberta McBride, 16 Sept. 1969, Archives of Labor and Urban Affairs, Wayne State University.

Jess Ferrazza interview by Jack W. Skeels, 26 May 1961, Oral History Collection, Archives of Labor and Urban Affairs, Wayne State University.

Oral History Collection, Archives of Labor and Urban Affairs, Wayne State University.

Government Documents

U.S. Department of Commerce. *Sixteenth Census of the United States: Characteristics of the Population.* Vol. 2, pt. 7. Washington, D.C.: Government Printing Office, 1943.

———. *Seventeenth Census of the United States: Characteristics of the Population.* Vol. 2, pts. 22, 46. Washington, D.C.: Government Printing Office, 1952.

U.S. Department of Labor, Women's Bureau. *Negro Women War Workers.* Bulletin 205. Washington, D.C.: Government Printing Office, 1945.

Secondary Sources

Alonso, Harriet Hyman. *The Women's Peace Union and the Outlawry of War.* Syracuse: Syracuse University Press, 1997.

Amott, Theresa. "Black Women and AFDC: Making Entitlement out of Necessity." In *Women, the State, and Welfare,* ed. Linda Gordon, 281–98. Madison: University of Wisconsin Press, 1990.

Anderson, Karen. *Changing Woman: A History of Racial Ethnic Women in Modern America.* New York: Oxford University Press, 1996.

———. "Last Hired, First Fired: Black Women Workers during World War II." *Journal of American History* 69 (June 1982): 83–95.

———. *Wartime Women: Sex Roles, Family Relations, and the Status of Women during World War II.* Westport: Greenwood Press, 1981.

Baker, Paula. "The Domestication of Politics: Women and American Political Society, 1780–1920." In *Women, the State, and Welfare,* ed. Linda Gordon, 55–91. Madison: University of Wisconsin Press, 1990.

Balbo, Laura. "Crazy Quilts: Rethinking the Welfare Debate from a Woman's Point of View." In *Women and the State,* ed. Anne Showstack Sassoon, 45–71. London: Hutchinson Education, 1987.

Baron, Ava. "An 'Other' Side of Gender Antagonism at Work: Men, Boys, and the Remasculization of Printers' Work." In *Work Engendered: Toward a New History of American Labor,* ed. Ava Baron, 47–69. Ithaca: Cornell University Press, 1991.

Blum, John. *V Was for Victory: Politics and American Culture during World War II.* New York: Harcourt Press, 1990.

Boris, Eileen. "The Power of Motherhood: Black and White Activist Women Redefine the Political." In *Mothers of a New World: Maternalist Politics and the Making of the Welfare State,* ed. Seth Koven and Sonya Michel, 213–45. New York: Routledge, 1993.

———. "'You Wouldn't Want One of 'Em Dancing with Your Wife': Racialized Bodies on the Job in World War II." *American Quarterly* 50 (March 1998): 77–108.

Branch, Muriel Miller, and Dorothy Marie Rice, *Pennies to Dollars: The Story of Maggie Lena Walker.* North Haven: Linnet Books, 1997.

Bredbenner, Candace. *A Nationality of Her Own: Women, Marriage, and the Law of Citizenship.* Berkeley: University of California Press, 1998.

Brodkin, Karen. *Caring by the Hour: Women, Work, and Organizing at Duke Medical Center.* Urbana: University of Illinois Press, 1988.

Brown, Elsa Barkley, and Gregg D. Kimball, "Mapping the Terrain of Black Richmond." In *The New African American Urban History,* ed. Kenneth Goings and Raymond Mohl, 66–115. Thousand Oaks: Sage Publications, 1996.

Brown, Michael. *Race, Money, and the American Welfare State.* Ithaca: Cornell University Press, 1999.

Campbell, D'Ann. *Women at War with America: Private Lives in a Patriotic Era.* Cambridge: Harvard University Press, 1984.

Capeci, Dominic, Jr., and Martha Wilkerson. *Layered Violence: The Detroit Rioters of 1943.* Jackson: University Press of Mississippi, 1991.

Carby, Hazel. *Reconstructing Womanhood: The Emergence of the Afro-American Woman Novelist.* New York: Oxford University Press, 1987.

Chateauvert, Melinda. *Marching Together: Women of the Brotherhood of Sleeping Car Porters.* Urbana: University of Illinois Press, 1998.

Clark-Lewis, Elizabeth. *Living In, Living Out: African American Domestics in Washington, D.C., 1910–1940.* Washington: Smithsonian Institution Press, 1994.

Cohen, Lizabeth. *Making a New Deal: Industrial Workers in Chicago, 1919–1939.* New York: Cambridge University Press, 1991.

Corrigan, Philip, and Derek Sayer. *The Great Arch: English State Formation as Cultural Revolution.* London: Basil Blackwell, 1985.

Davis, Scott C. *The World of Patience Gromes: Making and Unmaking a Black Community.* Lexington: University Press of Kentucky, 1988.

Dalfiume, Richard. *Desegregation of the U.S. Armed Forces: Fighting on Two Fronts, 1939–1953.* Columbia: University of Missouri Press, 1969.

Dittmer, John. *Local People: The Struggle for Civil Rights in Mississippi.* Urbana: University of Illinois Press, 1994.

Evans, Sara. *Born for Liberty: A History of Women in America.* New York: Free Press, 1989.

Fairclough, Adam. *Better Day Coming: Blacks and Equality, 1890–2000.* New York: Viking Press, 2001.

———. *Race and Democracy: The Civil Rights Struggle in Louisiana, 1915–1972.* Athens: University of Georgia Press, 1995.

Fehn, Bruce. "African American Women and the Struggle for Equality in the Meatpacking Industry, 1940–1960," *Journal of Women's History* 10 (Spring 1998): 45–69.

Feldstein, Ruth. "'I Wanted the World to See': Race, Gender, and Constructions of Motherhood in the Death of Emmett Till." In *Mothers and Motherhood: Readings in American History,* ed. Rima Apple and Janet Golden, 131–70. Columbus: Ohio State University Press, 1997.

Finch, Minnie. *The NAACP: Its Fight for Justice.* Metuchen: Scarecrow Press, 1981.

Fried, Richard. *Nightmare in Red: The McCarthy Era in Perspective.* New York: Oxford University Press, 1990.

Gabin, Nancy. *Feminism in the Labor Movement: Women and the UAW, 1935–1975.* Ithaca: Cornell University Press, 1990.

———. "Women Workers and the UAW in the Post-World War II Period, 1945–1954." *Labor History* 21 (Winter 1979–80): 5–30.

Gaines, Kevin. *Uplifting the Race: Black Leadership, Politics, and Culture in the Twentieth Century.* Chapel Hill: University of North Carolina Press, 1996.

Gavins, Raymond. *The Perils and Prospects of Southern Black Leadership: Gordon Blaine Hancock, 1884–1970.* Durham: Duke University Press, 1977.

Giddings, Paula. *In Search of Sisterhood: Delta Sigma Theta and the Challenge of the Black Sorority Movement.* New York: William Morrow, 1988.

———. *When and Where I Enter: The Impact of Black Women on Race and Sex in America.* New York: Bantam Books, 1984.

Gilmore, Glenda. *Gender and Jim Crow: Women and the Politics of White Supremacy in North Carolina, 1896–1920.* Chapel Hill: University of North Carolina Press, 1996.

Goodwin, Joanne. *Gender and the Politics of Welfare Reform: Mother's Pensions in Chicago, 1911–1929.* Chicago: University of Chicago Press, 1997.

Gordon, Linda. "Black and White Visions of Welfare: Women's Welfare Activism, 1890–1945." In *Unequal Sisters: A Multicultural Reader in U.S. Women's History,* 2d ed., ed. Vicki Ruiz and Ellen Carol DuBois, 157–85. New York: Routledge, 1994.

———. *Pitied but Not Entitled: Single Mothers and the History of Welfare.* Cambridge: Harvard University Press, 1996.

Hale, Grace. *Making Whiteness: Popular Culture and the South from 1880 to 1940.* New York: Vintage Books, 1998.

Hartmann, Susan. *The Homefront and Beyond: American Women in the 1940s.* Boston: Twayne Publishers, 1982.

Hicks, Cheryl D. "Northern Crime/Southern Parole: Working-Class Black Women, Their Families, and New York State, 1920–1935." Presented at the University of Houston Annual Black History Workshop, March 2001.

Higginbotham, Evelyn Brooks. "African-American History and the Metalanguage of Race." *Signs* 17 (Winter 1992): 231–73.

———. "Clubwomen and Electoral Politics in the 1920s." In *African American Women and the Vote, 1837–1965,* ed. Ann Gordon et al., 134–55. Amherst: University of Massachusetts Press, 1997.

———. *Righteous Discontent: The Women's Movement in the Black Baptist Church, 1880–1920.* Cambridge: Harvard University Press, 1987.

Higham, John. "Introduction: A Historical Perspective." In *Civil Rights and Social Wrongs: Black-White Relations since World War II.* University Park: Pennsylvania State University Press, 1998.

Hill, Oliver W., Sr. *The Big Bang:* Brown v. Board of Education *and Beyond: The Autobiography of Oliver W. Hill, Sr.* Ed. Jonathan K. Stubbs. Winter Park: Four-G Publishers, 2000.

Hine, Darlene Clark, "An Angle of Vision: Black Women and the U.S. Constitution, 1787–1797." In *Black Women in U.S. History: Theory and Practice,* ed. Darlene Clark Hine, 2:193–207. New York: Carlson, 1990.

———. *Hine Sight: Black Women and the Re-Construction of American History.* New York: Carlson, 1994.

Honey, Maureen, ed. *Bitter Fruit: African American Women in World War II.* Columbia: University of Missouri Press, 1999.

———. *Creating Rosie the Riveter: Class, Gender, and Propaganda During World War II.* Amherst: University of Massachusetts, 1984.

Hunter, Tera. *To 'Joy My Freedom: Southern Black Women's Lives and Labors after the Civil War.* Cambridge: Harvard University Press, 1997.

Janiewski, Dolores. "Seeking a 'New Day and a New Way': Black Women and Unions in the Southern Tobacco Industry." In *Black Women in American History,* ed. Darlene Clark Hine, 3:761–78. New York: Carlson, 1990.

———. *Sisterhood Denied: Race, Gender, and Class in a New South Community.* Philadelphia: Temple University Press, 1985.

Jensen, Joan. "All Pink Sisters: The War Department and the Feminist Movement in the 1920s." In *Decades of Discontent: The Women's Movement, 1920–1940,* ed. Lois Scharf and Joan Jensen, 199–219. Westport: Greenwood Press, 1983.

Johnson, Marilynn, "Gender, Race, and Rumors: Re-Examining the 1943 Race Riots," *Gender and History* 10, no. 2 (1998): 252–77.

Kelley, Robin. *Race Rebels: Culture, Politics, and the Black Working Class.* New York: Free Press, 1994.

Kerber, Linda. *No Constitutional Right to Be Ladies: Women and the Obligations of Citizenship.* New York: Hill and Wang, 1998.

Kryder, Daniel. *Divided Arsenal: Race and the American State during World War II.* New York: Cambridge University Press, 2000.

Ladd-Taylor, Molly. "My Work Came out of Agony and Grief: Mothers and the Making of the Sheppard-Towner Act." In *Mothers of a New World: Maternalist Politics and the Origins of the Welfare State,* ed. Seth Koven and Sonya Michel, 321–42. New York: Routledge, 1993.

Lawson, Steven. *Running for Freedom: Civil Rights and Black Politics in America since 1941.* New York: McGraw-Hill Publishers, 1996.

Lemke-Santangelo, Gretchen. *Abiding Courage: African American Migrant Women and the East Bay Community.* Chapel Hill: University of North Carolina Press, 1996.

Lichtenstein, Nelson. *Labor's War at Home: The CIO in World War II.* Cambridge: Harvard University Press, 1982.

———. *Walter Reuther: The Most Dangerous Man in Detroit.* Urbana: University of Illinois Press, 1995.

Lipsitz, George. *Rainbow at Midnight: Labor and Culture in the 1940s.* Urbana: University of Illinois Press, 1994.

Lutz, Frances Earle. *Richmond in World War II.* Richmond: Dietz Press, 1951.

May, Elaine Tyler. *Homeward Bound: American Families in the Cold War Era.* New York: Basic Books, 1987.

McClusky, Audrey Thomas, and Elaine M. Smith, eds. *Mary McLeod Bethune: Building a Better World.* Bloomington: Indiana University Press, 1999.

Meier, August, and Elliot Rudwick. *Black Detroit and the Rise of the UAW.* New York: Oxford University Press, 1979.

Mettler, Suzanne. *Dividing Citizens: Gender and Federalism in New Deal Public Policy.* Ithaca: Cornell University Press, 1998.

Milkman, Ruth. *Gender at Work: The Dynamics of Job Segregation by Sex during World War II.* Urbana: University of Illinois Press, 1987.

Mink, Gwendolyn. *The Wages of Motherhood: Inequality in the Welfare State, 1917–1942.* Ithaca: Cornell University Press, 1995.

Montgomery, David. *The Fall of the House of Labor: The Workplace, the State, and American Labor Activism, 1865–1925.* New York: Cambridge University Press, 1990.

Morris, Aldon. *The Origins of the Civil Rights Movement: Black Communities Organizing for Change.* New York: Free Press, 1984.

Mouffe, Chantal. "Feminism, Citizenship, and Radical Democratic Politics." In *Feminists Theorize the Political,* ed. Judith Butler and Joan Scott, 369–84. New York: Routledge, 1992.

Murray, Florence, ed. *Negro Handbook, 1946–1947.* New York: Current Books, 1947.

National Association for the Advancement of Colored People. *NAACP Annual Report,* 1951. Washington: NAACP Publishers.

National Urban League, *Fortieth Anniversary Yearbook.* New York: Urban League, 1950.

Ovington, Mary White. *The Walls Came Tumbling Down.* New York: Arno Press, 1969.

Payne, Charles. *I've Got the Light of Freedom: The Organizing Tradition and the Mississippi Freedom Struggle.* Berkeley: University of California Press, 1995.

———. "Men Led, but Women Organized: Movement Participation in the Mississippi Delta." In *Women and the Civil Rights Movement: Trailblazers and Torchbearers,* ed. Vicki Crawford et al., 1–12. Bloomington: Indiana University Press, 1993.

Polatnick, M. Rivka. "Diversity in Women's Liberation Ideology: How a Black and a White Group of the 1960s Viewed Motherhood." *Signs* 21 (Spring 1996): 679–706.

Pratt, Robert. *The Color of Their Skin: Education and Race in Richmond, Virginia: 1954–1989.* Charlottesville: University Press of Virginia, 1992.

Randall, Vicky. *Women and Politics.* New York: Macmillen Press, 1982.

Reed, Merl E. *Seedtime for the Modern Civil Rights Movement: The President's Commission on Fair Employment Practice, 1941–1946.* Baton Rouge: Louisiana State University Press, 1991.

Robnett, Belinda. *How Long? How Long? African American Women in the Struggle for Civil Rights.* New York: Oxford University Press, 1997.

Roediger, David. *The Wages of Whiteness: Race and the Making of the American Working Class.* New York: Verso, 1991.

Rogin, Michael. *Ronald Reagan: The Movie and Other Episodes in Political Demonology.* Berkeley: University of California Press, 1987.

Rose, Elizabeth. *A Mother's Job: The History of Day Care, 1890–1960.* New York: Oxford University Press, 1999.

Ruddick, Sarah. *Maternal Thinking: Towards a Politics of Peace.* Boston: Beacon Press, 1995.

Salem, Dorothy. *To Better Our World: Black Women in Organizational Reform, 1890–1920.* Black Women in American History Series, ed. Darlene Clark Hine. New York: Carlson, 1990.

Sassoon, Anne Showstack. "Women's New Social Role: Contradictions of the Welfare State." In *Women and the State,* ed. Anne Showstack Sassoon, 154–88. London: Hutchinson Education, 1987.

Scharf, Lois, and Joan Jensen, eds. *Decades of Discontent: The Women's Movement, 1920–1940.* Westport: Greenwood Press, 1983.

Schrecker, Ellen. *Many Are the Crimes: McCarthyism in America.* Princeton: Princeton University Press, 1998.

Scott, Lawrence, and William M. Womack, Sr. *Double V: The Civil Rights Struggle of the Tuskeegee Airmen.* East Lansing: Michigan State University Press, 1994.

Shaw, Stephanie. *What a Woman Ought to Be and Do: Black Professional Women Workers during the Jim Crow Era.* Chicago: University of Chicago Press, 1996.

Silver, Christopher. *Twentieth-Century Richmond: Planning, Politics, and Race.* Knoxville: University of Tennessee Press, 1984.

Silver, Christopher, and John V. Moeser. *The Separate City: Black Communities in the Urban South, 1940–1968.* Lexington: University Press of Kentucky, 1995.

Sitkoff, Harvard. "African American Militancy in the World War II South." In *Remaking Dixie: The Impact of World War II on the American South,* ed. Neil McMillen. Jackson: University Press of Mississippi, 1997.

———. *A New Deal for Blacks.* Vol. 1. New York: Oxford University Press, 1978.

———. *The Struggle for Black Equality, 1954–1992.* 1981. Reprint. New York: Hill and Wang, 1993.

Sklar, Kathryn Kish. "Historical Foundations of Women's Power in the Creation of the American Welfare State." In *Mothers of a New World: Maternalist Politics and the Origins of Welfare States,* ed. Seth Koven and Sonya Michel, 43–94. New York: Routledge, 1993.

Smith, Jessie Carney, ed. *Notable Black American Women.* Book 2. Detroit: Gale Research, 1996.

Smith-Rosenberg, Carroll. "Dis-Covering the Subject of the 'Great Constitutional Discussion,' 1786–1789." *Journal of American History* 79 (Dec. 1992): 369–84.

Solinger, Rickie. *Wake Up Little Susie: Single Pregnancy and Race before* Roe v. Wade. New York: Routledge, 1994.

Stack, Carol B. *All Our Kin: Strategies for Survival in a Black Community.* New York: Harper and Row, 1974.

Sugrue, Thomas. *The Origins of the Urban Crisis: Race and Inequality in Postwar Detroit.* Princeton: Princeton University Press, 1996.

Thomas, Mary Martha. *Riveting and Rationing in Dixie: Alabama Women in the Second World War.* Tuscaloosa: University of Alabama Press, 1987.

Thompson, Heather Ann. *Whose Detroit? Politics, Labor, and Race in a Modern American City.* Ithaca: Cornell University Press, 2001.

Tyler-McGraw, Marie. *At the Falls: Richmond, Virginia, and Its People.* Chapel Hill: University of North Carolina Press, 1994.

Weisenfeld, Judith. *African American Women and Christian Activism: New York's Black YWCA, 1905–1945.* Cambridge: Harvard University Press, 1997.

Weiss, Nancy. *The National Urban League, 1910–1940.* New York: Oxford University Press, 1974.

Welke, Barbara. "When All Women Were White, and All the Blacks Were Men: Gender, Race, and the Road to *Plessy,* 1855–1914." *Law and History Review* 13 (1995): 261–316.

White, Deborah Gray. *Too Heavy a Load: Black Women in Defense of Themselves.* New York: W. W. Norton, 1998.

Wilentz, Sean. *Chants Democratic: New York City and the Rise of the American Working Class, 1788–1850.* New York: Oxford University Press, 1984.

Wolcott, Victoria. *Remaking Respectability: African American Women in Interwar Detroit.* Chapel Hill: University of North Carolina Press, 2001.

Wynn, Neil. *The Afro-American and the Second World War.* New York: Holmes and Meier, 1993.

Zieger, Robert H. *The CIO, 1935–1955.* Chapel Hill: University of North Carolina Press, 1995.

Zinn, Maxine Baca, and Bonnie Thornton Dill. "Theorizing Difference from Multiracial Feminism." *Feminist Studies* 22 (Summer 1996): 321–31.

Index

MEGAN TAYLOR SHOCKLEY is assistant professor of history at Clemson University. A graduate of the University of Richmond, she has a Ph.D. from the University of Arizona and an M.A. from the University of Tennessee.

Women in American History

The University of Illinois Press
is a founding member of the
Association of American University Presses.

University of Illinois Press
1325 South Oak Street
Champaign, IL 61820–6903
www.press.uillinois.edu